The Self-Preservation Society

Also by Kate Harrison

Brown Owl's Guide to Life
The Starter Marriage
Old School Ties

The Self-Preservation Society

KATE HARRISON

First published in Great Britain in 2007 by Orion Books,
an imprint of The Orion Publishing Group Ltd
Orion House, 5 Upper Saint Martin's Lane
London, WC2H 9EA

1 3 5 7 9 10 8 6 4 2

A CIP catalogue record for this book
is available from the British Library

ISBN (hardback): 978 0 7528 7529 3
ISBN (trade paperback): 978 0 7528 8489 9

Typeset by Deltatype Ltd, Birkenhead, Merseyside
Printed in Great Britain by Clays Ltd, St Ives plc

www.orionbooks.co.uk

Fear is the prison of the heart
Anonymous

Prologue:

GREENHAM COMMON HIGH SCHOOL, 1982

Nucleomituphobia – Fear of Nuclear Weapons

This is how fear feels.

'... now, the theory of fight or flight originates from studies of animal behaviour.'

I don't mean the fizzy fear you get from things that go bump in the night, or watching *Halloween II* and *Friday the 13th*. Or even the moment in a dream when your feet turn to lead and the flame-throwing monster is catching up.

No, this is a nightmare I can't wake up from, because everything familiar in this world – from biology lessons to Adam Ant and pregnant giant pandas – is under threat. One day, maybe today even, it'll happen. And it'll kill anyone who hasn't prepared, and change life for ever for the lucky few who make it. And the really nightmarish bit? No one else seems to care.

'The term describes the physiological response to extreme stress, priming the body to attack or to run away, both responses which reflect the ultimate instinct for self-preservation.'

Lorraine has drawn a picture of a willy in the back of her exercise book, and is folding up the sheet of paper to pass to Steven Chubb. I suppose there are worse things to draw in a biology lesson. She's added pubic hairs with curly pen strokes. The only willy I've seen is my little brother's but

Lorraine has seen a real one ('OK, one in a dirty magazine, but it was on a real man. It was ginormous.') so her picture must be pretty accurate.

The probability that I'll die before seeing an erect penis is high, but it's not top of my worry list. I'd like to have kissed a boy, maybe, but I'm not too bothered about missing out on *intercourse*. It sounds like the most embarrassing thing in the world.

The second most embarrasing thing in the world will be having to use the toilet in front of my parents, but that's the price of survival. At least it'll be dark in the shelter.

'The body responds to stress by stopping non-essential functions. A human being may experience a dry mouth as salivation ceases, along with sudden evacuation of the bowels or bladder as gastro-intestinal function shuts down . . . '

Something hard hits the back of my head, like an air pellet. I reach under the wooden bench, and discover Steven's reply to Lorraine, screwed into a tight ball.

' . . . and the inability to sustain an erection.' Mr Jones, our biology teacher, is careful not to meet anyone's eye when he says 'erection'. 'These changes prepare the body for fight or flight.'

Lorraine unravels Steven's note. It says 'Suck on mine'.

'As if I would,' she whispers to me.

'The body instinctively prioritises muscle function to allow a rapid . . . '

And then it happens. A sound that would chill the blood even if you didn't know what it meant. But I do. That wavy wail is saying *take cover, the bomb's on its way*.

Mr Jones flinches, then begins to wave his arms around. His mouth is moving but all I can hear is a rushing noise, like the sound of a thousand seashells held against your ear. More urgent, my stomach contents feel like they're on a one-way trip out of my body.

This can't be happening. I should be at home, where the stockpile is hidden in the garage. Sixteen weeks' worth of pocket money spent on baked beans and evaporated milk and plasters and Dettol.

It'll take twelve minutes to run home. We only have four.

Mr Jones is lining everyone up by the door. I still hear nothing except whooshing but sweat has chilled my skin, and it feels like a huge fist is squeezing my heart.

There's meant to be a build-up, a two-week 'escalation of hostilities'.

I cast around the room, trying to remember the guidelines from *Protect and Survive*. You're safest in a downstairs room, with no outside walls.

Lorraine is pulling at my arm but I can't move. Or breathe. The science department is on the ground floor but there are draughty metal windows from floor to ceiling in place of two walls. They'll shatter in the first few seconds of the blast wave.

Oh my God. We're going to die. I told Dad we should have moved to Wales or New Zealand. I've survived a near-death experience involving a poncho and a slide, *and* a hundred childhood illnesses, only to be split into a million atoms and turned into a mushroom cloud.

Keep calm, Jo, remember to breathe. I stare ahead, try to think straight. And then I spot it.

Yes! The science prep room. The dizziness stops, though I'm still not at all confident I can hang on to the contents of my bowels. I let Lorraine pull me from behind the bench – we're the last to leave the classroom – and at the very last moment, I grab her blazer sleeve and drag her into the prep room. I take the key from outside the lock and then pull the door shut behind us, locking it from the inside. The cramped space stinks of iodine and mouse feed.

I grope for the light switch on the wall. 'Lorrie, put the plug in the sink and run the water. We don't have much time.'

My hearing is returning now: the siren's still sounding and Lorraine shouts above it, 'What the bloody hell are you doing, Joey? If there *is* a fire, we'll be burned to death in here, you nut-job.'

'It's not the fire bell. It's a *siren*. An air attack siren. There's a bomb on its way.'

Now her face is less certain. If anyone in school is an expert on the bomb it's me. And our fire bell has a reassuring ring, like a phone in a public call box. Not like this.

I hide the key in my pocket – I won't let her out, she's my best friend. I'm not going to think about Mum or Dad or Timmy or Misty. 'The water, quickly.' I spot a grey metal bin. Oh God, that's going to have to be our loo. On the bare brick wall, dog-eared posters show photosynthesis, native trees and the inner workings of the human body: maybe all three will be history, not biology, once the nuclear winter comes, and our organs mutate, thanks to radiation. The open wooden shelves are stacked with Pyrex flasks and disposable gloves and plastic bags big enough for corpses. The first aid kit is serious and satchel-sized. It's not a bad shelter, under the circumstances.

'You're wrong. You have to be.' But Lorraine begins to fill the sink. I push stacks of green paper towels against the bottom of the door and into the lock, to keep out fall-out. What will we eat? Lab mice? Humans can survive for weeks, so long as they have water.

The sink is almost full now. 'How long, Lorrie? Since the alarm started?'

'Buggered if I know.' She always swears when she wants to seem cockier than she's actually feeling. Her eyes are dark and wide, as if her Miners Special Effects black kohl has run. 'Three or four minutes.'

The fist tightens around my heart. 'Right. Switch off the tap. I'm going to have to put out the light.' My finger hovers over the switch. What if the gas supply for the Bunsen burners causes a fire? Shouldn't I have released the mice? I cut the light, and reach out for Lorraine. 'Shut your eyes and put your fingers in your ears.'

Oh God, I hope this isn't going to hurt. If we're going to die, let it be quick . . .

It begins, not with a flash, but with a rumble, and I wonder if the first missile has fallen somewhere far away, London or Oxford. Lorraine wriggles and I try to hold her still until she pulls my hands away from my ears and I realise that someone's pummelling on the door.

'JOANNA MORGAN! UNLOCK THAT DOOR THIS INSTANT!' It's Mr Jones.

'We can't let him in, Lorrie. There's no room and the bomb could be about to –'

'I said, open the door.' The banging continues. 'I don't know what you think you're playing at but you're holding up the entire fire drill and the whole school will have to stay outside in the freezing cold until you come out. And you're not going to be very popular.'

'Fire drill?' Lorraine finds the light switch. 'You *wally*. You complete and utter Joey. I knew it wasn't a bomb. We'll be in detention for a month now. Or on litter duty.'

She fumbles in my blazer pocket for the key and unlocks the door. Mr Jones stands on the other side, his left eye twitching in fury. 'What the hell were you thinking?'

My hands are shaking as I emerge into daylight, and I feel colder than ever, the sweat gluing my skin to my nylon blouse. I'm desperate for the toilet, because my insides seem to be made of water, but instead Mr Jones marches us down the corridor.

'I'm flabbergasted at this behaviour from you, Joanna. What was that about?'

'The siren . . . ' I say. 'It wasn't a fire alarm. It was an air raid siren.'

He stops. 'No, Joanna. The alarm was upgraded this weekend. This is a test.'

'But Mr Blake says . . . '

'But nothing.' He sighs. 'So you're in Mr Blake's class, are you? Bloody English teachers. There is such a thing as too vivid an imagination.'

And then we walk out of the main entrance to the field where 700 kids and sixty teachers are standing in shivering lines. My knees bend like Olive Oyl's as I stumble down the steps. Some fifth-formers start jeering and within seconds everyone is laughing and pointing, and I want to run for it, but Lorraine grabs my hand and we walk towards our tutor group.

As I pass Steven Chubb, he begins to whisper, 'Chicken, cowardy custard, scaredy-cat. Chicken, cowardy custard, scaredy-cat!'

And I know that I've just earned a nickname that I'll never shake off. But at least I'm still alive. Until the Bomb drops for real.

Chapter 1

Tyrannophobia – Fear of Tyrants

'Of course, the Tudors had it easy.'

The dead eyes of Anne Boleyn stare at me from behind the velvet rope as Dennis, my soul mate, warms to his theme.

'Think about it. No electricity, therefore no ineptly wired sockets capable of delivering hundreds of fatal volts. No gas, therefore no danger of leaks which could blow your house . . . or, in this case, your castle, to smithereens.'

He's only *half* joking.

Soggy families gather around us, forced indoors by a January downpour. They jostle for position alongside seen-better-days mannequins dressed as Henry the Eighth and his unfortunate wives. They clearly think Dennis is an official tour guide.

He looks the part. He took his anorak off before entering the Great Hall ('wouldn't want the rainwater to damage the historic tapestries, would I, Jo?'). Underneath, he's wearing a check shirt and chinos, as sported by younger Oxford dons in TV documentaries, an artfully casual uniform that proves they have weightier matters on their enormous minds than mere fashion. Quantum physics, maybe, or the preservation of relics of ancient civilisations.

Or, in Dennis's case, the preservation of civilisation in the small corner of southern England we call home.

Dennis couldn't care less about colour or pattern (unless the patterns are on the side of a lorry, warning of corrosive or explosive chemicals). But I do care, and I buy his clothes, so I chose a blue check that matches his eyes, and chinos the same sandy brown as his curly hair. He reminds me of an ageing cherub, the curls shot with grey, and the eyes wrinkled by forty years of trying to save people from themselves. A kind of suburban Superman.

He smiles at me. 'And no motor cars, so therefore no speeding accidents, no road pollution and no greenhouse effect. Those were the days, eh, Jo?'

'Utter bollocks!'

Disapproving eyes focus on the impertinent member of the tour party. Except it's not a member of any tour party. It's my dad.

'What about the dangers of bloody horses and carts?' my father says, delighted to have a captive audience. 'Toxic manure fumes. Crazed carriage drivers with road rage. Dick Turpin and his Merry Men lurking behind every tree to rob your gold bullion. Not to mention Jack the Ripper *and* the bubonic plague.' What he lacks in historical accuracy, he makes up for in enthusiasm.

Women are meant to fancy men who remind them of their dads, aren't they? No danger of that with me. My father thinks he's Michael Caine, but while his hero has grown old gracefully, Dad has not. He sports a year-round golf-club tan, and would rather die than countenance casual clothes. So apart from the security staff, he's the only man here in a navy blazer, but because it's a Sunday his bright white shirt is unbuttoned to reveal a wisp of chest hair, suspiciously dark for a man in his sixties.

What Dennis and my dad do have in common is a conviction that they're always right. In my boyfriend's case, that's true. He's incredibly well read, and shares my love of statistics: in a dangerous world, statistics keep you safe.

Whereas my dad is a dinosaur. Albeit quite a charming one.

'No drug-induced soaring crime rates,' Dennis counters. 'No hoodies. No crackheads. No nuclear, chemical or biological weapons of mass destruction.'

'What about those cannon things that propelled great balls of fire across the battlements? They were pretty destuctive.'

Anne Boleyn holds out her tiny plastic hands, which are peeling as if she's contracted some nasty Tudor skin disease. Alongside her, Anne of Cleves stares into the middle distance. Her wary expression seems familiar and it's only when I turn around that I realise why: my mother's face is composed in the same mask of careful neutrality.

Whenever life gets awkward, her eyes glaze over, as if she's teleported herself back home to her 'babies', the three Maine Coon cats that are Mum's reason for living. But she doesn't fool me. Every time Dad says something daft (i.e. pretty much every time he speaks), her pale lips purse, fleetingly, a dozen new lines of disappointment appearing like tiny needles around her mouth. Then they're gone: no one notices but me.

'A few cannons are nothing compared to the Ebola virus. Or sarin gas. Or DIY. Did you know that a thousand people a year end up in casualty from sandpaper alone?' Dennis considers this a killer blow.

My father shakes his head pityingly. 'I'm delighted to say that I didn't know that. And if I did, I wouldn't be showing off about it.'

The other tourists have finally realised that Dennis and Dad aren't an English Heritage-sponsored sideshow, but just two blokes having the kind of spat you could see in your local pub any night of the week. 'Torture chamber's this way,' a weary mother tells her ginger-haired twin sons. 'Whips and branding irons and a rack where they used to stretch little boys who refused to eat their greens.'

Dennis whispers, under his breath, 'There's a word for people who think ignorance is bliss.'

'And there's a word for people like you,' Dad says, not under his breath at all. 'Smart-arse.'

OK, so maybe today wasn't the best idea. It's Dennis's fault: his mother's idea of an outing for her eight-year-old son was to send him on a 'treasure hunt' around the local shops until he found one willing to sell him twenty Benson and Hedges to bring home. So he's never realised that wintry day trips to damp, draughty castles are simply the modern version of thumbscrews: torture for all the family.

Thank God for out-of-town superstores with Sunday opening: shopping beats heritage every time when it comes to domestic harmony.

Mum's lip needles appear again and I think it's time to change the subject. 'Maybe life wasn't too bad if you were King but somehow I doubt Henry's wives felt all that safe.'

My mother looks at me gratefully, her face relaxing enough to remind me how pretty she was, once. 'That's true. What was it we learned at school? Divorced, beheaded, *died*, divorced, beheaded, *survived*!' She nods in satisfaction. 'Funny the things you remember.'

I haven't exactly lightened the mood. We turn to stare at the crash-test-dummy wives, who surround the fat king, his codpiece obscenely prominent. Dad only agreed to come as research for his forthcoming role in the Operatic Society's production of *Henry – The Musical!* but the part of a womanising, gluttonous patriarch fits him like a glove.

I remember studying the Tudors at school, sitting at the back of the history lesson with my best friend Lorraine, trying to work out which queen we most resembled. I saw her eyes narrow and braced myself: to this day, Lorraine combines ruthless honesty with a bitchy streak. I kept my fingers crossed as she considered my Tudor *doppelgänger. Please, please don't let her say poor plain Anne of Cleves with her long nose and pointy chin, or sour-faced old Catherine Parr with her sulky lips.*

But she must have been in a generous mood, because she chose Catherine of Aragon. It wasn't a bad likeness: Henry's first wife and I share the same round face, big eyes and flushed cheeks (I wonder if hers, like mine, went red at the slightest provocation). And while neither of us could be described as skinny, we both got a decent cleavage as a consolation prize.

Lorraine wanted to be Jane Seymour, until she turned the page in *Kings and Queens for Secondary Schools* and realised Henry's third wife was distinctly beaky, had a double chin and looked nothing like the actress who did the ads for Le Jardin de Max Factor. In the end she settled for Anne Boleyn, 'because Henry the Eighth dumped Catherine of Aragon for her as Anne was prettier. Like me and you!' And then she giggled.

'... but what I don't understand,' my father is saying, 'is how come the most powerful man in the country had to keep getting *married*. One wife is enough for anyone surely?'

Mum's lips purse so hard that even Dennis notices, but Dad ploughs on regardless. 'I mean, sow his regal oats, sure, but wouldn't he get a nightly smorgasbord of ladies-in-waiting dying to lie back and think of England? Perk of the job and all that –'

'Talking of smorgasbords ...' I interrupt, spotting my chance, 'all this talk of death is making me hungry. It must be tea-time by now?'

While more sensible families are tucking into IKEA smorgasbords, their kids safely immersed in the children's ball pool, we're being royally ripped off. Dennis has paid £20 for four teas and four 'authentic Elizabethan cakes'. I love all cakes, but these taste as if they were authentically baked the same week poor Katherine Howard lost her head.

Rain thuds down on the corrugated iron roof of the King's Buttery (which my father keeps repeating in a silly, high-pitched voice, 'The king's buttery, he's covered in the stuff, that's why he's such a lard-arse,' and then laughing at himself). It's a modern building, if a Second World War Nissen hut counts as modern, and inside, you can see your breath in front of your face. The beige fan heaters produce very little warmth, but make the air smell scorched.

We've found a seat by the tiny window, and I wipe away the condensation with my fingers. Framed by the glass, the castle's like a drawing from a child's picture book, with stone walls washed grey by the rain, and a perfect ring of a moat to keep enemies out . . . or the women in. The castle windows are even smaller than the one I'm peering through and I wonder whether the occupants felt lucky to be there, or trapped.

Dad's fallen silent, and Mum's stirring her tea with the little plastic stick: the grey liquid whirls like filthy bathwater going down the plughole.

'Tuesday will officially be the most depressing day of the year,' I say, to break the silence. 'According to the statistics.'

Oddly enough, this doesn't seem to cheer anyone up, but Dennis tries to join in. 'Don't tell me . . . let me guess why. Is it because it's the beginning of the week?'

I shake my head. 'It's part of it, but not the main thing. Anyone else?'

Mum begins to fiddle with a knot-effect gold button on her pink fluffy cardigan, so she's obviously not playing.

Dad shrugs. 'The weather in January is the worst of the year. So is it to do with seasonal depressive pre-menstrual tension or whatever hypochondriacs get?'

'That's another contributory factor,' I say. 'But there's something more obvious. Dad, you definitely ought to get it, it's your specialist subject.'

My boyfriend and my father exchange looks of undisguised rivalry. Dennis tugs at the kiss-curl in his fringe, a sure sign of irritation. I'm already regretting the remark about specialist subjects, as Dad's main areas of expertise are: a) women young enough to be his daughter; b) the best tailors for bespoke suits in Bangkok; and c) the love songs of Rogers and Hammerstein. Whereas the area of expertise I was referring to was . . .

'Got it!' Dennis claps his hands together. 'It's credit card bills, isn't it? This is the week when the wages of Christmas sin come back to haunt us, in the shape of huge bills. Well, I say, us. I mean, anyone daft enough to rely on credit in the first place.'

Dennis has never had a credit card, or an overdraft facility. He even got through university (BA Hons, Social Policy) without going into the red and prefers the certainty of standing orders to fickle direct debits. Lorraine thinks that makes him 'the dullest man in the known universe, worse than Tim Henman or Prince Charles'. But I love his utter dependability. Surprises are seriously overrated.

Dad tuts and chews his cake with grim determination. After forty years as a bank manager, he's used to being in the right. 'Yes, January is dismal. Which is why we're taking the Caribbean cruise next month. What about you two? Any holiday plans?'

He folds his arms across his chest in triumph. He knows the answer to this one already. We don't *do* holidays. Not abroad, anyway.

'We might take a cottage in Cornwall at Easter,' Dennis says. His lazy mother never took him to the seaside, so he imagines *Famous Five*-style picnics on sunny beaches, rather than entire days spent in the car, chasing clouds from coast to coast, in the vain hope that it might stop raining for ten minutes.

'Far East's unbeatable at this time of year,' Dad says, sensing victory.

I sigh. 'Dad, stop it.'

Dennis takes my hand. 'The Foreign Office website is very insistent that no part of South East Asia is 100 per cent safe for British tourists.'

'As if *anywhere* is 100 per cent safe,' Dad mutters.

'Tenerife's lovely at this time of year,' Mum says.

'OK, OK,' I say, holding up my hand. 'Dad, you won't be happy till you've taken the piss so why don't I do it for you? I know I'm safer in the air than I am walking down the street. I know there's a whole world out there waiting to be discovered. I know I'm a great big cowardy-custard chicken scaredy-cat. But it's just the way I am, all right?'

Dad looks sheepish and I realise I must have been talking rather loudly as people are staring. 'Now, now, Bean. That's a bit harsh. What's wrong with wanting my only daughter to live a little?'

Dennis grips my hand more firmly. 'We like staying at home,' he says, 'and if other people followed our lead, the polar ice-caps wouldn't be melting, would they?'

It's not that I don't *want* to fly. I did it reluctantly when I was little, but the older I get, the more terrifying it seems. And however reassuring the safety statistics, I can't bring myself to travel in a tin box with no visible means of staying airborne. Not that it hasn't been frustrating. After university, I got endless postcards from backpacking college friends who'd been celebrating Christmas on the beach in Fiji, or swimming in Iceland's Blue Lagoon. Dad offered to pay for a course he'd seen advertised in the *Daily Mail* called 'Get High: Overcoming your Fear of Flying'. But then I met Dennis and he told me that fear was nature's way of preserving the human race, and that I didn't need to turn myself into someone else because he loved me exactly as I was.

That's when I knew we were made for each other.

'I doubt one trip to the bloody Canaries would be responsible for the end of the world,' Dad mumbles, but he knows he's defeated. We sit listening to the rain on the roof.

'Ought to start heading back,' Dennis says eventually, 'before the Sunday traffic gets too heavy.'

I look at my watch. It's two thirty in the afternoon.

In the car park Dennis averts his eyes from Dad's gas-guzzling 4x4, and Dad can't resist a sly chuckle at our mauve super-mini (chosen by Dennis because it tops the European NCAP safety league tables). As I kiss my parents goodbye, I realise I'm rather looking forward to the most depressing day of the year: at least at work, you don't have to pretend to be enjoying yourself.

Chapter 2
Ephebiphobia – Fear of Teenagers

'Keep it safe, keep it real, stay well cool, do what ya feel . . .'

There is nothing more cringe-worthy than adults trying to relate to the younger generation.

'We is safe . . . and we is sound.'

Especially when the adults in question all work in local government and would probably class the misuse of an apostrophe as the ultimate rebellion.

'We belong to da underground.'

There's a pause in the rap music and we hold our breath. I'm hoping that's the end of the Courtbridge Schools' Safety Group Young Person's Safe 'n' Sound Project hip-hop presentation. We wait, just to be certain it's over, before Mikey – the only member of council staff who could *ever* qualify as cool – starts applauding, then we all join in.

We're a pretty sorry line-up, the kind of people the tabloids love to hate for banning daisy-chains, or conker competitions, or coins in your Christmas pudding. I'm a foot soldier in the Killjoys' Army, as Community Liaison Officer (Accident Prevention, Public Protection and Civil Defence). Not that I've got the power to ban *anything*. The real clout lies with slutty Sheila Fothergill (mayor and chairwoman of the Civil

Protection Committee), and Dennis Diffley (Deputy Director, Public Protection and Civil Defence. And my soul mate).

Dennis winks at me and I hope the teenagers don't see, because they'd be horrified. To them, I'm sure he seems ancient, but he's only just turned forty. Our clothes don't help: he's in the suit he wears for photo-opportunities, the one that makes him look a dead cert for the Director's job. I'm wearing my grey suit. OK, the tailored jacket barely fastens across my chest, but once I've done it up, it seems to make my boobs disappear, which is just the way I like it.

Mikey high-fives the teenage lead rapper so hard that the boy has to clutch his palm to stop it stinging. Because Mikey has a tattoo (a rather small black Celtic pattern on his upper arm), one piercing (that we know of, in his eyebrow), and has been through rehab, the powers-that-be let him do precisely what he likes. He's spent an entire term on this peer safety project for the socially excluded, though the kids he's targeted with his workshops don't look particularly socially excluded to me. They have neat fringes and clean nails, and seem almost as embarrassed as the adults.

Mrs Fothergill gets to her feet, swaying slightly in her banana-yellow kitten heels. She steadies herself on the enormous oak table, her polished black talons leaving eight crescent-shaped dents in the Doomsday-old wood. I booked the council chamber for this special occasion, and the burghers of Courtbridge stare down at us from their gilt frames. They were moved from the Georgian town hall into the new-build council HQ in the 1970s, and they still look perplexed at their surroundings. Mrs Fothergill's portrait will join them before long, as the first female mayor in the town's history. No one stands in her way. She'd pierce their feet with her pointy shoes if they dared.

'Girls . . . and *boys*.' She lingers on the word boys, smiling at the lead rapper, who blushes so violently his spots look fit to burst. 'What a performance! As your democratic representative, and more importantly, as a person, I know what a terrible trial growing up can be. All those uncontrollable hormones ... No wonder accidents are so common among you youngsters.'

I catch Dennis's eye and we exchange sly smiles. Though menopausal, Mrs Fothergill is famously awash with uncontrollable hormones, and not shy of acting on them. Though I can't believe she'd take advantage of a teenager.

'That's why we're so grateful to Mikey. I have never met a man able to express himself so powerfully. He is willing to risk life and limb to engage the disaffected, and yet he bears this burden so lightly on those broad ... *capable* shoulders.' She pauses, licks her Juicy Tubed lips and winks in Mikey's direction.

I don't know whether to be scandalised at her cradle-snatching (she must be fifty-five, and Mikey's twenty-six), or relieved that she isn't targeting the students.

'So without further ado, that buffet's looking rather inviting so I think it's time to – what would you say, rap-style, Mikey? – ditch da bitch and get stuck into the food, yeh, mother-suckers?'

There's a pause as the kids look at each other, unable to believe what this old woman has just said, before Mikey steps in. 'Hey, Mrs F, we'd never diss you. But no messing, man, that grub's on borrowed time. Go, go, go!'

This time, they don't need any persuasion, and two dozen teenagers fall on the refreshments like a meeting of the Young Bulimics' Federation. They won't be disappointed: our subsidised canteen is one of the very few fringe benefits of working for Courtbridge Borough Council. The jam roly-poly won the traditional pudding category of the South-East Local Authority Catering Awards three years in a row.

'So, Mikey and Sheila, who'd have thought it?' Dennis whispers, creeping up behind me. 'Don't they make a charming couple?'

'Well, they would if she wasn't married.'

Dennis has a satisfied smile on his face. He loves knowing people's secrets. 'Never stopped her before has it? She even tried it on with me before we got together ... '

'You never told me that!'

'Oh, yes, she used to play footsie with me under the table during cabinet meetings . . . though thankfully our vandalism and accident rates in the borough are beginning to diminish in line with our Strategic Objectives.'

I'm just wondering whether the stress of his job has turned Dennis quite mad, when I turn and realise the *Gazette* reporter is earwigging.

I try to think of something supportive to add. 'Yes, I agree, it's a real achievement to engage all those troubled young –'

But my boyfriend cuts across me. 'Hi, Dennis Diffley, Deputy Director, Public Protection. I don't think we've met?' he says, addressing the reporter.

'No. I d-don't think we have, no,' the journalist stutters. He looks like the trainee, podgy and uncomfortable in his cheap jacket. The *Gazette* would hardly send their star reporter to this event. 'I wasn't quite sure who to interview.'

I smile reassuringly. 'I'm sure the kids will talk to you, once their noses are out of the trough.'

'Right. Better wait a mo then. And are you involved, too?'

'Well, I organise the schools programme so I suppose –'

But Dennis holds up his hand. 'Oh, Jo's one of the backroom girls. I'm sure you'd get a better quote from Councillor Fothergill.' He pushes the reporter a little too forcefully on the back, towards the fragrant Sheila. 'You don't mind, do you?' he mouths to me, but even if I did, I know he wouldn't turn back.

At first, when we started dating, it used to hurt like crazy when he ignored me at work or used my ideas in meetings, but when he explained why, it did make perfect sense. 'The think is, Jo, your ideas are brilliant, but you're so quiet that if I didn't tell people about them, they'd never be heard and never be acted on. We're a team, now, aren't we? If I get promoted, we both see the benefits.'

I never dreamed I'd end up with a high-flier like Dennis. Fifty per cent of people do meet their partners at work, but I've always been rubbish at flirting, and he seemed so out of reach. Until the Strategic Safety Partnership Christmas Dinner Dance, where my colleagues pulled snap-free, child-safe crackers (2350 Britons are injured every year by Christmas trees, lights and decorations) and congaed round the ballroom, while Dennis told me I was beautiful.

It's not as if he doesn't help me out too. He's banned from discussions about my pay rises or promotion, but he's nominated me for three different assertiveness courses (surely one day I'll get the hang of it?), given me new responsibilities (including the all-important Seasonal Safety Bulletin) and he agreed to come to the event today as a special favour – usually he's far too busy planning for major disasters to come to tinpot stuff like this. He came because he loves me.

There, I don't feel hurt at all. Except . . .

I stand in the centre of the council chamber and when I look down, my hands have formed fists. Chit-chat bounces off the walls, louder and louder, and I feel like there's a huge red arrow above my head, pointing to the loser who's so inconsequential that not even her boyfriend wants to talk to her. I'm considering bolting to the toilet when Mikey appears with a plate of crab pinwheel sandwiches. I could kiss him, except Mikey's such a tart, he might kiss me back.

'You look cheesed off,' he says, slipping out of street slang. 'Boyfriend's hob-nobbing I see.'

Dennis is already posing for a photograph with Sheila, who has snaked her arm around his back . . . no, hang on, it's lingering on his hips now. I turn away. 'I wish I could do all that schmoozing stuff.'

'Nothing to it. You've got to believe in yourself.'

'Hmm. Easier said than done.'

He raises his pierced eyebrow: the ring trembles for three seconds afterwards. 'Why? I mean, look at Dennis. He doesn't let his obvious shortcomings hold him back.'

'Oi! That's the love of my life you're talking about,' I protest, but not too strongly.

'Only kidding. All right, look at the teens. Seething masses of puppy fat and rampant oily t-zones, and yet there's no stopping them.'

I study the students in their little cliques alongside the buffet: there's a lot of pony-tail flicking going on, and that's just the boys. 'I wouldn't want to be that age again.'

Mikey raises his eyebrows. 'God, I would. Imagine all that sex to look forward to.'

'I was terrified of sex when I was a teenager. And adolescent girls are *horrible* to each other.'

Mikey frowns. 'But I bet you had the boys flocking round you when you were at school. What with your natural assests!' And he nods towards my cleavage.

I feel my face turn purple, and I pull the lapels of my jacket together. 'I'd have done anything to make them shrink when I was thirteen years old.'

'Really? What a waste.'

'It was like my boobs were the only thing about me the boys were interested in.'

'Don't be so hard on them. The boys, I mean. I bet they didn't know how to approach you. Shy girls are so forbidding. Such a shame. Harmless flitation is what makes life worth living.'

'Like you and Mrs Fothergill,' I say, desperate to change the subject.

He cringes. 'Oh God. I hope no one reads anything into that old bag's fantasies.'

'Now who's being judgemental, Mikey?'

'Fair point.' He scratches the stubble on his chin. 'Maybe I should give her one. To show willing. After all, Courtbridge Borough Council never discriminates on the grounds of age, gender, race, religion, sexual orientation . . . or wrinkles.'

I giggle. 'Or grey hairs.'

'Or receding hairlines.'

'Or support tights.' I am laughing out loud now.

'Stretch marks . . . '

Tears are rolling down my cheeks now. 'Liver spots.'

'Saggy boobs, varicose veins or haemorrhoids.'

I shake my head. 'You win. I can't think of any more.'

He nods over at Sheila, who is still lingering round my boyfriend, though the photographer has moved on. 'Oh, I've got the right horn now. She's such a temptress.'

'Stop it,' I say, feeling almost sorry for Mrs Fothergill. 'We'll end up that way, sooner or later.'

Mikey snaffles the final pinwheel, chewing it thoughtfully before declaring, 'All the more reason to make the most of our youth while it lasts, eh, Jo? I don't think you appreciate how special you are.'

And he smiles at me so kindly that for a moment I really believe I can change; joke, flirt and misbehave like I've always wanted to. Remembering a magazine 'party confidence trick' that recommended circulating with a bowl of nuts, I head for the buffet, grab a bowl of unflavoured corn snacks (Courtbridge is officially a Peanut-Free Anaphylaxis-Aware Zone) and scan the room for the least intimidating group of people.

Aha! The teachers are bound to be patient with me. I force my mouth into a confident yet friendly expression, and propel myself towards the corner, holding the bowl in front of me, like a Wise Man bearing myrrh.

'Corn snack, anyone?' My voice doesn't match the smile: it's more of a bleat. The teachers – two women nearing retirement, and a younger man with body odour – look a lot less friendly close up.

'No thank you.' The man's halitosis forces me to take a step back.

I try again. 'So what did you think of the performance?'

They sigh, clearly desperate to resume their discussion of detentions or the teachers' pension scheme or whatever is the topic *du jour* in staffrooms. The older woman eventually says, 'Bloody awful, of course. But on the plus side, that idiot Mike did agree to take our most irritating students, so what do you expect?'

The others nod agreement, then stare at me, waiting for me to go. I want to be assertive, stand up for my friend, but I can't remember any of the techniques properly: should I be using the 'broken record', or is this a good time for 'fogging'? I shuffle backwards until I am in the corner of the chamber, trying to merge with the wall. I was *stupid* to try.

I am a scaredy-cat. This is what I know. No gain but no pain either. Safe 'n' sound.

I peer at my flat Clarks shoes resting on the blue carpet, and wish I could disappear into the thick municipal pile. *Get a grip, Jo. Make yourself useful.* I look around for something to do. Hurrah! The remains of the buffet looks like a landfill site. I take my bowl of corn snacks – I seem to have eaten most of them without realising – and begin to stack stray plates and cutlery. No one pays me the slightest attention now they think I am a clearer-upper.

After all, isn't that what backroom girls are for?

From: Joanna Morgan
[mailto:JMorgan@courtbridge.gov.uk]
Sent: Wednesday 14 February
To: Dennis Diffley
CC: Courtbridge Accident Prevention, Public Protection and Civil Defence Team
BCC: LusciousLorraine@tramp.net
Subject: Valentine Safety Bulletin: Beware of Cupid's Arrows

Dear colleagues,
Here, as promised, is my latest research on seasonal health and safety risks. This month, as Dennis Diffley is giving the keynote speech to the Round Table Valentine's Day Lunch today, I've focused on affairs of the heart. Feel free to use these as you see fit! And remember, love is a dangerous business.

- Watch out for anonymous e-Valentines, which security experts say are more likely to come from hackers who are targeting your hard drive than from suitors targeting your heart (if you do fall victim, remember IT are on extension 34567).
- Roses are red, but they also have thorns which harbour deadly tetanus and several types of fungus that can cause severe damage to the body.
- 2.3 million Britons are allergic to perfume, so if you must *splash it all over*, keep an inhaler handy in case your paramour suffers an asthma attack.
- Sex-related injuries cost Britain £358 million a year in days off sick and insurance claims. Apparently, one in ten of us have claimed for damage to soft furnishings, and the most common injury is a carpet burn.

Keep safe, everyone,
Jo 'The Scaredy-cat' Morgan

Chapter 3
Gamophobia – Fear of Marriage

I'm late for Dennis's special Valentine treat.

It's all Lorraine's fault. I always copy her in on my safety bulletins, though she takes the piss out of them. She printed off the email and took it with her to work on the maternity ward, to keep her ladies entertained between their contractions. Though if anyone appreciates the hidden risks of romance and sex, then surely it's a woman in labour.

'I ONCE THGT ID BRKN A PENIS IN HALF ON A 1 NT STAND,' her first text informed me. 'BLOOD EVRYWHRE. ID ONLY BROKN SKIN BUT IT FREAKD ME OUT. MY TOP TIP 4 YR NEXT SAFETY BULLETIN – BEWARE OF OVERDOING THE FRCTION WHN WNKING A BLOKE OFF.'

The next text contained a list of the things her colleagues had retrieved from orifices while working in casualty, including 'PLICEMEN'S TORCH, PENKNIFE & A PRIMUS STOVE.'

I texted back: 'THAT MUST HV BEEN SOME CAMPING TRIP!

Lorraine has always been my expert on matters sexual but I'm not sure that spending her working hours at the sharp end of the birthing business, and her time off prowling the streets for men, has given her the most balanced approach to love.

The texts made me forget the time and when I get down to the foyer Dennis is pacing up and down, wearing a hole in the monogrammed Courtbridge Borough Council royal blue carpet custom made in 1972. The council architects must have come fresh from designing Eastern bloc airport lounges, because they completely ignored the beautiful mottled-honey Bath stone buildings that feature in all the local guidebooks. Instead they created a civic centre that looks like a stack of concrete shoeboxes.

'You're late,' he says.

'Only ten minutes,' I protest, though for Dennis ten minutes might as well be ten hours.

'I managed to be on time. I cut short my meeting with Wessex Water.' He pulls at the kiss-curl on his fringe.

'Let's hope no one decides to poison the rivers overnight, then, I wouldn't want dead fish on my conscience,' I say and he frowns back, as disapproving as a sitcom dad. I try again. 'So where are you taking me?'

'It wouldn't be a surprise if I told you.' He's striding ahead now, past the raised flower-beds which are dotted here and there with purple crocuses. Climate change has reached Courtbridge, no doubt about it.

I struggle to catch up in my heels. I'm normally a flatties girl, for safety reasons, but thought I'd make the effort for a special occasion. When I first moved in with Dennis, Lorraine warned me I'd have to put more work into keeping things *fresh*, that sharing a bathroom could prove the death of romance. 'Make an effort,' she advised, 'and I don't mean baking cakes.'

But two years on, I haven't yet had to buy a peephole bra and crotchless knickers, or greet him at the door wearing only a smile and a fur coat. Then again he's never needed any encouragement on that front. No one at work would guess that mild-mannered Dennis is a tiger in the bedroom. And the kitchen, the hallway, the living-room and the bathroom. Even the patio, though not at this time of year. Global warming hasn't quite penetrated his flagstones.

We cross the road, leaving behind the brutalist building, and darting down a cobbled alleyway that challenges my heels still further. I try not to guess where we're headed but the options for a Valentine's dinner in Courtbridge are limited.

There's the Pony and Trap, the town's oldest pub, now run by a national chain: the romantic menu will have been cook-chilled months ago in an Eastern European warehouse, and the red fabric roses on every table taken out of storage for their annual night of glory, before being packed away again, still in their little silver vases.

I'd have put my money on the Trap, but Dennis walks straight past and I catch a glimpse of the packed dining room, couples blinking under the fluorescent lights.

The Golden Orchid has a more intimate (i.e. pitch dark) ambience, mainly to conceal the food. The main source of lighting is the turquoise glow from the fish tanks, where doomed lobsters drift from one glass wall to the other. The Golden Orchid offers Chinese and English cuisine side by side, both loaded with monosodium glutamate, and neither remotely appetising. I know Dennis won't be taking us there. He is uncompromising on the topic of MSG.

He strides past as though there's a nasty smell. Well, actually there *is* a nasty smell, of chicken fried in old oil. Then he crosses the road.

He wouldn't be taking me to Matches, would he? Now that would be a surprise. Matches is the closest Courtbridge gets to trendy: it has Spanish-Bulgarian-Korean fusion tapas, a purple frosted-glass bar that runs the length of the room, and the most expensive cocktail menu in the county. In the year it's been open, I haven't ventured through its smoked glass doors, but the thought of a Slow Comfortable Screw is oddly tempting right now.

We don't mix drinks at home because *it makes it almost impossible to keep track of alcohol units.* I never exceed fourteen units in a week, and Dennis always stays the right side of twenty-one.

He marches past Matches without a glance.

'Slow down, please, Dennis.'

He turns, his forehead creased with impatience. 'Well, if you will wear ridiculous shoes . . . You know there are 8000 casualty admissions from high heels every year.'

I smile. 'Yes, I do know, because I was the one who compiled the footwear hazards bulletin. But if you remember, trainers cause 290,000 accidents, so surely stilettos are the wiser choice, statistically speaking?'

He gives me a dismissive look, unsure whether I'm teasing him, before turning down Canal Path.

I definitely know where we're going now. Courtbridge's very own floating restaurant: the Romantica, the number one location for illicit trysts and indecent proposals. But it has its legitimate side, too. I'd lay bets that nine out of ten couples within a ten-mile radius got engaged in the bobbing barge.

I stop in my tracks.

No. He couldn't be . . . not Dennis. Dennis isn't the marrying kind. He's too practical, too realistic. Moving in together is one thing – the bills are split, the chores are halved and the sex is on tap – but marriage is altogether too risky for the professionally cautious. A tiara, a vicar and a finger buffet don't exactly come with a money-back lifetime guarantee.

I shake the thought from my head and follow Dennis towards the gangplank. The Romantica looks charming in darkness: unlike in daylight, when you can't miss the rusty-brown stains on the hull, and the filler that's holding the windows in place. It feels like the boat's been here for ever, but apparently she began life on the Continent, perhaps cruising along the Seine occupied by elegant French couples, or floating past naked ladies in the red-light district of Amsterdam. Life in Courtbridge must be a let-down.

Through the window, I can see eight candlelit tables for two, most already occupied. Because of the date, these couples all fall into the legitimate category: you can tell by the bored way they're playing with the lettuce on their plates when they'd prefer to be playing footsie with the flirt from accounts.

Stop it, Jo.

It's dark inside the boat, and the smells of garlic and damp are competing with each other. Garlic is winning. My feet feel unsteady as I adjust to the movement of the water. 'Herr Diffley?' The owner appears from behind the fly-strips that conceal the galley from view. The Romantica is run by a spooky couple from somewhere behind the old Iron Curtain. I've never been inside the Romantica before, but everyone knows Karl and Kristina. They're always taking out ads in the *Courtbridge Gazette* to showcase their vampire-unfriendly menus.

The man who must be Karl looks like Wee Jimmy from *The Krankies*, dressed in full *maître d'* regalia. He shows us to the best table in the boat, at the back, facing the medieval bridge which gives our town its name. My eyes are adjusting to the gloom now, taking in the lacy tablecloths and the scratched crystal glassware. Our place-settings are an arsenal of dulled cutlery. Fish knives, butter knives, odd little pastry forks. Whatever's on the menu, I have a strong suspicion that every course, including dessert, is going to taste of garlic.

He hands the wine list to Dennis – 'is no choice of food, is set dinner we create to made ze heart and other parts leap' – and negotiates his way between the tables, flashing lascivious smiles at the women diners and raising his bushy eyebrow at the men.

'This is a nice surprise,' I say. Well, it's definitely a surprise.

'I thought it would fit the bill,' he replies, and gives me a meaningful look. 'It's a special night.'

He disappears behind the drinks list and I wish I had a menu to hide me. Could he *really* be about to propose? Dennis plans everything, with the exception of sex. Actually, I wonder if he even plans that during public protection meetings, mapping out the exact positions in his head to relieve the monotony of avoiding Armageddon.

I peer out of the window at the bridge: two teenagers are chasing each other. Their hoodies are black, and they wear drainpipe jeans that make their legs look as skinny as toothpicks. They weave in and out of parked cars, before the shorter one leaps up on to the narrow stone wall, placing trainered feet one in front of the other, like a wirewalker. The taller boy runs alongside, and I feel flushed with fear that Hoodie One might tumble off the side, into the water.

'Stupid little bugger,' Dennis whispers, following my gaze. 'Probably been sniffing glue. The canal's so shallow he'll break his neck if he falls.'

As he says it, the shorter teenager wobbles and I gasp, as he seems to hover in mid-air for seconds . . . it can't possibly be that long but that's how it feels, and then his friend reaches out and they both tumble back on to the bridge, the friend breaking his fall.

God, what a relief! But he fell from quite a height. What if the weight has injured him? I crane my neck, my nose so close to the cold glass that it gives me goosebumps, trying to see through the gaps between the stone balustrades. Nothing happens. I don't breathe. The clink of cutlery stops or, at least, I stop hearing it. I can see the two figures flat out on the bridge, there's no sign of movement at all, and I replay that fall in my mind. That boy could have broken his back.

'Dennis?' I'm about to suggest calling an ambulance when I see them, Hoodie One and Two, scrambling to their feet, unsteady enough for me to worry that they might be injured. But then I wipe the condensation from the glass and see that Hoodie One's hoodie has slipped off, revealing a great mane of long blonde hair . . . and now Hoodie Two reaches down, his head hidden by fabric, and the two Hoodies are snogging.

'Oh. It's a girl.'

Dennis pulls a face. 'Even more reason for her not to be out after dark. Kids like that are the reason Anti-Social Behaviour Orders were invented.'

I'm about to protest when Karl arrives at the table bearing a round white plate covered in . . . oh no . . .

'Snails in garlic butter,' Karl says triumphantly. 'Nothing better for putting ze lead in the pencil.'

Snails are more likely to make me throw up but at least

Dennis likes them. As he orders the wine – something French and expensive sounding – I wonder who on earth first decided that these flaccid rubbery creatures, which retreat into their shells at the slightest provocation, could be an aphrodisiac.

After three snails (cut into pieces small enough to gulp without chewing or tasting), one French onion soup, and half a chicken with 40 cloves of garlic, my tastebuds are screaming in surrender.

The booze and the gossip distract me from the food, though. Dennis is on form, telling tales from the disaster planning committee. He's surprisingly indiscreet when he's had a glass of wine, and now we're well into the second bottle, there's no stopping him. He seems to be on a mission to consume all our allotted units on one night.

Mrs Fothergill is apparently having affairs with both the fire chief *and* the ambulance control room supervisor, and the speculation's rife over which senior policeman she'll choose to complete her 999 hat trick.

Outside, incredibly, the Hoodies are still at it. Their lips must be numb but they only manage to detach from each other for long enough to take a few steps, before they're compelled to kiss again.

'They're not *that* fascinating, are they?' Dennis asks, sounding amused rather than annoyed.

'Do you think it's their first kiss?'

He smiles. 'And their second, third, fourth, fifth, sixth . . . ' he counts off on his fingers, 'ooh, they must be up to their thirtieth by now.'

'Novelty's not wearing off yet, though.'

'I should hope not,' he says. 'I've been at it twenty-seven years and it hasn't worn off for me.'

It's true: Dennis kisses like a teenager. Fervent and passionate. OK, and a tiny bit sloppy. But in a good way.

For a while, we stare at the couple, who're still joined at the lips. They're not even groping. They're clutching each other's hands, down by their sides, as if the kisses are so tumultuous that they need to hang on for balance.

Dennis reaches over to take my hand and grasps it hard. 'I wanted this to be a special night. A memorable night.'

Now my mouth is dry. Is this going to be *my* moment? My first proposal of marriage? From the only person in the world who is ever likely to offer?

'I was bloody nervous about us living together, Jo, I'll admit it.' He blushes, as he rarely admits to weakness. 'I'm not exactly a spring chicken, after all, stuck in my ways and with who knows what kind of bad habits. And as for your habits . . . ' He chuckles.

I try not to think about his bad habits: the way he scratches inside his ears and then inspects the wax on the end of his finger. The way he monitors my toilet roll consumption, and bites his lip over my excesses when we have to buy 'yet another family pack'. But compared to my dad, he's a paragon.

'No, to be fair, Jo, I have to say you're pretty house-trained. And the benefits of having you around – well, the bed's always nice and warm – do outweigh the disadvantages.'

'Dennis Diffley, last of the great romantics!'

He takes a sip of wine, then refills both our glasses. They are *enormous* glasses and we must be on ten units each by now.

'Now I never claim to be a New Man. It's taken me a long time to get my life *just so*. Well, you know how important being settled is to me, after my childhood. I like my own company. But I don't think I could ever go back to living alone.'

He's right: we did make the transition without any of the fireworks Lorraine had prediced. No arguments over cleaning the bath, or putting the rubbish out. 'Me neither,' I say. Though I do miss my little studio flat. Now and then. It's only natural to feel nostalgic occasionally.

'I've been thinking about it a lot. You know I'm not a man

to rush into things, but there comes a time when one needs to think about the future and . . . Oh, *good* timing.'

Karl is carrying a large spiky pudding which, as it looms closer, I realise is a heart made from meringue. None of the other diners have had a heart-shaped meringue. We've been earmarked for special treatment.

'Shall I do ze honours?' Karl asks, his alarmingly large kitchen knife poised above the meringue.

'No, no, leave it to me,' Dennis says, waving him away. 'Now where was I? Oh yes. Commitment.'

There are pointy brown peaks on the meringue, where the heat has toasted the sugar. It looks delicious: meringue is one of my favourite things. But I can't imagine ever eating again. Because Dennis is about to propose marriage.

He gives me a special lingering look, one that's usually a prelude to sex. I feel ever so slightly queasy. Must be all that garlic, because this is the happiest moment of any girl's life, surely, even now we're liberated and assertive. I love Dennis. He's a good man, the nearest to my twin on earth, the only bloke I've ever found who will tolerate my warped view of the world.

It's definitely the garlic.

I take a deep breath. OK. Maybe I feel a teeny bit nervous. Perfectly natural. It's not like I've ever been one for impulsive leaps in the dark. I was scared when we agreed to move in together, after all. If it hadn't been for the lease on my studio running out and the landlord wanting to flog the building to a developer, I'd have stayed there till my dotage.

'Jo,' he says. 'I know you won't be expecting this, but . . . '

I look down, avoiding his sincere gaze because I don't want him to notice my queasiness when he pops the question. I *knew* I should have passed on those bloody snails.

By the bridge, the Hoodies are no longer kissing. There we are. Nothing lasts for ever, not even hormonal teenage passion. Other things matter more. Compatibility. Attitudes.

Fear of being alone.

Where did *that* come from?

The Hoodies are coming towards us now, not realising we can see them. They stop a few yards from the boat, and Girl Hoodie stops and traces her finger down the side of Boy Hoodie's face, as though he's made of marble.

There's a dragging feeling in my stomach, like lust, but then I recognise it. Envy. I don't want Boy Hoodie, but I want the feeling Girl Hoodie has, whatever it is that's transforming her face – glowing under the street lamp – into radiance.

'Jo . . . ? Oh bloody hell, I don't see what's so fascinating about snogging teenagers. When did they come back?'

'They were there all the time.'

'Idiots. They must be frozen. Anyway . . . what I wanted to ask . . . '

I prepare myself for my big moment.

'Jo, would you like to get a joint bank account?'

I snort with laughter – it comes out before I can stop myself. He stares at me, with the same irritated expression he gets when our Head of Department talks over him in a meeting. 'Sorry, Dennis! But . . . ' I can't tell him that I'm laughing out of relief. 'I just wasn't expecting it.'

'Well, I think it's time. And it's also the fairest way of doing it. Of splitting the bills. And I know we both want everything to be fair.'

'Hmmm, yes,' I say, nodding until my neck's sore. A bank account! Hooray. 'Great idea. But the thing is, Dennis . . . '

He's raising his knife to pierce the meringue and down it comes, in the centre of the heart, and there's a hiss and out pours a pool of blood-red sauce, followed by a melted pool of egg-yolk-yellow vanilla ice cream. Baked Alaska. I've always wanted to try it. He slices right through the meringue, adjusting his knife carefully so our portions are of identical size, exactly half a heart each. 'The thing is, what?'

'Nothing,' I say. The Hoodies have gone. 'So long as we can have one of those cheque books with animals on them. Otters and badgers and stuff.'

He raises his eyebrows. 'Well . . . it's not what I'd choose but if that's the deal . . .' and he reaches out to shake my hand, as though we're business partners. But then he reaches across and whispers in my ear, 'We'll ratify the merger later, eh?' before kissing me briefly on the lips.

I *do* fancy him. I really, really do. And I'm excited about spending the rest of my life with Dennis. We're made for each other. It's just odd that when I transfer the meringue and the ice cream and the raspberry sauce from my spoon to my mouth, all I can feel is the heat and the cold.

It doesn't taste of anything at all.

Chapter 4
Alliumphobia – Fear of Garlic

This morning I feel new empathy with the chicken cooked with forty cloves of garlic. Our bedroom is hot thanks to the early sunshine and Dennis's energy efficient central heating. As a result, our garlic-infused sweat has soaked into the bedding and the curtains and the walls, and I know that however many showers I have, the stink will linger for days.

But I do need to make at least a token effort to banish the miasma of garlic, so I clatter into the bathroom, making as much noise as I like because Dennis left an hour ago. I climb into the shower using the grip handles, avoiding the emergency pull-cord. The water is on the chilly side, so at least there's no danger of getting scalded, but I wish the Man of the House would turn the temperature up a few degrees, like he keeps promising. I think he secetly likes the icicle effect. He's a little bit strange that way.

I don't mean that he likes to dress in giant nappies or craves six of the best with a garden cane. Or at least, if he does, he hasn't asked me yet. Maybe that comes once we've set up the joint account, and are bound together by standing orders . . .

I take the loofah (fairly traded of course) and scrub away at my garlicky body. The last time I put this much effort into exfoliating was when I was eight and Lorraine told me everyone was born with freckles and I wasn't washing hard enough to get rid of them. I ended up taking the top layer of skin off my arms and legs, but when it grew back – painfully – the freckles were still there. A couple of years after that, I grew breasts and Lorraine didn't, and she stopped going on about my freckles. She's been much happier since she bought herself double-Ds for her twenty-fifth birthday present.

Dennis likes my boobs. And my bottom is 'nicely proportioned and entirely lacking in cellulite'. My legs are 'well toned, if very slightly too short'. Might not sound like the most generous compliments, but he's scrupulously honest, so I couldn't really ask for higher praise. And in bed, he's as ardent as any Hollywood lover. Last night our clothes were off before we'd got out of the entrance hall (though Dennis folded them away after we'd finished).

He's quite bossy in bed: not in a pervy way, just making all the decisions about, well, you know, what we do. Suits me. Sometimes sex is so daft that you need at least one of you to be taking it seriously or you'd get a fit of the giggles and that wouldn't be the right thing at all.

He's also *deadly* serious on the topic of contraception, with a belt-and-braces approach, involving ultra-safe condoms, spermicidal jelly and his uncanny knowledge of the safest phases of my menstrual cycle. The condom failure rate (up to fourteen pregnancies per one hundred users) gives him sleepless nights.

The shower goes cold, so I leap out. I brush my teeth and then use the special water pump that jets away food debris like a high-pressure car wash (though I'll confess I don't use the safety goggles that Dennis insists upon in case the water hits my eyes). I aim the jet at my tongue, too, but the garlic's burned into my mouth, so I can't taste my coffee or my hurriedly buttered toast. All the scrubbing's made me seriously late for work.

Outside, the sharp winter sun makes my head ache, and my poisonous breath forms a thick mist that follows me as I leave our bungalow, number 64 Salzburg Avenue, and head towards real life. That'll teach me to consume all my alcohol units in one go (hangovers cost the UK £2 billion in lost wages every year).

As usual, the wide road is deserted, an asphalt river with bungalow-tugboats evenly spaced along its curves. All the bungalows have a nautical feel. Number 64's side walls curve gently like the bow of a ship, the downstairs toilet window is a porthole of stained glass and inside every surface is panelled and polished, awash with mahogany and oak.

When I first moved here, I couldn't get used to the quiet. I didn't miss my studio flat, which always made me feel like Gulliver, thanks to its miniaturised kitchenette and its three-quarter-sized bath. But its location was great, right in town, near the marketplace and a paper shop and late-night convenience store. I've never had the wildest of social lives, but I loved sitting in the big Parker Knoll granny chair, looking out of the window. At Christmas I'd watch families weaving around the stalls looking for the gaudiest decorations, eating the oily fresh doughnuts I could smell from two floors up. Or in the summer, I'd wait for darkness to tempt out the skateboarders, all in black like bats. And I'd gawp at the impossible manoeuvres that became more daring with every bottle of strong cider.

Lorraine used to laugh at me. 'Life isn't as bloody spectator sport, Jo. Let's get down there and join in.'

But she didn't understand: I'm no good at joining in. You can divide people in this life into doers and spectators – and Lorraine, of all people, should know that the doers need an appreciative audience.

There's nothing to see in Salzburg Avenue. Estate agents call our area Little Austria, but everyone else knows it as the blue-rinse ghetto. The neighbours are friendly enough: the weekend I moved, Mrs Cronin from next door came round with a bottle of sherry which she obviously hoped to share with us. Dennis took it before she could take a step over the threshold.

'I had my fill of snooping neighbours as a kid,' he said.

Dennis doesn't talk much about his childhood, but it's left him with a pathological hatred of prying eyes. I knew I couldn't argue. But, whenever I see Mrs Cronin through the kitchen window, clods of soap suds dropping from her pink flowery rubber gloves, she looks away. And I can't say I blame her.

I walk out of Salzburg Avenue, down Vienna Way, and towards the Old Town. I move slowly because of the hangover: my pupils are slow to respond to light, so when the sun emerges from behind a cloud, my surroundings seem bleached out. And when I step into the shade, it's like there's been an eclipse and I'm falling . . .

I get as far as the cobbled pedestian area, where the street is so steep I need to lean on a postbox for support. I watch the people who pass by. There's not exactly a rush hour in Courtbridge. That's for city folk. We have a bustle hour. Imagine Women's Institute stall-holders trying to secure the best tables in the church hall, sharp elbows at the ready. *Oh, excuse me. No, excuse ME, I'm so sorry*, they say, almost always meaning the exact opposite.

Today people seem as weary as me, moving more languidly than usual, yawning from lack of sleep and wincing from muscle strain after spending last night in traditional style, i.e. getting pissed enough to sleep with their partners. I wonder if Lorraine went home with the cross-dressing barman from the hospital social club at the end of her shift.

I look down and realise I've forgotten my fluorescent bib: Dennis gave it to me when the clocks went back in October. It's the same design the rescue services wear on the hard shoulder after an accident. I remember what Dennis told me about Mrs Fothergill and wonder if she likes her 999 boys to put theirs on in bed. Or perhaps she keeps them as trophies.

The thought makes me giggle, and the giggle turns into a laugh, and then as I cross the road my eyes seem to be playing tricks because there's a flash of fluorescent green and it's the same shade as my bib and I wonder whether I haven't somehow put it on after all, and then the flash gets brighter and that lime green is all I can see and then I feel myself falling and my face is reflected in the time-polished mirrors of the cobblestones, my mouth in a ragged 'O' and then . . .

Chapter 5
Gnosiophobia – Fear of Knowledge

'Jo . . . Joooo?'

Disinfectant catches in my throat and stings the inside of my nose. But however much the cleaners use, it still never disguises the twin smells of the school toilets: Impulse – men just can't help acting on it, or so the girls in the fifth form say – and drains.

'You're bloody miles away again,' Lorraine calls from outside the cubicle. 'Come on, you moron, we'll be late.' Her insults echo round the room, bouncing off the tiles.

I straighten my skirt over my goosebumpy legs, and try to get the loo to flush. Always a high-risk activity in this cubicle, but the one next door is worse, a bubbling volcano of dark blue toilet roll and urine that's spilled across the brown floor. Parents are impressed by the pristine paintwork and modern signs welcoming them to Greenham Common High School ('Working with Common Purpose') but after three months here, I know it's more a case of 'Common as Muck'. Not one of the toilets has escaped some form of vandalism. Broken seats, cracked cisterns, handles repaired with yellowing Sellotape and metal coat hangers. I don't need any persuasion to Now Wash Your Hands. Except the water's always freezing and the liquid soap dried up circa 1976. As it's now 1981, this place must be germ heaven.

'Jo. We'll be late. I'm not waiting no more.'

I open the door in time to see Lorraine wiping the back of her hand across her mouth, to remove ninety per cent of the Rimmel Toffee Apple lipstick she's applied so she doesn't get detention for wearing make-up. She coloured her hair at the weekend with a Shaders & Toners so the brown lipstick clashes with her plum-coloured fringe, but I'm not saying anything. Wouldn't dare.

Alongside her in the age-mottled mirror, I frown. Why can't I be pretty too? My fingers sting under the running water where I've bitten them, while Lorraine's fingers are long and perfect, like a hand model's.

'Oi, grumpy. Come on.'

Lorraine pokes out her tongue at me in the mirror and I smile. I pick up my khaki schoolbag, with its Biro-ed graffiti promising devotion to bands I'm not allowed to listen to: the Sex Pistols and the Boomtown Rats. In the other hand, I'm carrying wellies in a green St Michael bag.

The corridor's already empty as we run upstairs to the English department, pushing past prefects to race into Mr Blake's classroom.

He's not there yet, but the rest of my tutor group is more hyper than usual: Harriet the class bitch is spitting chewed balls of paper at Steven Chubb, the heart-throb. Everyone's carrying wellies. Some have already put them on, and are stomping about, leaving footprints of dried mud on the lino.

'Good morning, 1G!'

That voice makes me blush and I hope no one's noticed. It's like dark chocolate and crumpets dripping with butter. Melty and rich but edgy too.

I dare to look up, then away again as the blush spreads. He's wearing a brown suit and brown penny loafers and his black hair is uncombed, with soft sleepy peaks. I wonder if he slept alone.

I've gone bright red. Lorraine nudges me. 'Reckon it's all off. Wouldn't be wearing a suit if we was off to the farm, would he? Dragged the bloody wellies in for nothing.'

'Settle down, 1G. I have bad news, and good news . . .'

He waits for this to sink in. He comes from Liverpool, like the Beatles and Kenny Everett and Keith Chegwin. On our first day, he explained that people from Liverpool were either known as Liverpudlians *or* Scousers, and that seemed so sophisticated. There's not a single special name if you come from West Berkshire.

'The bad news is . . . the farming project has been brought to a rather unexpected halt. And that means we won't be going on the field trip.'

The farming project is nothing to do with geography: no crop rotation or 'compare and contrast the benefits of arable over dairy herds'.

There's a moan, and he nods back at us. 'I know. I think you can draw your own conclusions about why Mrs Henderson decided to stop us going to the abattoir. Censorship is never a positive step. But I think the quality of work you produced after our visit to the cattle market is a powerful statement in itself.'

I'm sure he's talking to me: he read out my poem to the whole class. I called it 'Bite to Eat' and it was about the journey to market of a calf taken from its mother and the meadow where it eats fresh grass. I showed my dad my exercise book, with the comment Mr Blake had scribbled in the margin: 'Remarkably moving and insightful, A-minus'. Dad read the poem several times, but all he said was 'So we've got your bloody English teacher to thank for this vegetarian fad then? Just what we need – some lefty teacher filling your head with mad ideas. Not like you haven't got enough of your own to begin with.'

I didn't think that was very fair. Yes, Mr Blake is a vegetarian, the first I've ever met, and yes, he explained about factory farming and battery hens. I hadn't known what an abattoir was before then. It sounds too nice a word for something so horrible.

But these are the things people *should* tell children. We're the ones who can change the world.

Not that the boys were going to the abattoir to change the world. They wanted to see lots of blood, so now they're annoyed. But most of the girls look relieved. I know I am: I'd hate to break down in front of my favourite teacher. And I bet abattoirs are freezing in November.

'I understand you're disappointed – but it simply means we'll be moving on to the next project that bit faster . . . I hope you're ready, because this is the big one.'

We wait. There are stories that Mr Blake's been in trouble with the head teacher before after parents complained, but at least it means English is never boring. He pauses again, his face – which is usually moody and pale, even in the summer – is pink, and I can see he's excited, so I feel excited too.

'It's war.'

He lets the reaction ripple around the room – nudging and jostling by the lads at the back, nervous giggles from the nail varnish wearing mob immediately behind me. Lorraine pulls a face. 'Bor-ing . . . I get enough about the war from me nan.'

The room has gone quiet again. 'Leave your wellies here, but bring your exercise books. We're off to the hall to see a movie.'

We drift out in crocodile formation, with that giddy feeling that always bubbles up when we're allowed out of the classroom in lesson time.

We find our seats as the scent of baking gingerbread comes through in waves from the school kitchen.

It's my least favourite of all the cakes the dinner ladies mangle. As it cooks, it smells boggy, too much flour dragging down too little stale ginger. When you stick your spoon in it, it smells of damp laundry.

Lorraine and I sit next to each other in the front row. Mr Blake has already set up the projector – this is a real *reel*, not a flickering Betamax video in the cramped TV room.

'There's no sound on this, so I am going to play some music. I want you to concentrate on the images, and jot down your first reactions.'

He presses 'play' on his Alba cassette recorder. The clunk and settle of the needle into the vinyl groove echoes round the speakers: I imagine Mr Blake at home, in frayed denims, kneeling at the side of a turntable, making the tape for us.

The first notes on the piano make me wince as I realise what it is. 'Imagine'.

I scowl. *How could he?* I took against The Beatles last December, when Mum and Dad went into mourning over the death of John Lennon. They played the records so loudly that the house seemed to shiver from the waves of guitar music. And Mum kept singing along, while Dad grasped her hand, more affectionate than I'd ever seen him. 'We've lost more than John. We've lost . . . our youth.'

It takes Mr Blake a while to get the reel loaded, but finally, the film is sucked up into the projector. The screen fills with light, and then shades of darkness, as a title appears: 'Hiroshima, 6 August, 1945'.

I've heard of Hiroshima, of course. A big bomb in Japan. Didn't it mean the end of the war?

'It was a clear morning,' says Mr Blake, in the deadpan voice he usually saves for poetry. At primary school, Mrs Fitzpatrick spoke like a xylophone, veering from high shrieks to low growls to keep our attention. But Mr Blake speaks as though he doesn't understand what he's saying, no emotion, just words. Except somehow that means you can't stop listening.

'A perfect morning for flying.' A plane in black and white cuts across a grey sky. I wonder if the sky was blue in real life. On the tail of the aircraft, the stars and stripes, again in black and white.

'The *Enola Gay* left the Tinian airbase at 2.45 a.m. Its mission was straightforward – to drop a single bomb.'

The plane rumbles silently through the grey-blue. I can hear the clanging of tins from the kitchen, one of the dinner ladies has heard the record and is singing 'Imagine'.

'La-la-la . . . all the people . . . '

'The bomb was called Little Boy.'

Lorraine starts to fidget. They're catching, fidgets, like hiccups, so I sit on my hands to stop myself. She reaches into her bag to pull out a tube of Spangles and offers me one. Its fizzy orange flavour makes me feel sick.

'Whoay-whoay-whoay . . . '

The screen goes white again, and I turn round, expecting the tail-end of the film to be spinning off the reel, as it does when something goes wrong with the projector. But it's still whirring, and Mr Blake is staring at the screen. 'The bomb exploded at 8.15 a.m., in the air above Hiroshima.'

The screen is still white. Then a picture begins to melt through, like a photograph appearing in a tray of developing fluid. At first it looks like fabric rags hanging in strips off a football. It's being held by a woman in a cap with a cross on the front, a nurse's cap.

'La la la today . . . '

And then I realise: the ball with rags attached is a person's head, on a body with skin peeling away. A moment later, there's an odd noise from Lorraine, not a word, but a croak from her throat. She begins to cough and I think her Spangle's gone down the wrong way.

Mr Blake says, 'The people who survived said the bomb was like a second sun. The people in the centre of Hiroshima died instantly. They were the lucky ones.'

The picture changes, to a silhouette of a houseplant. My eyes stretch open, trying to process what they're seeing.

'The explosion caused a light so bright that for miles around, the patterns of objects in its way were burned into stone . . . you can see the shadow of the leaves on the pillar . . . '

He pauses, and another image replaces the plant. A child, wearing a patterned kimono.

'It had the same effect on skin.'

The child is naked. The patterns are burns. I've seen enough. The smell of ginger is in my nose like sneezing powder.

'Imagine . . . la la la . . . '

'The people who could run, couldn't see. The flash had blinded them. The ruined city was an obstacle course.'

The film shows a dome, its tattered roof now open to the sky. What colour was the sky now?

'But they had to run. Because what was left of the city was going up in flames, and so they tried to find their way to safety by sensing the heat on their skin.'

I can't take my eyes off the screen, but I want to run too. The middle of my Spangle has dissolved, and I stick the tip of my tongue into the sharp gap to stop myself crying out.

Pictures of people with no clothes on, streetcars reduced to metal skeletons.

'Some of them tried to find their way to the river, where they could bathe their wounds, where the water might act as a break between the flames and safety . . . '

His voice is slower now.

'But when they got there, the water was boiling. They had a choice. Wait for the flames, or jump in.'

'Lah lah lah a dreamer . . . '

'Oh, belt up singing, Glenda, you're not exactly Sheena-bloody-Easton.'

I drag my eyes from the screen, but the pictures are burned in, like the flowers on the kimono, the leaves on the pillar.

I blink as the lights come on, my hands wedged between my legs and the underside of the chair. When I pull them out they're red and the dimpled pattern of the plastic is imprinted on my palms.

'And that, 1G, is what war will be like for us. Or rather, much worse, because the bombs that are trained on Newbury, *right now*, are hundreds of times more powerful than the one used on Hiroshima. Shortly to be joined, literally in our backyard, by American weapons at the airbase, aimed at Russia. You might have seen it on the news, the women who arrived at the beginning of the month, on a peace march?'

I do remember. Dad laughed at them. 'Deluded fools. As if the Soviets care about a bunch of hairy-legged women!'

Mr Blake's not laughing. 'This is a threat to all of us. To the survival of the human race. Our parents and our grandparents had it easy, with battles where you could be a hero, or could get lucky. Well, our luck has run out.'

He flicks his eyes up at the hall clock, as the second hand counts the last moments before midday. 'Thank you for your attention, 1G. A little food for thought before lunch. We'll talk more of war tomorrow afternoon. Meanwhile, isn't that spaghetti bolognese I can smell from the canteen?'

He stops speaking one second before the bell sounds, jolting me into reality. My classmates are subdued as they file out, but once they're in the corridor, queuing for dinner, the chatter starts up again. For them, Hiroshima is a long time ago and a long way away . . .

But I can't move. Mr Blake fusses with his precious reels of film, and the caretaker is wheeling tables into position for the dinner sitting.

'Jo,' Lorraine punches my arm, 'you're behaving like a right dipstick. I'm starving and if we get in the dinner queue now we might get chips before the fifth years nab them all.'

I look up, but I can still see the pattern of that kimono.

'Come *on*, Jo. You're being weird. Jo. Jo . . .'

Chapter 6

Nosocomephobia – Fear of Hospitals

'Jo . . . Jo . . .'

I'm falling, but before I hit the ground, it melts away. Everything's bright white and I feel like I'm outside, cold and dazzled by sunlight and there's a crunch as I hit cobbles. I don't feel anything but I *know* it's my bones making that noise and then all I see is rubies and diamonds . . .

'Come *on*, Jo. I bet you can hear us.'

It isn't Lorraine any more. It's a man's voice, a Welsh voice, the vowels soft as double cream and the consonants brittle as toffee.

Rubies and diamonds glitter in the sunlight, tiny fragments against the cobbles, but more rubies than diamonds now, a wash of red spreading, changing colour . . .

'It's a crucial time,' the voice continues, more matter-of-fact now, 'the sooner a patient emerges from this stage, the better the long-term prognosis.'

Someone's sweeping the diamonds away, but the red wash is still spreading.

'Is she going to be brain damaged?'

My father . . .

My father's voice is dragging me to a place where I don't feel weightless and where nothing sparkles. Gradually my mind reacquaints itself with my body, part by part, each area mapped by a different sensation: throbbing down my left side, as though someone is twisting my hip-bone slowly in its socket. My torso feels scrambled, nothing quite where it should be, churning as lost organs try to find their way home. Stinging in my groin. Heaviness in my hand, like I'm tethered.

'It's always a waiting game, I'm afraid. I don't think we're going to have to operate to reduce the cranial pressure, which is good news. And she's young. Do you hear me, Jo? Fancy trying to open those eyes?'

My head pulses, as though my brain is too big and trying to escape the confines of my ridiculously small skull, but the skull is like a vice and ... shit, that *hurts* ...

'Was ... was that a blink?' My mother. Not daring to trust her own eyes. I wish I could reach out to her, but even if I could work out how to raise these leaden eyelids, I'm too scared it'd trigger new waves of pain.

'You probably imagined it,' my father says.

'If she did blink, it might only be a reflex,' the warm voice says. 'We still know very little about what triggers a patient's emergence from coma.'

Coma? Is that where I am? My body's definitely here, feeling a thousand years old, yet moments ago I was at school. And twelve again. With bitten nails and a monster crush on my English teacher.

'And whatever you've seen on TV, if ... *when* she begins to respond again, it's rarely a miraculous overnight recovery. Two steps forward, one step back, is the mantra with brain injury.'

'Could I hold her hand?' It's Dennis.

Please don't, Dennis. Don't touch me, touch equals pain ...

'That's fine, but be gentle. And don't be too disappointed if she doesn't respond.'

No, *don't*. I want to shout out but I can't and the words of protest reverberate in my brain like howl-round on speakers and I tense in anticipation of the agony of Dennis's hand on mine and everything begins to fade away ...

*

'Tell you what, I didn't fancy her chances one bit when they dragged her in.'

Where am I now?

'Right dent she had in her scalp, measured it on my fingers, three centimetres deep, even though it hadn't hardly broke the skin.' The voice is gossipy and female, belonging to someone who is used to being listened to. A teacher? But I'm not back at school. And I can't open my eyes which means I must be . . .

'You *didn't* stick your fingers in there?' The other voice is little-girly, enjoying being scandalised.

'Course I *didn't*! But you could see. Like a boiled egg when you tap it with your spoon and it caves in. Only time I seen a head that bashed before, we lost 'im.'

'Oooh,' says the scandalised voice. They must be nurses. God help me. 'Doesn't look too bad now, does it?'

'You never can tell what's going to happen next, Kylie, you just can't. But still I wouldn't be betting my bingo money on this one regaining all her marbles, put it that way.'

You're wrong. Anger makes the pressure in my brain hum because I can't tell her she's wrong. *Isn't she?*

'Such a shame,' says little-girl. 'Can't be much older than me.'

'Shoulda looked both ways, shouldn't she, eh? You all right to wash her? Last thing she needs is bedsores.'

'OK.'

Rubies and diamonds flash before my eyes again. And I sense a familiar taste in my mouth. It feels gritty and dirty . . . Is this what fear tastes like? Because I ought to be afraid, surely? I ought to be terrified.

'Leave you to it, then.'

But I'm not. Floaty, yes. Muddled, definitely. But frightened . . . for the first time I can remember, I'm not afraid.

'One more thing. Am I meant to talk to her, like the doctors tell us to? In case she can hear us?'

The other woman tuts. 'Not sure there's much point. Mind

you, if it got me into Dr Williams' good books, I'd sing her the entire Take That back catalogue.'

I feel a cold breeze as someone lifts the sheets away from my body, followed by a hesitant hand on my leg. 'Shoulda looked both ways.' But I *always* look both ways. What the hell's happened to me?

'H . . . hello, Jo,' the girl says. 'Um . . . I'm going to clean you up a bit, OK?' And I hear a trickle of water followed by a wet stroke, like our old dog Misty licking me. As exhaustion descends like a heavy, scratchy blanket, I taste that taste again and I *know* that on some level that taste is connected to what I am doing here. And then I work out what the taste is.

Garlic.

' . . . I would have expected better of the police, given my connections.'

Dennis. And other people. I can hear their breathing. My mother's doll-sized intakes of breath, as if she's frightened someone will tell her off for taking more than her rightful share of oxygen. My father's deep inhalations more than making up for it. And a fourth pair of lungs, producing a whiny wheeze so high-pitched that perhaps only the comatose and dogs can hear it. Surely it can't be . . .

'Well, let's face it, mate. Courtbridge's finest plods are hardly Inspector Morse, are they?'

My brother. That voice, complete with the estuary drawl he's adopoted to get ahead in advertising, is unmistakable.

So I'm still in the hospital. I check for pain but my body feels as insubstantial as cotton wool. Maybe it's the drugs. And then I check for fear: *nothing*.

'I'm sure they've been trying their best, Timmy.' Mum, the human emollient, tries to keep things nice. Dennis's breaths become more laboured.

I don't need to open my eyes to picture the gathering: my dad pacing the room, wondering how long before he can go and flirt with the nurses. His face will be creased with just enough lines to show deep concern, without making him look his age. Occasionally he might run his fingers through his thick hair, blonder and shinier now than it was in his twenties, thanks to fortnightly dye-jobs at the caressing hands of Savannah, the hairdresser to whom he's entrusted his locks for twenty coiffed years.

As you'd expect of the perpetually leading man of Newbury Amateur Operatic Society, he'll have agonised over his costume for the role of anguished father. I'd guess at a sober black suit, *Love Story* meets *The Godfather*. Or smart and dignified like his idol, Michael Caine. Ted Morgan, the ultimate chameleon.

Dennis will be in casuals: a garish rugby shirt bought from a Sunday supplement, and . . . God forbid he's come out in jogging pants. I can only hope they're not the ones with the hole in the crotch, because the more defensive he's feeling, the more inclined he is to spread his legs wide, like men on trains.

My mother in a size 8 baby-blue twinset, the uniform all women pensioners wore in the 1970s, before they began shopping in Gap and going on superannuated hippie trails to smoke hash in Marrakesh and Goa. Poor Mum. She hasn't quite caught up. And no doubt my condition has added a dozen new wrinkles of disappointment to her face.

And then Timmy. He's inherited my father's awareness of the dash he cuts, but he'll have aimed for 'grief casual'. Good jeans from a label too trendy for me to have heard of, hugging his ridiculously skinny frame. Perhaps a preppy Henry Winkler zip-up cardigan, but with some kind of twist, like a Serbo-Croat swear-word knitted into the back. Handmade shoes. A gold ring. Hair tousled with £25 styling gel, to suggest sleep disturbed by his elder sister's plight. A look designed to get tongues wagging at the nurses' station: hetero, metro, homo or bi? My little brother likes to keep them guessing.

'I can't help feeling that a spate of thefts of penny chews from a newsagent would have your local bobbies calling for reinforcements.'

'And I suppose London policemen are all masters in the art

of detection?' Dennis says, instantly switching sides from criticising the local bobbies to defending them.

'How masterful do you need to be, exactly, to solve a hit-and-run perpetrated by a Lycra-clad individual on a *push-bike*?'

I hear *another* person's breathing then, speeding up, and wonder who's joined us before I realise: that's *my* breathing. And the hit-and-run . . . that's *me* they're talking about. I search for a scrap of a memory to make sense of it.

Nothing.

'It's not as if bikes have registration plates,' Dennis says, 'though I'm planning to lobby our MP to present a motion arguing the case for them.'

'What? Would you have them for tricycles, too?' My brother's enquiry is deadpan.

'There'd be an exemption for three-wheelers or child-specific models.'

I must remember something. But all I can summon up is that revolting taste of garlic. Don't nurses brush the teeth of people in comas? Or is my injured brain producing a mirage in my mouth?

'Ah, but how will you define a child? I reckon most street crime is committed by under-sixteens on Raleigh Choppers anyway,' Timmy sneers. 'Hey, I know. What about licensing clothes? Lycra licences only issued after a body scan to ensure no unsightly wobbly bits. And no hoodies permitted unless the wearer has been cleared by local magistrates.'

Hoodies? I grasp on to a fragmentary image, of two kids wearing hooded jumpers on Court Bridge. But it doesn't seem to connect to push-bikes or accidents, and the effort makes my head ache. It's exhausting.

'. . . and I hardly think that making jokes as your sister lies critically injured is appropriate.' Dennis's lecturing tone is so familiar, it's almost reassuring.

'What do you suggest, Herr Commandant? That we sit here miserable as sin waiting for her to flatline?'

'Timmy!' My mother's warning is whispered, as if she doesn't really mean it.

'Or maybe you're expecting some emotional scene where she wakes up, we all cry, and suddenly she's able to recite Shakespeare's sonnets or see visions of the Virgin Mary?'

'You're upsetting your mother,' Dad says.

'As if that's ever bothered *you*,' my brother spits back.

Well, don't mind me, chaps. I'm only the one who's hovering on the edge of life here.

'Bloody hell, Tim, you've been here five minutes and you've started,' Dad snaps. 'You're not helping. Why don't you bugger off back to London where you're needed for your oh-so *vital* work? Because we don't need you here.'

'Ted,' Mum bleats, on the edge of tears.

This is beyond a joke. Aren't they meant to be wafting aromatherapy oils under my nose? Playing compilations of my favourite songs, or a tape from a pop star begging me to return to consciousness? Since when have coma patients been tempted to come round by a full-blown domestic?

' . . . Lynda, don't defend him. He's taken two bloody days to get here and now he's lording it all over us as usual. Can't he ever learn to put someone else first?'

Huh. Like Dad would know anything about that.

Enough's enough. I concentrate hard on remembering where my eyes are, on trying to recall what it feels like to open them, how each little muscle works to lift a millimetre of skin on my lids. It feels like lifting up a double-decker bus.

'Um . . . I don't know if you remember, but the doctor did say that even if we don't think she's fully here, Jo might be able to hear us,' Dennis says.

No kidding, buster. Remember me? The patient you're all here to help? Now I'm determined to shift these sodding eyelids just to show 'em.

My brother sniffs ferociously. He's been doing it since childhood, and I'm sure his outstanding nasal control comes in extremely handy at ad agency parties. 'Well, it'd probably be more of a shock to her if we were all getting on like a house on fire. Eh, sis? If you can hear me, give me a dirty look like you always do . . . '

My eyes are still weighed down, but lifting them feels achievable now, somehow. I try to remember what they taught me when I joined a gym (for precisely one session). Are you meant to push on the in-breath, or the out-breath?

Pop.

The weight shifts and I feel cold air on the whites of my eyes. For a moment I can't see a thing, and just as I'm panicking that I've gone blind, my family swim before my eyes. They're bleached out at first as though I've been staring at a lightbulb, but gradually the scene settles, the colours return. Dad in his navy suit, aggressively flicking through a magazine. Timmy languid on the edge of the bed, picking at an imaginary spot of dirt on his laundry-fresh jeans. Mum, in rose-pink knitwear (I was nearly right), peering down at her hands, tightly coiled in her lap.

And Dennis in his rugby shirt and – thank God – decent cords, looking back at me, more tired than I've ever seen him, my clean-shaven boyfriend covered in whiskers that make him look like Captain Birds Eye.

'Jo?' he sounds hesitant at first and I try hard to widen my eyes in response, but I don't think it works. 'Look, her eyes. She's waking up.'

'Typical Jo,' my brother turns quickly, and his face is so uncharacteristically soft that it makes me want to cry. 'Just in time for dinner.'

I've been focusing so hard on my eyes that it's only now that I smell food.

Mum and Dad turn to stare, but already the tiredness is weighing down my eyelids and I begin to drift to a place scented with roast dinner and overcooked vegetables and overripe oranges . . .

Chapter 7
Russophobia – Fear of Russians

Gravy and bacon and the bitter scent of Brussels sprouts boiled into submission. The sickly sweetness of clove-studded oranges, already going rotten. And the farmyard tang of wet Labrador.

The perfume of Christmas at 17 Greenham Lane, Newbury. If you bottled it, you'd have to call it Eau de Desperation.

'There was no hot turkey and crackers on offer at the camp today, but the protestors, almost all of whom are women, insisted that missing out on Christmas dinner was a small price to pay.'

'Ruddy lesbians,' my father says, enjoying his outrage.

'Ted!' my mother scolds, but it's too late.

'Mummee, what's a lesbian?'

'It's another word for a kind of lady, Timmy. But not a very polite one,' Mum says, then whispers to my dad, 'Now look what you've done.'

I try to zone out. I'm sitting on the floor, leaning on the radiator, which is so hot it stings my skin, although I'm wearing a T-shirt under my new dog's-tooth batwing jumper. I trace the pattern of the carpet with my finger: thick golden rope against an emerald green background. If I focus hard enough, maybe I can forget where I am.

'The pastry's *soggy*, Mummy, I can't eat nothing *soggy*.'

'I know, darling.' Mum and Timmy are wedged together on the sofa, sharing a plate of cold sausage rolls. She begins to remove every speck of pastry so that the bare sausages resemble the babies' willies we saw in the RE module on religious rituals. Timmy won't touch them uncircumcised.

Dad is fiddling with the huge remote control for the new TV, which is his present to himself, though he claims it's 'for all the family'. It comes with a new invention, Teletext, and we're the first people in our street to get it. Dad is a bank manager, after all, so must always be one step ahead of the neighbours.

He presses some buttons and the image of tired, dirty women disappears from the screen, replaced by coloured electronic squares.

'Look, it's an advent calendar,' Dad says, before Timmy can ask about lesbians again.

It doesn't look much like an advent calendar to me. I try to decipher the picture on the screen: crude blocks of green and red in a primitive cone-shape . . . 'It's a Christmas tree!' I say, pleased I worked it out faster than my brother.

The TV sound is still playing behind the advent calendar, and a woman is being interviewed: 'We'll definitely be here past new year into 1982. We'll stay till 1992, 2002, if the world's not been blown up by then. This is deadly serious. We won't let them bring in the missiles. It's a matter of life or death.'

I realise it's the peace camp down the road at Greenham. 'Dad –' I wave my hands, trying to get him to flick back to the news.

'And look what happens when I press "reveal",' he says. The tree lights up with yellow cubes, flashing on and off like cursors on the two ZX Spectrums in the computer room at school.

'Dad, let me watch the news.'

'For God's sake, Jo, not that again. It's Christmas.'

'But it's important . . .' My news fixation is the latest

family joke; hot on the heels of my hilarious crush on the footman in *Upstairs, Downstairs*, and my craze for collecting gonks (which I now see are ugly as sin), I am officially obsessed with doom and gloom.

Mum looks up from the plate of naked sausages. 'Let her watch it, Ted.'

He sighs then points the remote at the TV. The black background disappears, but the green tree remains, like the Cheshire cat's smile, hovering over footage of enormous warheads.

'That's the mix function,' Dad explains, before pressing another button.

'Meanwhile, government ministers insist that Cruise is an essential part of allied defence strategy. They point to the situation in Afghanistan, still unresolved two years after the Russian invasion, as evidence that the threat of nuclear aggression is as acute as ever.'

'Nuclear aggression?' I feel shivery, so I push my body against the radiator, before realising I'm not really cold. I'm scared. Since Mr Blake's movie, I see flower-patterned burns whenever I close my eyes. And sometimes I dream I'm standing by that super-heated river, trying to choose whether to be roasted or boiled alive.

A look passes between my parents, a kind of shutting down, and Dad rearranges his face into the relaxed expression of Terry Wogan interviewing Shakin' Stevens, while Mum takes refuge in the kitchen.

'Load of fuss about nothing,' Dad says.

'But they said –'

'It's the news,' he insists tetchily, 'that's their job, making everything sound as bad as possible. It's not bloody *Jackanory*. They're hardly going to say, "The Ruskies are welcome to wander through some country none of us have heard of, we're all going to live happily ever after." But that's the truth, Jo. We've lived through much, much worse.'

'But . . . ' I stare at the ceiling now, counting the cracks in the Artex, knowing Dad's wrong, that this is the most dangerous time in history, but unable to find the right words to persuade him.

'But nothing . . . you need to grow up, Jelly Bean,' he says, and his voice softens as he uses my nickname. 'Having daft crazes for toys or pop stars is one thing. Even that bloody vegetarian phase was better than this. It's abnormal for a twelve-year-old to be into current affairs. No boy is ever going to fancy a girl who likes warheads, you know.'

I bite the inside of my cheek to stop myself crying from frustration. I know I should be more like Lorraine, worrying about whether it's cooler to fancy Andrew Ridgeley or George Michael. But how can I do that, when my parents have their heads buried in the sand? We're one nuclear button away from annihilation and all Dad cares about is the auditions for the Operatic Society's production of *My Fair Lady*. And all Mum cares about is Timmy.

The dog waddles in from the kitchen. She nuzzles my face with her nose and her eyes meet mine. We called her Misty because of those eyes: even though she's *only* a dog, when I look into the blackness, it makes me think of infinity, of staring into the sky and wondering what exists beyond the stars and our galaxy. I asked Dad once and he couldn't explain what was beyond infinity. Or what happens when we die. Whenever I think of either of those questions, it makes me dizzy.

'Hey, daydreamer? Wakey wakey?' It's Mum, holding out an extra large slice of chocolate yule log. 'This should take your mind off the end of the world.'

Chapter 8
Nostophobia – Fear of Returning Home

They don't know much, doctors.

After three weeks and six days in hospital, that's my staggering conclusion. Not that I remember much of the first week, except fragments of eavesdropped conversations that I shouldn't have heard (it's amazing what people say when they think you're half-dead).

Dr Williams is right about one thing: coma isn't like it is in the movies. There's been just one Tinseltown moment: my miraculous awakening after forty-nine hours of absence. I've heard four different accounts of this touching scene now, from Dennis ('I was the first one to notice you'd come round!'), from Mum ('Your eyes were shining, it was like you'd been reborn.'), from Dad ('I've got to be honest, Jelly Bean, I thought you looked like you weren't all there! Sandwich short of a picnic or something.') and from Timmy ('All very moving, but don't go getting a taste for the limelight, sis, it's not you.'). I've no way of knowing which version is nearest to the truth, but I think there's been a fair bit of rewriting history, in true Hollywood style.

The rest is pretty un-showbiz. The catheter to drain my bladder and the itching sensation I can't quite shake off although it's been gone two weeks. The bird-like legs where my plump thighs used to be. The scaly patches wherever my skin met starched NHS sheets.

My face is now the colour of those sheets. But looking on the bright side, my features are sharper, because hospital food is inedible and Dennis's food parcels – health-enhancing, will-to-live draining dinners, full of Omega-3 oils, to assist brain function – are even worse. The bruising on my face took for ever to disappear, but now all that's left is a grey shadow on my temple and, above it, a dent I can't stop touching. Oh, and a bald patch.

Yep, I have gone bald before my dad.

I've always known that the human body is vulnerable. I hadn't understood quite *how* vulnerable.

'You all set, Bean?' My father smells of cologne and wears a spiv-sharp grey suit (very *Alfie*). He takes my holdall while I carry the movie-star bouquet of pink roses and gerbera that Timmy had couriered over from his favourite Notting Hill florist yesterday. He's kept up an ambush of impressive floral arrangements in lieu of visits, and I think he forgot I was going home.

'Whatever,' I mutter. *Going home*. Nearly four weeks in hospital, yet I haven't had my kidneys removed for sale on the international organs black market. I haven't been suffocated by a murderous medic with Munchausen's. I've even escaped the superbug (well, I won't quite believe I'm out of the woods till I've checked the incubation period for MRSA on the internet).

'Shall I have them bring you a wheelchair?' Mum suggests.

'I'm perfectly *fine*. Can't you lot ever stop fussing?' I snap back, and the guilt kicks in instantly. Pills and physio sessions in the chilly hospital gym have begun to unfurl my locked limbs and restore some muscle tone, but my brain . . . let's just say I'm not myself. I seem to have developed temporary Tourette's: time after time, my mouth responds before I have time to censor it.

My parents exchange glances that say *we're lucky to have her at all* and *we need to give her time*.

They don't know the half of it. The confusion. The sentences I start and can't finish, because I lose my thread. And the flashbacks.

The only person who knows about my flashbacks is Dr Williams. I steeled myself to mention them a few days ago, when he called me in to talk about what happens when I leave hospital, i.e. what to expect from the rest of my life. Sitting in his shabby office, I felt underdressed: it's hard to pull off a grown-up conversation when you're in your nightie.

'What I really want to know is, will I ever return to *normal*?'

'Normal! Now why on earth would you want to be that?' He leaned back in his chair, feet on the desk.

I was shocked the first time I saw Dr Williams. His mellow voice suggested a beefy rugby player with a cauliflower ear. Instead he's what Lorraine would call 'a lanky streak of piss': tall and wiry, like a medical Morrissey. He has floppy brown hair and his face is a network of lines, though I'd guess he's younger than Dennis. But he also has the gentlest brown eyes I've ever seen and a sense of humour that makes brain injury seem almost bearable: no wonder the nurses swoon. The unluckiest pedestrian in Courtbridge has somehow landed the best doctor in the world.

'OK, I grant you that I probably never was all that normal in the first place. But will the moods ever go?'

'Moody's normal, too, remember. Let me find those statistics I dug out for you . . . ' He rifled through his in-tray. I told him early on that statistics make me feel better, however grim they are. I like to know what I'm up against. 'Here we are. Twelve months after a moderate head injury, forty-eight per cent of patients report problems with anxiety, pressure, depression, irritability or temper.' He paused to let this sink in.

'So I've a one in two chance of staying this way?'

'Yeah, but then again,' he turned the page, searching for another figure, ' . . . ninety-eight per cent of women without a head injury are moody.'

'You made that one up, didn't you?'

He grinned. 'I like to call it extensive field research with the female gender.'

'Can't you ever be serious?'

'In this job? No way.' He scratched his head. 'Look, Jo, I appreciate that the lack of answers is irritating.'

'You mean maddening.'

'Could we compromise on *a little trying*?'

'Absolutely totally bloody exasperating is my final offer,' I said, arms folded.

'No problem with your vocabulary, then. OK. I'll confess, I get frustrated too sometimes. But it's so fascinating: the brain is the world's last uncharted territory. My job is all cliff-hangers. Why would a blow to the head turn a sweet girl like you bad-tempered? Will the old personality ever reassert itself?' He frowned. 'Would you want it to?'

'Of course I . . . ' I stopped. There were benefits to being permitted to snarl, though I wished I could discriminate more: Dad and Timmy were definitely overdue for the odd tongue-lashing, but Mum and Dennis didn't deserve it. 'It's not just the moods.'

'Go on.'

I blushed. 'I know it sounds crazy . . . '

'Nothing you can say to me will sound crazy, Jo. I love symptoms. Clues to what's going on up here.' And he knocked his knuckles against his head.

'I keep . . . going back. In time.' I looked up, waiting for him to press the secret panic button that would summon the men in white coats.

'How far back in time, exactly?' he asked, evenly.

'Eh? I don't follow.'

'Second World War? Stone Age? I've had a few French Revolutions. Marie Antoinette's very popular with women who're fond of cake.'

'Oh.' I giggled. 'No, not like that. In my own time, my own memories . . . Things that have happened to me. Flashbacks, as though I'm back, in the past, watching myself.'

'Watching yourself? Like an out-of-body experience?'

'Sort of.' I felt relieved that he was taking me seriously. 'Not that I'd mind having that body again. Not a trace of cellulite. Didn't know I was born.' Then I blushed. He'd already seen my body, cellulite and all.

'I'll ignore that,' he says, 'though it's my duty to point out I've seen more cellulite on a supermodel. So how often do the flashbacks happen?'

'I know it's definitely happened twice, though I suppose it's possible I've forgotten some other ones. But those two flashbacks are so clear. So detailed. Flicked fringes, high-necked frilly blouses, the works.'

'Were you the same age, in the flashbacks?' He'd begun to take notes. 'And you don't have to tell me this, Jo, but were they traumatic occasions?'

'Hmmm. I was eleven, twelve. And I suppose, well, they weren't traumatic as such but . . . ' To my surprise, I realised tears were running down my face.

'But not very happy either?' he said, passing me a tissue.

'No . . . sorry.' I gulped, really crying now and feeling the pressure of more tears behind my eyes. It didn't used to hurt to cry. 'I used to feel *frightened* a lot of the time. Sounds silly, doesn't it? I mean what does a kid have to be afraid of?'

'It's OK, Jo. There's no hurry, we can take our time with this. You can make a follow-up appointment, whenever you need one.'

'I . . . Is it bad? What I've told you?'

'Not really. Everyone responds differently to head injury. An out-of-body feeling, floating above yourself, that's a commonly reported experience. Often people who've been in a coma have . . . ' he hesitated, 'what laymen call Near Death Experiences. Some surveys say it's as high as thirty-seven per cent.'

I smiled at his statistic, though my throat had tightened. 'Thanks for that.' My voice was croaky: the word death hadn't been spoken by anyone I'd met in hospital. When Mum or Dennis alluded to the times they'd been most afraid, they tended to trail off or talk in euphemisms about 'slipping away' or 'fading'. But I had the haziest memory of nurses standing at my bedside, rating my chances in more down-to-earth language.

'Typically patients imagine themselves on the cusp of this world and another.'

'Another world. Like heaven?'

'Mainly heaven, yes. Hell's not popular at all. Generally people report bright lights and clouds and soft voices behind them, offering them a choice between following the voice or returning home. Sometimes it's a river, with the patient on one bank and their loved ones across the water.'

'Sounds . . . nice. Peaceful. Trust me to get the smelly girls' loos at school.'

'I've always wondered what females talk about in the toilets.'

I ignored his distraction attempt. 'So . . . does that mean I've officially been *near death*?'

He hesitated again. 'The visions don't, in themselves. Personally I think the bright lights may be produced by coma-specific brain activity.' He took a breath. 'But you *were* near death, Jo. We don't dwell on this when patients are recovering, but as you've mentioned it, well, I wouldn't have staked my car on your chances of emerging. And *pretty much* unscathed.'

'Right.' I made no sense. The original glass-half-empty girl had a stroke of luck. Jo Morgan, ultimate scaredy-cat, an against-all-odds *survivor*?

'You're in bloody good shape, Jo. I mean it. I can see why the flashbacks are disturbing, but there were only two. Maybe you won't have any more.'

I sighed. 'There's nothing you can do to make sure?'

'We could try medication, but it'd be a sledgehammer to crack a nut. I'd pefer to let you heal in your own time. Hey, don't look so sad. Not many of us get a second go at adolescence.'

'I'd have preferred the angels and harps and flouncy nightie stuff.'

'You're a one-off, Jo. Too smart for angels and all that

bollocks,' he said, then tapped the side of his nose. 'But don't you dare tell anyone I said that. You'd get me struck off.'

If I wasn't a whey-faced invalid, I could have sworn he was flirting with me. 'I'm going to miss having you to make me feel sane,' I said. 'And safe.' That was the strangest thing about hospital: despite the monitors and the smells and the sounds, I never once felt afraid. For a while I hoped perhaps I'd put my fears behind me, that the knock on the head had turned me into a bionic woman, fearless and feisty. But as soon as I thought about life *outside*, I realised I was the same old cowardy-custard.

'Aha. That's another thing I wanted to talk to you about. It doesn't have to be goodbye . . . '

I blushed again. Surely Dr Williams wasn't going to ask me out? After he'd seen my devoted Dennis visiting me twice-daily (boring me rigid by reading out Sudoku hints, but at least he was there). 'You know I've got a boyfriend but if I didn't . . . '

He shook his head, blushing himself now. 'Oh no, no, not like that. Not that you aren't my loveliest patient, of course, but . . . I know you'll be coming in for physio and occupational therapy, but I wondered if you'd also like to come to my rehab group?'

I stared at him.

'Listen, it's a laugh. You'll love the Monday Club. Bingo. Board games. Free drinks. Well, free Ribena and decaffeinated tea, anyhow. And the best company you'll find this side of Swindon.'

'I . . . the others, are they very disabled?' I whispered the last word, already feeling guilty at my seemingly lucky escape.

'They're just *people*, Jo. Nothing to be afraid of. Maybe you'd call them . . . eccentric, some of them.' He spread his fingers. 'OK, I won't fib. Some of my patients are never going to enjoy the quality of life they had before. They can be difficult and unpredictable. But so can I. I think it could help you. Give it a go, Jo!' He winked.

I know patients always fall in love with their doctors, and

maybe I have, a little bit, with mine. So I must have said yes to keep him happy, because I don't have *any* intention of hanging out with a bunch of head-cases.

'I had to park miles away,' Dennis says, puffed from his walk. As he kisses me briefly, hot panting breaths on my neck, I remember the last time we made love. Valentine's night. Garlicky sweat forming wherever our bodies met. His weight, his passionate clumsiness, had felt as reassuring as usual. Even his slight selfishness – coming before I did, as he tends to after a few drinks – made me feel irresistible and alive. Yet hours later, I nearly wasn't alive at all.

They've told me the story now, what they know of it. I was in the wrong place at the wrong time, as a cyclist ploughed down the hill. A racing bike, a flash of Lycra (most witnesses agreed lime green, though one insisted it was more of an acid yellow), and I hit the deck, my head taking the force of the impact on the hard cobbles, my body sliding after it. The bike went down too, briefly, but its rider wasn't hanging around: as the Good Samaritans of Courtbridge came to my rescue, Lycra-man was back in the saddle and steaming off like Lance Armstrong. All he left behind was a pile of broken plastic from the light on the front of his bike.

Rubies and diamonds . . .

That's what I remember: shards of plastic in a pool of my own blood. They said it was pouring from my head, though it was only a shallow flesh wound. What was going on inside that would cause me *much* more trouble.

Eight people called an ambulance. That's the kind of place Courtbridge is. As I was being strapped onto a stretcher in case of spinal injuries, the speculation was beginning: was the cyclist blinded by sunlight? In such a state of shock that he'd fled without thinking? Or in the wrong place at the wrong time, perhaps an adulterer on his way home from a Valentine's tryst.

He still hasn't been found and the smog mask he was wearing means it's becoming less and less likely that he will.

Dennis seems more aggrieved about that than anything else, 'A smog mask? In Courtbridge? Didn't he know we've made greater strides towards improved air quality than any other local authority in the south of England?'

Apparently my case provoked endless headlines about the 'Tragic Valentine Coma Girl', 'Lycra Louts' and 'Cycle-Ogical Warfare' (nine pedestrians killed and 1000 injured by cyclists in the last five years). Dennis has saved the cuttings but I am in no hurry to read them. Yes, the bloke was stupid to run away, but I was stupid to cross the road without looking. I don't think I've ever done that before, I'm like one of those teenagers who fall pregnant the first time they have sex.

Accidents will happen. Even to me.

'You off then, Jo?' says the Sister, in that irritating way of stating the obvious that seems to pass for chit-chat on the ward. I'm sure she's the one who was writing me off when she didn't think I was listening. 'You take care of her!' she tells the others. 'She might not be so lucky next time.'

That word again. *Lucky* Jo.

Dennis cups his hand round my elbow, like a solicitous grandson leading his elderly nan across the road. 'Will you stop pawing me, please, I *can* walk on my own,' I snarl and his eyes narrow before he gives me a tight smile.

'Of course you can.' His voice is tolerant and I feel like a total bitch.

Once we're out of the ward, turning left towards the car park rather than the familiar route I've taken for weeks towards physio, I wish I hadn't been so fast to brush him off. The corridor is long and low, with lights that make my hands look like a corpse's. The smell of lukewarm beef stew and disinfectant is stronger than it ever seemed on the ward. Grey lino stretches ahead of me and it begins to swim before my eyes and I have to lean on the wall.

'You OK?' Behind me, three anxious faces are lined up, watching for the signs of mental meltdown.

'Never felt better,' I lie.

They don't look convinced. Something tells me that my accident might have turned them into scaredy-cats too.

Chapter 9
Soteriophobia – Fear of Dependence on Others

According to breakfast TV this morning, the secret of happiness is counting your blessings, ideally six a day. After two long weeks of miserable house arrest, I'm willing to try anything. So . . . blessings. Um.

Got it!

Blessing number one: we live in a bungalow.

When I announced I was moving into Dennis's place two years ago, Lorraine thought it was the funniest thing in the world: in her eyes, single-storey dwellings are strictly for the over-seventies.

The first night Dennis brought me here, after the legendary Strategic Safety Partnership Christmas dinner dance, I was unusually giggly and made some remark about how at least he'd never have to put in one of those Stannah stairlifts.

'That's why you're different, Jo,' he whispered to me, 'no one else but me has ever thought ahead like that, planning for inevitable infirmity, but *you* understand.' I was about to protest, to explain I was joking, but then he kissed me for the first time. And after that, it no longer seemed important.

Now, like the other residents of Salzburg Avenue, I'm finding our one-level living a blessing. No stairs to topple down if I have a funny turn. Who'd have guessed infirmity was so imminent?

The net curtains twitched when I came home from hospital, but now they're still again. I suppose I could try to bond with the neighbours, but my family aren't keen for me to go out on my own just yet. They've tried to lock down every moment of my day, no room for accidents. Lorraine is banned from visiting because she might over-excite me, like a toddler exposed to preservatives and trashy cartoons.

It seems strange, but I think my head injury has affected them more than me. If you are a scaredy-cat, you always expect to become a statistic one day. But they were unprepared for the worst and it's hit them hard.

Whereas in my case . . . it makes no sense at all, but now that the worst *has* happened, a newly hatched reckless streak keeps telling me, *you've beaten the odds once, Jo, maybe you could do it again. Why not take a risk or two?*

I ignore it, of course. That way madness lies.

Blessing number two: every day is a duvet day.

Though actually my life now is more timetabled than when I was twelve. At 07:00 hours, Dennis gets up, accidentally on purpose brushing against me to make sure I'm still warm to the touch. Some mornings – and I know this isn't nice – I stay still, like a child playing statues. Not because I want to frighten him but because . . . actually, I don't know why I do it. I used to be such a good girl.

07:49 Dennis leaves the house, but not before he's stood for a full minute at the foot of the bed, watching me. He doesn't say anything but I know he's there, I can hear his breathing. I became very good at reading noise in hospital: you can learn so much when you're feigning sleep. Eventually he'll lean over and plant a kiss on my lips, like the prince in the fairytale. It's a solicitous kiss, the kind you'd give a hairy-cheeked granny on visiting Sunday, when you don't know whether she'll still be there the next time you come. He hasn't kissed me *properly* since we came back from hospital.

Sometimes I wonder if he ever will again.

08:30 The phone will ring: either my mother or my father at the other end. I daren't ignore it as that would cause a

110mph Berkshire–Wiltshire mercy dash. Dad drives like he's in *The Italian Job* under normal circumstances and he can't afford any more penalty points on his licence.

I prefer it when Dad rings. I always answer with the sprightliness of an actress in a cereal commercial. He'll ask how I am and I will say I feel great. He'll give me a weather report from the electronic monitoring station in his shed, along with an account of what the pretty weather woman on *Breakfast News* was wearing. Then, occasionally, he'll forget to put my mother on and hang up and *then* I can ignore the phone because I can pretend I was in the shower.

Of course, four out of five times it's Mum on the line, her hesitant voice expecting the worst.

I crank up the *joie de vivre*, in the hope that they might decide to leave me alone for *one bloody day* but it never happens. Tuesdays and Thursdays are unavoidable, because I need ferrying to physio and occupational therapy sessions and, of course, I can't drive since my injury. But on the other days, her excuses are increasingly imaginative. 'I need some upholstery fabric I can only get from that lovely shop near you,' she'll say, though she's shown no previous interest in soft furnishings. Or, 'the cats need their space', which is equally unconvincing, as she mollycoddles them more than she ever did Timmy.

08:45 I shower. The best time of day. When I first came home, I was terrified of getting my head wet (in hospital I'd survived on strip washes and the occasional excruciating bathtime supervised by a nurse) so for four days I pretended to shower, running the water, and splashing shower gel around so the room smelled Ocean Fresh.

I did this until I realised I was no longer smelling Ocean Fresh myself and my latest craziness was bound to be discovered. I looked up phobias on the internet and found a site saying that if you sing at the top of your voice whenever you're terrified, it blocks the bit of the brain that produces fear and – three verses and choruses of 'My Favourite Things' later – I was clean.

Now I look forward to the only moment in my day when I can guarante to be alone. And I sing my little heart out, adding rude words as I go . . .

'When the bike hits, when my head splits, when I'm feeling shit . . . I simply remember the booze and the fags, And then I feel less of a tit!'

09:00 Breakfast. The accident's taken away my appetite, but I force something down before Mum arrives, otherwise she'll insist on watching me eat, mumbling, 'Oh, you must have more, Jo. Keep your strength up,' as I struggle to swallow a few mouthfuls. Things don't taste the same; I used to hate coffee, but now I crave it, because the bitterness masks the tinfoil-flavoured jam on my cardboard toast. Not that I'm allowed the real thing, of course: Dennis thinks I haven't noticed that he's swapped our normal brand for the organic fairly traded, single bean, decaffeinated variety (the caffeine removed by the water method, rather than noxious chemicals, of course).

10:00 Typically, Mum, Dad or, worst-case scenario, both, will arrive just after the Courtbridge bustle hour is over. If there's an OT or physio sesion, then it's easy: I zone out of Mum's chatter on the way there, and on the way back I pretend to sleep again, as a result of all of my 'hard work' in the therapy room.

In truth, it's a doddle. The OT woman who did my assessments seemed almost disappointed at my competence. Of course, I didn't tell her about my showerphobia, because I knew she'd adopt this caring-sharing Cabbage Patch Doll expression, tell me it's normal and then try to 'devise some strategies for adapting and managing the challenge'.

I don't want to adapt! I don't want to manage the challenge – we're talking about a bloody shower, not climbing Everest.

I did try to convince her that there must be *truly* sick people who were more deserving of her valuable time. And she smiled at me, oh so bloody patiently, and told me that, 'Physical progress is certainly easier to map, but the mind needs time to heal, too.'

'I don't see why,' I whined, 'everyone says I've been so lucky.'

'Well, that's great,' she said, still saintly. 'And are you feeling lucky?'

It was strange, but when she said that, I was hit by this awful urge to wail. Not a delicate dab at the eyes with a tissue, but a full-on, ear-busting wail that would echo through the clinic. Hoping she wouldn't notice my eyes bulging with kept-back tears, I managed to say, 'Of course. I had a miraculous recovery.'

She didn't smile that time. Instead she said, 'Yes. You have done well. But what looks like a miracle from the outside doesn't always feel like one on the inside, Joanna.'

I pouted. 'It's not Joanna, it's Jo.'

Physio's easier. The woman knows I don't want chit-chat, and I'll let her know if anything hurts. I'm a good girl, I do my exercises, and I can see I'm getting stronger. Sit-ups haven't put any hairs on my bald patch, though.

Blessing number three: my newly toned thighs now fit into size ten jeans.

13:00 Lunchtime. *Bad* time. It's like being three years old, except I don't have a highchair. And if they did them in my size, I'm sure Mum would have bought one. She tries so hard to pretend we're haivng a 'girls' lunch' (though we never had them before), or that she's 'dying to try this recipe', but we both know that there's only one objective, and that's to get me to consume calories, preferably wholemeal organic ones but, failing that, empty calories will do. Even Dad's in on the act. He takes me to non-smoking gastro pubs and orders real ale that he forgets to drink because he's too busy monitoring what I leave on my plate.

14:30 Afternoons are the worst. No comedy emails doing the rounds in the office, no nodding off at your keyboard when no one's looking. I suppose it'll be different when I go back. *If* I go back. No one's talked dates yet. I'll need a medical and there'll doubtless be more counselling than was offered to an entire battalion of shell-shocked Second World

War veterans. 'But don't worry about rushing back, we'll muddle by without you,' Dennis says, which is a nice way of saying, 'your job is so inconsequential that it barely matters whether you're there or not'.

Usually I sit in the living-room, playing Monopoly or Cluedo with my parents. Mum never suggests Scrabble, because she's read all the booklets, and knows brain-injured patients sometimes have trouble with words and self-expression.

Last week, she arrived with a carrier bag full of crusts.

'You're not *seriously* going to suggest we feed the ducks, are you, Mother?'

She blushed. 'I thought it would be nice to get out of the house. Fresh air.'

'I am not a *bloody toddler*, Mother. I had *an accident.*' I jabbed my finger in her face and the more she recoiled, the louder my voice grew. 'I haven't entered my *second childhood.* And the last thing I want in the whole bloody world is to *feed the bloody ducks! I hate ducks. Creepy fat buggers!*'

Blessing number four: evidently I'm not having too much trouble with self-expression.

I felt so guilty afterwards that I threw everything I had into feeding those lucky ducks, for her sake. I stood at the edge of the pond, a giant among small children in Boden rainwear, trying to make sure every bird, regardless of size, had at least one crust. I engaged in sophisticated decoy activity to stop the geese demanding bread with menaces from the moorhens. I grinned manically at Mum, pretending I was enjoying myself and, after a while, I almost was.

'Where's *your* child?' A small boy in crocodile wellies, who had tired of kicking water at his younger brother, poked me in the knee.

'She must have swum off,' I said, without thinking. The boy stared harder.

'I didn't see anyone swimming,' he mumbled. 'I'm not *stupid.*'

'She's awfully fast,' I told him. 'And she has her own diving suit, so she can stay underwater for ages and ages.'

He began to back away from me. '*Not* true.'

'And then, right at the last minute she will jump up out of the water, grab any boys wearing crocodile wellies – which she hates – and push them over, head first, into the mud. And then the ducks will peck at them. Quack, quack! Quack, quack!'

He ran off so fast that he tripped over his own feet and for a moment, I felt terrible. At least the wet earth made for a soft landing. I heard him whispering to his mother, but she ignored him, irritated at having to abandon her gossip and take him home to change.

I couldn't stop quacking under my breath all the way home. If Mum noticed – and I can't see how she wouldn't have – then she was discreet enough not to say anything.

Blessing number five: these days, I can get away with anything.

16:20 Peace. Mum doesn't like driving in traffic, so she leaves after *Countdown*, urging me to get some sleep, as Dr Williams insisted it was *the* most important factor in my recovery. I comfort myself with the knowledge that, according to statistics, 4.20 p.m. is *the* peak time for nervous breakdowns in the UK. Although of all the figures I've researched in my time, this is the one I find hardest to believe. Surely it's the wind-down time of day: only an hour or so before you and your neuroses can skip off home to hit the bottle or watch snuff movies or whatever keeps you sane. 4.20 p.m. is when I'd most like to be back at work. Our office was directly above the canteen, so our afternoons were punctuated by the sounds and smells of institutional catering: the clattering and sloshing of the post-lunch clear-up, followed by the first sensory clues in our daily guessing game: what was Bella, the canteen's expert baker, making for tea? If it was lemon drizzle cake (my favourite), the acidic citrus aroma always gave the game away early, as Bella and her ladies pulverised enough fruit to satisfy 400 hungry council staff.

But most of the other bakes began with a vague, warm waft of sugar and butter and flour, before one of us took a first wild guess. *Macaroons!* No, no, caramel crunch, I can smell burned sugar. *Aha but how do you know that isn't just one of the cakes left in the oven too long?*

No sugar-loaded cake for me at home, though. Just one hundred minutes of surfing the net for weird statistics (well, it passes the time) before . . .

18:00 Dennis returns. I usually spray on some perfume and apply lipstick, in the manner of a 1950s' housewife (amount of lipstick consumed by average woman in a lifetime: six pounds). But he never notices; instead, he inspects me for *symptoms*. He works his way down my body, checking for twitching or odd rashes or tremors or paralysis. Then he instigates some pointless conversation and I can tell he's not listening to my words, but to my speech. Am I slurring? The lights are on, but is anybody home?

He used to eye up my body like a hungry wolf about to devour me. Now he's like an anxious farmer, convinced his prize cow is about to succumb to a bout of foot-and-mouth.

I told him exactly that last week.

'Don't be so daft, Jo. What a stupid thing to say.'

'I've watched *All Creatures Great and Small*, Dennis. I've seen the look on Christopher Timothy's face just before he went to his car to fetch the shotgun.'

'Oh for God's sake! If I'm getting a shotgun it'll be to shoot myself,' he said, storming out. But within a few seconds he was back, that social-worker expression on his face. 'Let's sit down, Jo,' he said, and led me gently towards the sofa.

'I *can* manage!'

'Yes, yes, you can, I know that,' he soothed. 'And I'm sorry for being short-tempered with you. This isn't your fault. It's what they said might happen.'

'What is?' I hissed back.

'Well . . . ' he pulled on his kiss-curl, 'the irritability. The irrational thoughts. It's all to be expected and sometimes I forget that. The report I read in *BMJ Online* said that both patients and relatives underestimate the time it takes for the brain to heal fully.'

'Fucking hell!' I shouted, and it felt good, so I shouted it again.

'*Please*, Jo. The neighbours.' He placed a firm hand on my arm.

'Sod the sodding neighbours. They'll understand. Of course they will, because everybody bloody sodding fucking understands, don't they? I don't want to be sodding understood! I want to be normal!'

And then I did the worst thing possible. I burst into tears. Instantly Dennis switched back into sympathy mode, all soft murmurs and strokes to the head, like you'd comfort a baby, and half of me wanted to wriggle out of his arms, but the other half made me bury my face in the long-hard-day-at-the-office crumples of his shirt, sobbing until he was soaked to the skin.

'There there, Jo Jo,' he repeated over and over, until the words no longer made sense. 'It's all going to be all right.'

That night, I fell asleep there, in his arms, and only woke up when he was putting me to bed.

I seem to be short of a sixth blessing. But all I need to do is remember the figures Dr Williams gave me: fewer than fifty per cent of people who've been in a coma survive. I might be a bit eccentric, but I'm alive . . . even a scaredy-cat can see that blessings don't get much bigger than that.

Chapter 10

Phengophobia – Fear of Daylight or Sunshine

Today, Mum's call never came. I waited by the hall table (Dennis is not a fan of cordless handsets, due to the potential health risk of all those signals bouncing round the house), willing the phone to ring, so I could get on. Not that I really have anything to get on *with*, but even so . . .

I amused myself by flicking through the *Civil Protection Chronicle*. I'd got all the way to the classifieds – some poor bloke is trying to flog a load of Cold War era prefabricated fall-out shelters, suggesting they're 'ideal for storage or as a den for children and stressed-out dads' – and Mum still hadn't rung. 08.51. My body felt itchy because my shower was overdue.

I made myself a cup of tea. It's the key task the occupational therapy woman asked me to perform on the first session, and now I wonder if I made some basic error that proved I required months of intensive rehab. Did I put the milk in before the water? I could never remember the 'right' order *before* the accident. Though, uselessly, I have no problem remembering that thirty-seven people a year are injured by tea cosies.

09.04 and I was starting to panic, which couldn't be good for my neurological health. My imagination, fired up by tannin, pictured Mum and Dad suffocated in their beds by the over-affectionate Maine Coons. Or murdered by one of Dad's many bits on the side: beaten with a putter by Mindy the golf club receptionist, or snipped to death by Savannah from the salon.

09:12. I was about to call Dennis in a panic when the phone *did* ring.

'What time do you call this?' I said.

'Oh, Jo,' Mum said feebly, 'we've come down with a bug.'

'Bug?' I computed the implications of this sentence. If the bug was bad enough to interfere with phone-call timings, surely a half-hour car journey was out of the question.

'Only a twenty-four-hour thing, I'm sure. We've certainly had a good clear-out, if you know what I mean.'

'Yes, thanks, Mum –'

'It's been both ends at the same time, half the night. Your father took the en suite, of course, so I've been on my knees in the main bathroom, and he never did get round to fixing the radiator in there. I've nothing but bile left, now, I swear, but still it keeps on coming.'

'Right. Thanks. Really wanted to know that. Have you taken a pill to stop it?'

'No, let it all out, is what I say. But it does mean . . . Jo, I can't see how we can possibly come over.'

'Ah. No, I understand. I'm sure I'll cope,' I said, trying to sound sad.

'Why don't I ring Dennis? Couldn't he work from home?'

'I'm a grown woman, Mum. I can be left Home Alone for a few hours without burning the house down or having a wild party.'

'Hmmm.' She sounded doubtful.

'Anyway, Dennis is on a Nuclear, Biological and Chemical Threats awayday at a five-star hotel in Hampshire,' I said. It was only a little white lie. 'I can't interrupt that. It could put everyone in Courtbridge at risk.'

'I suppose so. And you'll definitely be OK?' There was an urgency in her voice now that suggested she needed to bring our chat to a swift conclusion.

'Yes, Mum. Now why don't you ring off now? Don't you have an appointment with the big white telephone?'

'The big white . . . ? Oh, I see what you mean. Yes. In fact, now you mention it . . . bye, Jo. Ring later, I promise.' And she hung up.

I walked into the kitchen and peered out at the daffodil-filled garden, which seemed, like the day ahead, to shimmer with freedom and opportunity.

But the shimmer was a mirage. So far I've made and consumed three teas and two decaff coffees; polished off an entire packet of plain chocolate digestives; and watched several makeover shows and a schools programme about the fight or flight response.

I've also answered the phone to three cold-callers and had fascinating chats about no-step bath cubicles, panic buttons mounted on a tasteful necklace that will give me the confidence to live independently for longer, and the free Scandinavian cruise I've won (all they need from me is my credit card number).

As I don't have a card – the woman from the cruise company couldn't believe I survive without one – I then went on to Dennis's laptop and applied for one. Well, more than one. Six, actually. It's all very well for him to say that credit is the last resort of the financially incontinent but as my jailers, sorry, parents, haven't been dishing out pocket money, I don't have much alternative.

I also sent some emails to the sites run by personal injury solicitors, after the woman from the panic button company mentioned that I could probably get compensation for my accident (I'd told her all about it and she'd ooohed very gratifyingly in all the right places). I wasn't sure, what with it being a hit-and-run, but she thought it was worth a go.

But I haven't gone outside.

My courage failed me. It's been seven weeks since I went anywhere on my own, and though I loathe being watched all the time, *out there* now seems impossibly dangerous ... So much for the new adventurous me.

I've moved the net curtain aside in the lounge so I can watch the comings and goings in Salzburg Avenue, logically the most unthreatening 'outside' in the world. A tortoiseshell cat lies in the middle of the road, its body splayed out to capture as many rays of weak April sunshine as possible. A turquoise blur whizzes past the window – it's the woman opposite, a retired whirlwind who lives with her sister. Today she's been jogging: as she turns up her path, her tight-fitting vest top has rings of sweat around the armpits. The cat, intimidated by her sense of purpose, lolls away.

After that flurry of activity, nothing happens. Not a single car enters the cul-de-sac. The postman and milkman have already delivered. There's no breeze so even the leaves on the trees are motionless.

Still life.

Oh dear. I'm Sleeping Beauty, trapped in Dennis's bungalow for ever. In the kitchen, making myself yet another cup of tea, I remember Dr Williams' club. He's written to me since I was discharged, reminding me of the times and dates, but I threw the letter in the bin. It's bad enough being an invalid without sitting around drinking endless cups of tea and achieving nothing.

Oh.

The heavy panting of a diesel engine breaks the hush. I cradle my hot mug and tiptoe back into the lounge, which has gone quite dark. A dirty great lorry is parked right outside.

What starts as a niggle about the way it's reduced my right to sunlight turns rapidly into full-blown irritation, and I fly out of the front door in my bare feet to give the driver a piece of my mind. Only when I get out there do I notice the lettering on the side of the lorry, 'Courtbridge District Council Neighbourhood Cultural Resource – Working for U, with U and in UR Community.'

It takes me a moment to realise that this is the mobile library. And one more moment to feel the cold on my soles, and remember I don't like *outside*. Just as I turn to go back inside, the little door on the side of the truck opens, and a stout woman in a gaping red wrap-dress pokes her head out.

'Oooh, a non-member!' she cries. 'Can I sign you up?'

'No, you're all right,' I say without slowing down, 'I thought you might have been delivering something.'

'But we are! We're delivering cultural resources, the joy of learning and some surprisingly explicit romantic novels!' She's out of the truck now and heading towards me.

'I'm not much of a reader, to be honest.'

'Oh, go on! I get brownie points for signing people up, especially if they're from a disadvantaged group. Are you?'

'I don't think so.'

'Didn't think so. Shame. What about kiddies?' Her smile, I notice, is on the hungry side.

'Nope.'

'Disability?'

I glare at her. 'Don't you think it's rather intrusive to ask all these questions?'

She narrows her eyes. 'Sorry . . . It's ME isn't it? I can always spot it. I've got a great title on alternative remedies come back in. Woman in Venice Grove had the book for a fortnight, could barely get out of her bed except to see me, and since she's been growing her own wheatgrass, she's training for a half-marathon.'

'I don't have ME.'

'But by the look of things, you don't have much to do either. And you really ought to put something on your feet, at least,' she says, and this time she's got a point. Bare feet, uncombed hair, unironed clothes. 'Listen, why don't you sign up anyway, see if there's anything you fancy? That way I get those brownie points, and I promise I'll leave you alone after that.'

I can tell she's not giving up. 'All right. I'll join. Let me get something on my feet.'

By the time I comb my hair and force my feet into some old

trainers, the library has filled up. Not that it takes much. The pushy librarian, whose name is Penny, only just fits into the narrow aisle running the length of the truck, so the decision to move from Sci-Fi to Misery Memoir is not one to be taken lightly.

'Got a great one in,' Penny calls across to a very elderly woman who is browsing the Noir Crime shelf, her neck sunken into her shoulders. 'Woman was born in Stoke-on-Trent, sold as a sex slave to a Russian mafia boss and now runs her own porn studio in California. Won the Godalming Book Club's best non-fiction of the year.'

'Lovely,' says the woman, reaching out a gnarled hand to take the book for a closer look.

'Not a word of it's true, but that's never bothered anyone,' Penny whispers to me. 'Now then, what do you fancy? Nice bit of fluffy chick lit, take your mind off your troubles?'

'What troubles?' I snarl back.

'Now, now, don't fret. Mrs Hastings here –' she nods at the hunchback – 'was telling me all about your accident. Goodness me, you could write a book yourself. Miraculous recoveries always go down well. Though you do still look a bit peaky.'

I frown at the old woman in the corner. How the hell does she know about the accident? Must have read about me in the paper, I suppose.

'What about this one?' Penny continues, '"Fifi's life as a PA to dashing concert pianist Christophe is every girl's dream – until she's accused of stealing his earnings. Left with only the Manolos she stands up in, Fifi must clear her name and try to win the heart of her man in a million".'

'I'd rather read the phone book.' It's very hot in the library now; the tiny windows above the tall bookshelves barely let in any light.

'Yes, it does sound awful, doesn't it? All those books with pink covers, I'm sure they're written by trained monkeys. What about something a bit heavyweight then? This one's surprisingly interesting: *Greased Lightning: How Lard Changed the World*.'

She holds out the book and her perfume hits me: a Gothic scent like tropical flowers dying in a cave, blending with the musty smell of books that have been pored over by thousands of sweaty fingers.

'I'm sorry but I feel a bit . . . '

I'm swaying and it feels as though the shelves are going to topple on top of me, like Alice, and then . . .

Chapter 11
Bibliophobia – Fear of Books

'I heard . . . ' the girl behind the counter lowers her voice, 'that they're testing them for the bubonic plague.'

'Never!'

The queue isn't moving and I look nervously over at Dad and Timmy, in the corner of the library that's reserved for Little Readers (or Little Bleeders as my father calls them). Dad's chatting to Charmaine from the Operatic Society, and she's giggling a lot as usual, flicking her stupid ginger hair.

Every Saturday, Mum does the washing, while Dad drags Timmy and me round town to do the shopping. The library is always the last stop before we go home to spend the evening working out Ted Rogers' stupid clues on *3-2-1*, and inventing disgusting new fillings for our Breville Cut 'n' Seal sandwich toaster.

Timmy is sitting in the corner with a stack of Smurf cartoon books and 'practical jokes to play on your big sister' manuals, while Charmaine's five-year-old daughter Crystal stares at him as though he's the most beautiful person on the planet. He ignores her completely.

I always hide in the Teen Fiction section. I won't be a teen for six more months, but I've had it with stories about ballet and ponies. I like proper novels, about hostage-taking and weird ageing diseases that wipe out the entire population except a couple of fourteen-year-olds who will snog on the last page. The girl who stamps the books is only sixteen herself and recommends the gorier ones, turning a blind eye to the age limit.

'It's *true*. It's because the women are so filthy. Did you know it's apparently against their feminist rules to actually wash?' She flicks back her Lady Di fringe in disgust. She's getting into her stride now and showing no sign at all of stamping the borrower's Jilly Coopers.

I wish she'd hurry up. Today my illicit borrowing is riskier, because between my Robert Cormier and my John Wyndham, I have three adult books. And even if she lets me take them out on a child's ticket, I need her to do it before Dad comes over because he definitely won't let me borrow these.

'I didn't know they had a set of camp rules,' says the Jilly Cooper reader. 'My Tony was thrilled to bits when they arrested some of them the other day. Send 'em to bloody Russia, see how they like it in the salt mines, that's what he says.'

You can't go anywhere in Newbury these days without *Them Women* coming up in conversation. No one sticks up for them, even though they're the most exciting thing to happen round here since I was born. They've been here seven months now and there's no sign of them leaving.

'Russia wouldn't have 'em,' the girl says, finally lining up the books. 'Because they're smelly –' stamp '– weirdo –' stamp '– perverts!' Stamp. 'There you go. Oh, I like that one. I swear it's the raunchiest one of hers I've read.'

The borrower leaves happily, anticipating a night of posh rumpy-pumpy. I approach the counter nonchalantly, checking that Dad and Charmaine are still lost in discussion about their roles in *My Fair Lady*, before I hand over my five choices. She stamps the Cormier, then stops.

'Oh, now, *Joanna*,' she says disapprovingly. 'What do you think you're doing with these?'

I blush. 'I'm doing some research. For school.'

'Come on. We never did this at school and I'm not that much older than you.'

'Well, we do. You were never in Mr Blake's class, were you?'

'*Flaky* Blake? Well, that makes more sense. But you know I shouldn't let you take them out on these,' she says, holding up my five green tickets, which mark my subhuman status as a child borrower.

I can hear the weary rumble of my father's voice from the kiddy corner: he's tugging at my brother's arm. 'Time to go, Timmy.'

'*Please*,' I beg the girl. 'I can read them in a week, and I'll make sure I return them back to you next Saturday, then no one else needs to know. It's *important*.'

She folds her arms across her large chest. 'I don't get it, I really don't. Rude books I understand. I learned everything I know from novels.'

There's a howl from the corner. Timmy! My brother's always threatening tears, but rarely lets himself cry in public. Everyone in the library, including Counter Girl, looks up.

At first I wonder if he's play-acting to get noticed, but the howling continues and my father's face is white.

'Can anyone . . . is there anyone who can . . . ' his voice gets louder and louder, as the head librarian races over from Large Print Historical Fiction. She's followed rapidly by Counter Girl, who can't resist a drama.

I seize my chance, scooping all my books into my carrier bag. The Cormier, the Wyndham, *Effects of Radiation on the Human Body*, *Cold War Targets in Western Europe*, and *Home Sweet Home: Fall-Out Shelters for the Armageddon Age*. If no one else will take the threat seriously, it's down to me to save our lives.

Holding the bag behind me, so Counter Girl doesn't notice, I jostle my way to the front of the crowd surrounding Timmy. 'That's my brother, let me through.'

When I get there, I wish I hadn't. Charmaine is quite pale,

despite her mustard-coloured instant tan, and Dad seems paralysed, his mouth wide open in shock. And Timmy . . .

The first thing I notice is the blood streaming from his nose. Then the tears that are tumbling down, diluting the shockingly red blood that covers his face. And his Muppets T-shirt. And a section of the space rocket patterned carpet.

He's had nosebleeds before – I'm sure he can bring them on, to get attention – but this is different. It's not stopping. If he carries on like this, he'll run out of blood. And human beings can't survive without blood.

Much as I hate my brother, I don't want him to die . . .

The head librarian swings into action now, pouncing on Timmy's nostrils and pinning them together, despite my brother's howls. 'Will you all move away from the boy, this isn't story-time,' she barks at the onlookers. Then she turns to Counter Girl, 'And Jessica, stop gawping for once in your life, and call an ambulance.'

Chapter 12

Xenophobia – Fear of Strangers or Foreigners

Dr Williams couldn't quite keep the satisfaction out of his voice when I rang.

'Oh, that's excellent. I knew you'd come round in the end.'

'I've only said I'll give it a try. Once,' I said.

'Once tried, never bettered.' I pictured his sharp smile. 'So what made you think again?'

'I suppose . . . ' I hesitated, unsure how much to reveal about my current state of mind, 'I'm surrounded by people who want to help but it feels more like being under surveillance. I thought strangers might be more laid-back company.'

'My bunch are so laid back they're almost horizontal,' he said. 'And how are you feeling generally?'

'Better,' I lied. Well, it's only a half-lie: physically I am better, in fact probably in better shape than I was before, thanks to all the exercises. But I don't mention the peculiar incident in the mobile library van, that horrible tiredness that took me back to 1982 again. Or the fact that Dennis has begun to ask questions about the avalanche of junk mail offering free holidays, free money and very expensive medical appliances, that followed my web surfing and heart-to-hearts with friendly cold-callers. Or the split personality that I've developed, which means *I want to be alone*, but get totally wobbly as soon as I am left to my own devices.

'So will you be bringing anyone with you? Only, if it helps, you can tell them that it's doctor's orders that you come alone. Part of the rehabilitation process, step towards independent living, blah blah blah.'

How did he know? 'That does help,' I said, feeling an unfamiliar bubbling sensation in my stomach, and then remembering that this is what it's like when you have something to look forward to.

Of course, the excitement doesn't last. In fact, by the time Mum drops me off outside the hospital gates, I feel more like a shy four-year-old about to start school. And on that particular occasion, I wet my knickers before I made it into the classroom.

'I'll be back at one,' Mum says bravely. 'Have a lovely time.'

She's wrapped me up warm against sharp April winds; I'm almost disappointed she hasn't also given me a ham sandwich and a Kia-Ora. At least clutching a packed lunch would give me something to do with my hands. But head injury patients travel light: my mother wouldn't trust me with house keys, and like the Queen, I don't carry cash.

I walk through the grounds, past the redbrick Victorian ward block, past the physio and OT departments, past the brand new buttercup-yellow maternity unit, past A&E. I pass a woman in a wheelchair, snoring in her sleep as an orderly pushes her across the lumpy concrete. Then there's a man so old his clothes look fossilised, and a flushed young girl whose belly is so extended I don't know how she stays upright.

This is *my* world now. At least the pregnant girl is only a temporary member of the In-Firm, but the rest of us are going nowhere fast. Or, very slowly, in the case of the fossilised man.

I follow the signs for Brain Injury Rehabilitation: through the car park, behind ENT and Ophthalmology, past the wheelchair repair centre, and there it is. Tucked away, as if the hospital authorities are ashamed of it. Even the building looks apologetic, a slumped hut, with a balding felt roof and pock-marked pebbledash walls.

It's not quite 10.30, and I don't want to be the first in, so I take my mobile out of my pocket, to make it look as if I have a life. The phone is the only valuable Mum lets me carry, and then only because she fears I will collapse somewhere. She even conquered her lifelong technophobia to program in an ICE 'In Case of Emergency' number so that kindly strangers can give her a tinkle if further disasters befall me.

I text Lorraine, 'AM ABOUT TO ENTER LION'S DEN. WISH ME LUCK.'

She's still banned from Salzburg Avenue, which I suspect suits her just fine. And the sad truth is that her phone calls exhaust me, making me dizzy with gossip and overly gory details of her recent deliveries.

She responds straight away, 'U R THE SEXIEST, BRIGHTEST HEAD-CASE I NO. STAY COOL.'

I smile, despite the complete uselessness of her advice. But 'Head-case'? I quite like that. Makes me sound wilder, more rebellious than before: the girl who beat the odds.

'Now you *are* a vision in blue jeans.'

I look around for the source of the poshest voice I have ever heard, richer than treacle tart.

At first, all I can see is a cloud of cigar smoke, condensing thickly in the cold spring air. Then a pocket of clear air appears, revealing a racing-green tweed jacket . . . then a pink shirt . . . a purple Paisley cravat . . . a lizardy neck and, finally, a pink wrinkled face with grey eyes so bright I instantly know they've seen more than I might in ten lifetimes.

He's leaning on the bicycle rack. A slow, confident smile lifts first his lips and then multiple folds in his cheeks, a concertina of skin folding all the way up to his eyes, like a fancy Austrian blind. On top of his head are vanilla-ice-cream-coloured curls. He takes another puff of his cigar before he speaks again.

'Did I startle you?'

'No. Not really.'

He smiles again, raising an eyebrow. 'Shame. You look a little startled. And, you know, when you're my age, being able to surprise a beautiful young woman really would be something to celebrate.'

I manage an embarrassed laugh. The smoke dissipates again and I dare to look more closely at his face, to attempt to carbon-date this strange figure. He's short – no more than five foot eight or nine – but not stooped. The hands that hold the cigar are mottled yet powerful, but when I catch a glimpse of the palms, they're scarred, the colour of farmed salmon.

I have never seen anyone like him before.

He takes a step forward, politely transferring the cigar to his left hand and moving it behind his back. 'I'm Roger. But everyone calls me Frisky.'

'Right,' I say, pulling a face before I can stop myself.

He shrugs. 'I *know*. The nickname seemed appropriate when I was a young man but it's faintly grotesque on a wrinkly old bugger. The trouble is, I'm rather too used to it now to change back.'

'I didn't mean . . . '

'Oh, my dear, I know you didn't. You seem a very well-brought-up young lady. Although there is *one* thing.'

'What?'

'It is customary to return the favour when a stranger offers his name.'

'Sorry. I forgot. I'm Joanna Morgan. Jo.'

He holds out his hand to shake mine and I avert my eyes: the texture of his palm is like Barbie doll plastic. He looks unimpressed at the weakness of my handshake and I sense he's already bored.

'And you're . . . don't tell me, let me guess. A *social* worker?' He bares his teeth – so shiny-white and straight, they must be false – in a sneer.

'God, no.'

'A volunteer?' This is said with less contempt.

I blush. 'No. I'm a patient.'

His eyes narrow in surprise and then he beams again. '*Really*. Oh, excellent news. About time we had a little feminine influence at the Monday Club. You know,' he whispers now, letting me in on a secret, 'the trouble with the bloody brain injured is they tend to be male and distinctly oafish, because it's mainly men who are daft enough to end up with a blow to the head. What a refreshing change it will be to have a young *lady* in our midst.'

I flinch at the implication that only stupid people end up here. 'I'm coming to try it out, that's all.'

His face softens now and those eyes, again, draw me in. Looking into them makes me feel understood, somehow. 'Oh, that's what everyone says, Joanna. But you know, there's a camaraderie among head-bangers that can prove a hard habit to break.'

'Head-bangers? Isn't that a bit offensive?'

'What would you prefer? Brain injured sounds rather feeble. Without being too presumptuous, Joanna, would I be right in assuming you're new to all this?'

'Yes. It was only two months ago.'

'Right. Well, what the doctors don't tell you – even our lovely Dr Williams, who's a pretty decent sort – is that you're in a different world now. One where we tend to be direct. Speak our minds. It saves time, which is what some of us are short of.'

I nod, feeling still more terrified of the people I'm about to meet. I'm tempted to run away, except I'm pretty sure this Frisky would come after me. 'I have felt *odd* since it happened.'

'Well, compared to the rest of them, you look *smashing*, if I might say so, Joanna Morgan.' He takes a drag on the cigar, the end burning red, then orange, before producing a perfect smoke ring.

'Take no notice of this miscreant! Whatever he's said it's an outrageous lie.'

'Dr Williams!' I'd recognise his warm voice anywhere. 'Actually, he was singing your praises.'

I turn to see him; he's in 'civvies' – a black shirt and skinny jeans that make him look more like Morrissey. Outside the ward, it's easier to see that he's *very* cute.

'Jo! I am so pleased you made it. So what's the Air Vice-Marshal been telling you then?'

I turn back to Frisky. 'Air Vice-Marshal?'

He blows away the last of the smoke and raises his eyebrows. 'My dear, take no notice of our Welsh friend. Young people today have no concept of military ranks. A few dogfights, half a century ago, that's all.'

Dr Williams winks at me. 'A few dogfights? Not what I've heard, Frisky. And not like you to indulge in false modesty, especially when there's a lady present.'

Frisky steps alongside me and touches my arm, to guide me towards the door. 'Lady? Joanna isn't a lady. She's *one of us*.'

And, as I let myself be led up the rickety steps into the rehab unit, the words repeat in my head. One of us. *One of us*.

I never thought I'd be so pleased to be labelled a head-banger.

Dr Williams unlocks the door and switches on a bank of strip lights, which flicker alarmingly. Aren't flickering lights meant to trigger fits? Not advisable in a room full of the brain injured.

The hut is ninety-nine per cent youth club, one per cent family planning clinic. There's a game of table football, a dartboard (with Velcro darts, of course, no sharp edges allowed), piles of car and motorcycle magazines and a set of foam easy chairs coated in a livid green and black print. An ancient coffee machine in the corner, one of those that also offers soup and squash so that each drink tastes more of the previous one than the flavour you asked for. Plus orange plastic stacking chairs, wood-effect laminate tables, and a tall bookcase stacked with battered boxes of Monopoly, Mouse-trap and Operation. I know already each one of them will have some vital piece missing that renders the entire game redundant. Still, it's not the winning, eh?

But the rack of books and leaflets on the wall isn't fun and games. *Why Did I Have a Stroke?* nestles next to *What to Expect after Brain Injury*.

Dr Williams looks at me anxiously. 'Now I know it doesn't look much . . . '

'Oh, it looks *fun*, doctor,' I insist. And it definitely beats Salzburg Avenue.

'You're not still calling him doctor?' Frisky says scornfully. 'Everyone is equal at the Monday Club.'

Dr Williams' face flushes, redness spreading from his neck through his cheeks. 'Well, yes, that is the whole idea. That there's no hierarchy. No experts.' He holds out his hand. 'So, in the spirit of the club, I'm Nathan.' And he blushes more deeply.

'Hello, Nathan,' I say and I find myself blushing too at the strangeness of saying his name.

Frisky sighs. 'Don't mind me. I feel like an extra in *Dr Kildare*.'

Dr Williams – Nathan – steps away quickly and switches on the radio, Classic FM, which is presumably the station of choice for patients with dodgy brains. Motorhead would be asking for trouble. The strip lights have stopped flickering, but the string quartet doesn't quite mask the hum from the bulbs.

I sit down on one of the spongy chairs. 'So what *exactly* happens at the club?'

'Well, if you get here early, *Nathan*' – Frisky says the name in a slightly mocking tone – 'will treat you to one of his *special* coffees, reserved for those of us he thinks are able to handle the neurological consequences of caffeine exposure.'

I look over my shoulder and, sure enough, Nathan is retrieving a travel kettle from a locked cupboard. 'You've spoiled the surprise, Frisky. Caff or decaff, Jo?'

'Caff, please.' It'll make a nice change from the insipid stuff at home.

'Better do it fast, Nathan, or the boys will get jealous,' Frisky says. 'Mind you, they're going to be so distracted by our new recuit, I doubt they'll notice.'

'So who else comes along?'

'There's usually about a dozen of us, plus the volunteers.'

'And . . . ' I hesitate, struggling to find a way to ask the question. 'The others. Are they . . . well, what are they like?'

Frisky pats my hand. 'They're just a bit more direct than most people. I always think a head injury magnifies your existing quirks, maybe adds a few more.'

'Very well put,' Nathan says, handing me my coffee.

Frisky winks at me. 'Of course, there are people here I'd normally cross the street to avoid. But I think they were always like that, even without a bang on the head.'

I nod nervously and suss out my escape routes. I can't help thinking that it's nice and cosy with only the three of us. Then we hear a noise like a herd of elephants on the steps outside.

'Better hide the coffee,' Frisky says, 'because that sounds like Monster to me.'

'Monster?' I say, gripping the mug.

'Long story,' Frisky says. 'But don't worry, I'm sure he'll tell you himself.'

Two hours later, and I do indeed know all about Monster: the fight outside a nightclub at Christmas five years ago, the drunken kicks and blows to the head that made his face swell so dramatically that his then-girlfriend couldn't recognise the 'monster' in ITU. By the time Monster's face had returned to its former boy-band glory, albeit with a long, neat scar along his hairline, the girlfriend had shacked up with his best friend. And in the time it's taken him to recover sufficiently to find a part-time job in a factory, the girlfriend has married and had two kids: the family Monster always wanted.

Then there's Falsie. Falsie lost his left eye and his living in an accident at the tiny under-the-arches garage he owned. His speech is difficult to decipher at first, and he knows it, so he simplifies the story into a few key phrases. His wife sits next to him at the centre, they travel everywhere together now they've sold the business. In two weeks, they're off on a Nile cruise. Frisky tells me later that when Falsie's had a couple of drinks, he takes out his eye and passes it around. It's a work of art, apparently: the hazel colours match his real eye exactly.

Slasher is an ex-Hell's Angel who came off his bike six months ago. After me, he's the newest head-banger. He made a beeline for the sofa without saying a word to anyone, picked up a *Motorcycling News*, and within seconds, tears were rolling down his tattooed cheeks. I nudged Frisky.

'Shouldn't someone go and help him?'

He shook his head. 'He needs his space. At home, his parents won't leave him alone so this is his safety valve. He'll be OK in a few minutes.'

Frisky introduces me to everyone, and I try to keep track of who's who. The men all have aggressive, matey nicknames, but the two women, Liz and Deidre, are called by their proper names. Liz is barely out of her teens, and nearly died in a pile-up on the M4; she sits in a corner, clutching her brown plastic cup of tea, reading magazines and looking fed up. And Deidre is in her late sixties; she had a stroke a year ago and though the only outward sign now is a slight downturn on the left-hand side of her mouth, she comes back every week to play cards. 'Gives me something to look forward to, dear. Before the stroke I never used to go out, not since my husband died. Now I have quite a social life, what with this and moving into the sheltered housing. Stroke of luck, I call it.'

Nathan works the room, chatting and joking like a holiday rep. I eavesdrop on a few conversations and realise that with each anecdote or casual remark, he's collecting information, without them suspecting a thing. He asks about Monster's new job and explains how his employer could get cash to make the workplace more Monster-friendly. He listens to

Falsie's wife's concerns about making new friends on the cruise, and role-plays what they might say about the accident. And with Slasher, he waits until the tears have stopped, then offers him a biscuit and a chance to talk.

When he comes over to me, I'm instantly on guard. 'What's the prognosis, Doc? Am I going to lose my marbles?'

He smiles. 'I think the fact you've hung on to them so far is a good sign. So how are you finding the club?'

'It's . . . ' I look around the room, thinking it over, 'great. Not what I expected, though.'

'In what way?'

'I thought the people would be, well, scarier. Does that sound awful?'

'No, not at all. Humans very quickly accept other humans with missing limbs and horrible injuries but there's something about the brain that makes us extra wary.'

'What made you want to spend your life with *us*, then?' I say, surprised at the strange solidarity I feel with Slasher and Liz and Frisky: us against the world.

'Oh, I've always been contrary. And it's what I said to you in hospital: the brain is one of the last uncharted territories. As a boy I wanted to be an explorer, but let's face it, I don't have the physique. You don't need crampons to enter the dark world of the central nervous system.'

'That makes you the Edmund Hillary of the mind then?'

'More like Phileas Fogg,' he says.

'Around the brain in eighty days?'

'Eighty days wouldn't begin to cover it,' he says, then stops. 'You've got me on my hobby-horse, Jo. Sorry. This is meant to be about you.'

'I'm a bit bored with me, though. Especially because me these days means illness and amnesia and paranoia and bad temper.'

'That's not how you come across to me, Jo,' he says, then coughs. 'And bear in mind that the people here are the ones who still feel the need for some support. There are hundreds more who've come for a short time, then moved on. So what about you? Will you be coming back? Next time there's a talk about memory tricks. And we'll decide where to go on the summer outing.'

I look around the room at the nicknamed people, and the shoddy furniture, and the low-tech games, and it occurs to me that two months ago, I couldn't have imagined spending time here, never mind choosing to. But this is also the first place in two months where I have been able to relax, to stop caring what other people think.

'Well, so long as my Mum lets me out to play,' I say, surprised at myself.

Nathan beams. 'Terrific. I *knew* you'd like it. I knew it. That calls for a drink – can I interest you in a criminally weak cup of tea to celebrate? Daren't get the coffee out in public.'

'You make it sound so tempting,' I say. 'Go on then.'

Nathan heads for the machine, still grinning. I feel someone brush against my arm.

'Well, well, well. Haven't you made our young doctor's day?' It's Frisky, his face more wrinkled than ever in amusement.

'I expect he's on commission from the hospital, to get people to come here,' I say. 'Like pyramid selling.'

'Hmm. If that's what you want to believe. Never mind him, what are *you* doing later?'

I giggle. 'Are you propositioning me, Frisky?'

'Oh, if only, my dear. If only. The spirit is just about willing, but the body . . . however, I did wonder if you might like a spot of very late lunch? Some of the chaps go to the WRVS, but it reminds me of the NAAFI. I don't live far away, and I can guarantee you'll be quite safe. Unfortunately.'

'My mother's coming to pick me up,' I say, realising I sound more like a four-year-old than a grown woman. 'She's not wanted to let me out of her sight since the accident.'

'All the more reason to spread your wings, wouldn't you say?' And he chuckles. 'There comes a time for every chick to fly the nest.'

I weigh up the options. Beans on toast with Mum

scrutinising my every move in case I've over-exerted myself. Or lunch with a mysterious – yet too old to be dangerous – stranger.

'Give me a minute to make a phone call.'

Of course, my mother thinks I'm having some sort of brainstorm and the only way to convince her otherwise is to introduce her to Frisky. I've told him to meet us in the hospital car park, after I've had a few minutes to prepare her.

'Mum, I know it's a bit sudden, but Frisk . . . um, Roger is a total gentleman.'

She folds her arms across her chest. 'Is that so? I mean, how do you know he hasn't preyed on young women like you before?'

'He's not preying on anyone.'

'Really. Well, it seems very fishy to me.' She's straightened up and seems taller than usual. This is a side of my mother I barely recognise: the last time she stood up to anyone was two decades ago. But despite the mint-green trouser suit, and the pink frosted lipstick, she now looks like a force to be reckoned with.

'He's a harmless old chap who wants some company,' I say, hoping Frisky can't hear me from his hiding place behind a St John's ambulance.

'Harmless? Don't you think it's rather peculiar for a man to hang around a group of people with head injuries? Waiting for someone vulnerable.'

'Mum, he's not a weirdo. He's a patient himself,' I say, and then regret it. This is not going to reassure her one bit. And actually, I still don't really understand why Frisky keeps coming to the club. I'm sure he'd have much more fun at a tea dance or bridge night; a man like him would be mobbed by oversexed grannies.

Mum's eyes nearly pop out of their sockets. 'What, you're proposing to slope off with some potential psychopath? There's no way of telling what someone like that might do . . . ' She trails off, realising what she's said.

'Really?' I say, simultaneously angry and more determined to spend time with Frisky, even if he does turn out to be an axe murderer. At least he doesn't judge me. 'Well, I'm glad that's out in the open, Mum.'

'Joanna, I didn't mean that *you're* like that.' She's shrinking back into herself before my eyes, mortified.

'Whatever, Mum. But I want to go with Roger and I'm a grown woman and there's nothing you can –'

And then Frisky appears from behind the ambulance, more dashing that David Niven. '*Hello* there. You can't be Joanna's *mother*.'

Mum stares at him.

'No,' he says, shaking his head in a brilliant show of disbelief. 'You must be Joanna's *sister*.'

This has to be the corniest line ever, one even my father wouldn't attempt, yet my mother actually flutters her eyelashes. 'No,' she says, a girlish quality to her voice. 'Definitely her mother and don't I know it.'

'They can be such a *worry*, can't they?' Frisky says, switching into caring, sharing parent mode.

'Oh!' Mum says. 'Oh, it's been quite, quite the most stressful time lately. I thought she might not make it and now . . . ' her hand darts to her mouth. 'Sorry. I'm usually more discreet.'

But then usually no one bothers to listen to my mother.

Frisky holds out his liver-spotted hand. 'Roger Freeman Van Belle. A pleasure to meet you.'

Freeman Van Belle? What kind of a name is that?

'I'm Lynda,' my mother says breathlessly.

'Lynda. I know it's hard to let Joanna out of your sight while she's so *delicate*, but I'd very much like to treat her to lunch. It's important, don't you think, to widen her horizons gradually?'

'Oh,' she says, as if this is a surprise. 'Well, I don't doubt you'll take care of her.'

'But?' Frisky raises his curly white eyebrows, which knit together momentarily.

'But . . . ' Doubt and then shame cross my mother's face: she can't bring herself to ask Frisky if he's *OK*, if he can get through an afternoon without a seizure or a naked romp up the frozen food aisle in Sainsbury's.

He steps in front of her, well inside the exclusion zone she always maintains with strangers, and touches her shoulder. 'Lynda. I *promise* I won't let her come to any harm.'

And I don't actually care what Mum thinks because *I* believe him. This wrinkly old man with a ridiculous name and mysterious past makes me feel completely safe.

'All right,' my mother says. 'You look after her, though, Mr Freeman. I'm trusting you with my baby.'

He nods solemnly and waits while she clambers up into Dad's 4x4, waves at me and drives off.

'Now, Joanna,' he says, smiling, 'I think it's time for you and I to get roaringly, steamingly drunk!'

Chapter 13
Cibophobia – Fear of Food

Frisky's house is ten minutes' walk from the hospital, in a tree-lined avenue of tall Victorian villas. His is semi-detached and, like its owner, gently decaying. Next door has a stone façade the colour of Cornish sand, ornate detailing as sharp as the day the mason took a chisel to it, and paintwork that zings, from the black lacquered railings to the white sash window frames.

Frisky's stonework is discoloured, his masonry aged into soft focus, his railings rusty and his woodwork peeling, revealing a dozen different paint shades. But the house has a certain dignity, as a four-storey home should, and inside it smells of fresh flowers and emulsion.

'The kitchen is in the process of redecoration,' he says, rather unnecessarily, as we enter a high-ceilinged room with a Belfast sink, a range cooker and a dozen doorless cupboards. The walls are bare plaster, still drying from the edges inwards. Under my feet, the original black-and-white herringbone tiles display a century's worth of wear and tear.

'And how long before it's finished?'

'Ah, now, there's a question. Not sure a house like this is ever *finished*, Joanna. Especially not when one's relying on the grandson to do it. Wonderful boy, of course, such a perfectionist, but I wouldn't bet my shirt on it being finished within my lifetime.'

I look at Frisky, wondering how much longer that lifetime might last.

He catches me looking. 'Since you're clearly speculating on my appalling old age, I'm eighty-five. Twenty years younger than the house.'

'Sorry, I didn't mean . . . '

'Nonsense. It's natural to wonder. Frankly I wake every day utterly astonished to have been granted more than my three score years and ten. But thrilled, of course. Absolutely thrilled.' He touches the bare walls tenderly. 'The more time I have to see her restored to glory, the better.'

'Your grandson's a builder, then?'

'More of an enthusiast, like me. Except considerably better up ladders than I am. Vertigo, you know. But Luke . . . ' he pauses, looking at me intently, 'is a good boy to his grandfather, all things considered. And he loves the house as much as I do, and not only because he'll inherit it one day.'

Before I can reply, my stomach growls so loudly that it echoes around the room.

'My dear! I am being the most *appalling* host. Take a seat in the conservatory while I knock up a little something for lunch. We can't starve you when you're still convalescing, can we?' And he shooshes me out of the kitchen.

The conservatory dates back to a time before double glazing: it's possibly the prettiest room I've ever seen. The ironwork seems organic, ornate curls and tendrils wrapping themselves around thick glass. Though many of the panes are speckled or cracked with age, they still seem to trap what little sun there is today, so that my skin feels caressed by unfamiliar warmth.

Beyond the glass, the garden is thawing after the long winter and bluebells are scattered across the lawn. Two enormous oak trees stand like ancient sentries at the far end of the plot guarding the ugliest of caravans. It is large, brown and derelict, with a hideous corrugated roof and small mean windows.

'Here we are. Not too early for a snifter?' Frisky brings in a tray with two tumblers full to the brim with ice, lemon segments and a shot of unidentified spirit. 'I take it you do drink gin?' he asks, and from his tone I know the only acceptable answer is yes.

'Well, um, of course, I *used* to. But I was advised that after the accident, I ought to avoid alcohol, for the time being.'

Frisky's eyes narrow. 'Oh dear. Do you know, it's one of the things I loathe most about having survived into the twenty-first century. This quite ludicrous *obsession* with being sensible.'

'Well, I suppose people like that are only being careful.' People like that? Who am I kidding?

'Careful. Yes. And do you think we won two World Wars by being careful? Invented vaccination? Electricity? Space travel?'

'No, but this isn't really in the same category,' I say, sensing the end of a beautiful friendship. 'I just don't believe in taking pointless risks.'

'That all depends,' Frisky says, pausing to swallow an enormous slug of gin from his glass, 'on whether you perceive pleasure to be pointless.' He sighs. 'You know, gin is distilled from juniper. So it's virtually a herbal remedy.'

'Even so,' I say, 'I think I'd prefer water.'

He sighs again. 'Goodness. Have you heard the phrase, youth is wasted on the young?'

I smile, feeling rather foolish. He disappears again, and I hear loud bangs and crashes. I've made him angry now. Why can't I stop being such a coward? I've been given a second chance, but I seem incapable of taking it. Water fills my eyes so I stare fixedly at the bloody caravan, willing the tears away, and suddenly I see a face at the window.

'Oh! Frisky?'

Frisky comes through with a terracotta bowl of olives, and a crystal glass of iced water. 'What's the matter?'

‘I think there’s someone in that deserted caravan,’ I whisper, though the interloper must be at least sixty feet away. ‘Should we call the police?’

He begins to chuckle. ‘Oh, dear me, no. That’s just Luke.’

‘Your grandson?’

‘Yes. He lives in the caravan, you see.’

‘But this house is massive.’

‘And a massive mess. There’s only one bedroom fit for human habitation and that’s mine.’

‘Couldn’t he sleep in the kitchen? It must get freezing in the caravan.’

‘Ah yes but . . . ’ Frisky tails off slightly. ‘Wildlife. Yes. That’s it. Luke is *awfully* into wildlife. Wiltshire’s answer to St Francis of Assisi, really. Loves all creatures great and small. And there’ve been some terrible cases of cat-napping in the area. So he sleeps in the caravan, to keep an eye out. Wonderful boy.’ He chews thoughtfully on an olive, before spitting out the stone. ‘And do you like cats, Jo?’

‘They’re all right, I suppose. More of a dog person, really.’

‘Oh, I thought all women liked cats,’ he says, sounding disappointed. ‘There’ve been some dog-napping incidents too. Frightful business. But they’ve gone right down since Luke decided to do his pet policeman thing.’

‘Right . . . ’ The whole thing sounds unlikely. ‘So will Luke come over for lunch then?’

‘Possibly. He’s a little shy, you know, the way people so often are when they’re at one with nature. All he needs is someone to bring him out of his shell. Do you know what I mean?’

‘Ye-es,’ I say, crossing my fingers that this cat-loving hermit won’t be joining us.

Frisky disappears again. I’m starving, the first time I’ve felt properly hungry in weeks. I hate olives but they look so succulent against the terracotta dish. I reach out for a small green one and chew carefully, afraid I might break a tooth on the stone.

The sharp lemony tang hits my tongue, then makes my

nose twitch. It's delicious, the first food that tastes *better* since the accident. I try a juicy purple one the size of a grape, which tastes of coriander.

I'm reaching for a black one when Frisky returns from the kitchen with another tray. There's a plate of sliced tomatoes, garnished with pink crescents of onion; a dish of feathery rocket, with Parmesan shavings curled on top; a wooden board with French bread and a huge wedge of runny cheese that's already melting on to the knife; two wishbones of red-brown marbled sausage, tethered with string; a flash of yellowy-green oil; and a carafe of wine the colour of resin.

'These olives are great.' The black one is intensely herby. 'What's this got in it?'

'Ah, thyme. My favourite. Reminds me of Crete, during the war. It grew wild, you know, just the thing for livening up our bloody awful rations.'

'Is that where you learned to cook?' I say, my mouth watering as he spreads the plates out in front of us.

'Oh, this isn't *cooking*, Joanna. I'll show you cooking, one of these days. But I certainly learned a lot about self-sufficiency. Now are you sure I can't tempt you to wine?'

He pours himself a glass and a summery smell of cut grass wafts towards me. 'I would, but . . . '

'The doctors warned you, I know. But do you always do as you're told, Joanna?'

'Ummm. Well.' I can't quite bring myself to admit it. 'Not *always*.'

He looks at me for so long that I feel uncomfortable. Perhaps he's developed a sixth sense for when someone's fibbing.

'OK, most of the time,' I admit, eventually.

'And has doing what you're told stopped you landing up in a coma? Made you cram in as much fun as you can, in case there really is no tomorrow?'

'No,' I say, sulking now.

'It's not for me to tell you how to live your life, Joanna. God knows, I've mostly made a hash of my own. But at least

I've enjoyed making mistakes. It strikes me you're too worried about getting things wrong to do anything at all.'

My sulk is turning into full-on anger. 'Don't patronise me. What am I meant to do – go without a seatbelt? Or, I don't know, go for a jog along the hard shoulder. Or maybe I should go home with strange men!'

He looks shamefaced. 'You know, you're absolutely right. Sorry. The war, that's my excuse. Turned me into such a bore, telling everyone to seize the day.'

His climb-down takes the wind out of my sails. 'What *did* happen to you, Frisky?'

'Terribly unspectacular, alas. No heroic dogfight over the Channel defending the White Cliffs and Vera Lynn's honour. I was travelling between bases when my engine failed. Brought her down in a field, and the buggers were more worried about the bloody plane than me. I took a bit of a knock, everything seemed fine and then the fits started.'

That must have been how he burned his hands. 'Fits? As in epilepsy?'

He shrugs, takes a bite of sausage. 'Well, I called them funny turns. Less clinical. Happened all the time to begin with, pretty alarming, but then they eased off until, bingo! Last year, I woke up on the Post Office floor, surrounded by nosy parkers.'

'All these years later?' I ask, shivering. Will it be the same for me?

'Well, who knows if it's connected? What the docs described as a "cerebral accident". But a happy accident, too, as it's how I met the charming Dr Williams. Began coming to the club because my friends were dropping like flies and a chap gets lonely at home.' He sees my hesitating over the cheese. 'It's very good, that one, but potent. Try a little bit if you're not sure.'

'It's not that. I was wondering if it's pasteurised?' Dennis and I once went on a long weekend to a food safety conference in Ipswich and I still remember the slides ...

'Oh I shouldn't think it's safe for a second. Absolutely

teeming with bacteria, listeria and little green men from Mars, I'd imagine. A truly scary dairy product.' He takes a spoon and ladles the gooey cheese on to his bread. 'Luke likes that horrid plastic cheese, though, let me look in the fridge.'

He leaves me alone, eyeballing the pool of cheese. A surprisingly enticing smell of ammonia rises from the plate, challenging me: if I close my eyes I can recall the microscope image, little wormy tubes of listeria dyed turquoise so they showed up better, criss-crossing the screen, longing to invade my gastro-intestinal system.

When I open my eyes again, the cheese is oozing further out of its rind and, without thinking about it, I take a slice of the bread, initially to stop the liquid running off the side of the plate. It slides unctuously into the pitted dough, and smoothes over like self-levelling concrete. It has a life of its own.

And so do my hands because they lift the slice to my lips and without really thinking, I take a bite. My teeth sink into the soft cheese and then the chewy bread, and then my brain and nose and tastebuds process the texture and the taste and the mushroom-and-perm solution smell, and as Frisky emerges from the house bearing a piece of cheese the colour and shape of a Lego brick, I sigh deeply.

'Joanna, are you all right?' He stares at the piece of bread in my hand, my toothmarks giving the game away. 'By God, you've eaten the cheese.'

I nod, slowly, as a smile spreads across my face. 'I have eaten the cheese. Tempted by forbidden fruit. Frisky, it's *wonderful.*'

He beams. 'Oh I am thrilled to have led you astray, Joanna. What fun.' He lifts up his wine to chink against my water glass. 'I think we should drink to listeria. You know, I always thought it'd be a lovely name for a little girl.'

'Hang on,' I say, the cheese making me reckless. 'Can I change my mind about the wine?'

Frisky looks ecstatic. 'My dear, it's a woman's prerogative.'

*

Sometimes you only realise how cold you were when you warm up again. The wine spreads through my body like a sunset and I swear I can even feel my bone marrow defrosting.

'That tastes so . . . ' I take another sip. 'It's beyond words, Frisky.'

'Let me try.' He picks up his glass and sniffs. 'Pine and thyme. Olive groves. A hint of smoke and the faintest whiff of donkey doo-doo.'

I giggle. 'And you can get all of that from *smelling* it?'

He closes his eyes. 'Well, I am cheating a little bit. It comes from the vineyard near where we were stationed in '41, before we got thrown out by the Germans. Those of us that made it out. I have a case sent over every year.'

'Wouldn't you rather forget those times?'

He holds his wine up to the sun, sloshing it around, before drinking. 'It's still the most beautiful place I've ever seen. And I have always been more of a glass-half-full kind of chap.' He grins. 'Though I can't help noticing yours is nearly empty. Top up?'

I hold my hand over the rim. 'Better not, I feel quite tipsy already and I don't want to end up comatose again.' Frisky chuckles and I realise it's the first time I've been able to joke about what's happened. Mum and Dennis would be horrified.

'Do you remember much about your accident, Jo?'

'No. I keep expecting the details to come back to me, but nothing.'

'Maybe it never will,' Frisky says. 'Nature's way of protecting you from horrible memories. Good memories are the ones you need to hang on to.'

'Frisky?' I hesitate, then change my mind. I don't want him to think I am a loony. 'Oh, it doesn't matter.'

'In my experience,' he says, all serious now, 'whenever a woman says "it doesn't matter", she means the exact opposite. Out with it!'

'It's what you said about memories. Ever since the accident, well, I've been having these flashbacks. Memories from when I was little.'

Frisky looks serious. 'What kind of memories? Traumatic ones?'

'Not really. Though they wouldn't rate in my top ten great moments either,' I say, wondering as I do whether I could name ten great moments in the Life of Joanna Morgan. 'They're pretty mundane. Christmas. School. A trip to the library.'

'How peculiar.' Frisky nibbles contemplatively on an olive. 'I did know a chap who had waking nightmares after a close shave. Tumbling to earth in the wreck of his place, flames lapping round his ankles, that sort of thing. He bailed out, but being a glass-half-empty sort of fellow, he never remembered *that* bit.'

'Poor bloke. But at least his flashbacks had a reason.'

He puts his feet up on the table, wincing slightly at the creaking of his knees. 'Annoying perhaps, Joanna, but I'd say you've got off pretty lightly with a few flashbacks.'

I look out at the garden, where two young squirrels are putting on a show, jumping up onto the bird table and chasing the nuts around. They're not eating any, just doing it for fun. 'Yes, I know. But they feel so *real*. Creepy.'

'I bet there's a connection somewhere,' Frisky says. 'A deeper purpose.'

'Maybe.' The first one, the Hiroshima movie, did change the way I saw the world. I've always thought that I was born a scaredy-cat, but the flashbacks have made me wonder. And if I wasn't born a coward, could I learn to be brave all over again?

'What does the good doctor say?' Frisky asks.

'Give it time.'

He rubs his hands together. 'Ha! I love it when the doctors don't have a clue.'

'He says I should write it all down, to help me understand what triggers them.'

'Never mind that, Joanna, he probably wants the material

for a piece in *The Lancet* or *Head Shrinkers' Quarterly*. Sure I can't tempt you? Only a tiny dribble left anyhow.'

He holds the carafe above my glass. 'Oh, all right then, Frisky.'

'So … what the devil could be triggering the strange memories of Miss Morgan? Overdoing it, maybe? My funny turns came on when I was shattered.'

I shake my head. 'Don't think it's that. I'm tired all the time.'

'Something nice then? Music? The old tunes always take me back. *Just direct your feet, to the sunny side of the street …*'

'No. The first flashbacks were when I was in hospital, and the only sounds in ITU were pumps and beeps and whispers.'

'OK. All a case of narrowing it down. Getting closer. So let's think, what else do we get in hospials?' Frisky says, scratching his chin.

'It's probably a wild goose chase.' I'm starting to feel tired again now. Before the accident, I'd forgotten how it felt to *collide* with tiredness, the way a child does, so it almost knocks you flat.

'What if … ' a smile begins to spread across Frisky's face, 'the missing ingredient was smell?' He stands up, pacing the cracked tiles, working it through. 'Think about it, Joanna. It's a powerful sense. One whiff of wine instantly conjures up a few spring days six decades ago. And they pump the smell of baking bread through the fans in supermarkets to make you feel warm inside.'

I try to focus, to test Frisky's theory. The first flashback began in the toilets, didn't it, that smelled of … well, the obvious, but also disinfectant. Just like ITU.

Then there was Christmas and the smell of hospital roast dinner. And wasn't it the mouldy scent of old books and old lady lavender perfume that transported me back to the library? 'Frisky, you're a *genius*.'

He nods. 'Maybe I am. It does make sense, doesn't it? I

mean, we all respond to smell, but the accident could have made you super-sensitive.'

'But . . . ' the euphoria is short-lived, 'it doesn't solve my problem. If anything, I'm more afraid than ever. Either I wear a clothes peg on my nose, or *anything* could set it off. A chip shop. The perfume section of a department store. It's a jungle out there.'

Frisky looks hurt. 'Come on now. Think how many million smells you've smelled since the accident, and you've only had three funny turns.'

That I can remember. I could have forgotten a dozen more, like I've forgotten the accident itself. My memory's shot to pieces.

'You're probably right,' I say, struggling to keep my eyes open. 'I'd like to go home now, Frisky, if that's all right.'

'Oh dear. I've upset you, haven't I?' He perches on the edge of the table.

I slump further into my chair. 'It's not you. I've overdone it today, I think. That's the trouble with us head-bangers, eh? One minute we're all *normal* and the next . . . '

'The doc's right about one thing, Joanna. It takes time. It will get better, I promise.'

I shrug. 'Time. Yeah. Shame you can't get that on prescription.'

'I'd be queuing for extra, that's for sure,' he says.

'Sorry to be so whiny,' I say but he flicks his hand to dismiss it.

'What's a moan between head-bangers? Now, let me see if I can get young Luke to run you home,' and he hops off the table, heading out towards the garden.

'No, really, I can get a minicab,' I protest, though I can hear Dennis's disapproving voice in my head, 'honestly, Jo, do you know how many women are assaulted every year by bogus taxi-drivers?'

'Oh no you don't, Joanna. Besides it'll do my grandson good to talk to a woman for a change. He can talk to the animals but he's pretty hopeless when it comes to girls.'

I laugh, though I'm not entirely sure he's joking. My craving for bed is uncontrollable and I close my eyes as he disappears to fetch Doctor Dolittle . . .

I must have fallen asleep because Frisky's hand on my arm makes me jump.

'Your carriage awaits, Joanna. This is Luke.'

He hovers behind his grandfather like a shy toddler. If toddlers grew to six feet tall. As he steps forward, I do a double-take. Frisky must have looked like this when he was young . . . combined with the RAF uniform, and more charm than my little brother, Frisky would surely have had his pick of land girls.

Luke has hair so dark it soaks up the light. His eyes are grey like Frisky's, though in the bright conservatory, they look violet. His high cheekbones are so sharp they're almost Slavic: both these men were born to be filmed in black and white, challenging the camera with broody, moody smoulders.

But Luke is *not* Frisky Mark II. That becomes clear within seconds. He won't meet my eye, preferring to run his left foot up and down the loose grout between the conservatory tiles. His trainers are mud-coated, as are his loose black trousers. This is not a man who thinks twice before getting dressed: even his T-shirt looks like the kind you'd get free with a crate of beer. He does fill it rather well, though.

'Come on, Luke. Joanna's our new friend!' Frisky says.

'Hi,' Luke mutters, still not looking up.

'My grandson says he'll be happy to take you home. He's completely safe.'

Luke glares at Frisky. He doesn't seem happy at all, but I have a strange sense that there's more to it than a disagreement over my transport arrangements.

'I'm parked out the front,' he says, shuffling past me. His voice has a transatlantic twang to it, but none of Frisky's confidence. I half expect a whiff of body odour or, worse still, cat piss from all these pets he's supposedly guarding, but instead he smells of sleep, that biscuity aroma of duvets. He must have been woken up to play taxi-driver.

Frisky and I follow him out – this time it isn't the grand entrance hall that I notice, but the brown freckles of damp on the walls, and the enormous gaps between the floorboards that a rescued kitten could fall through. Back outside, I scan the street for Luke and his car.

'Where's he gone?'

Frisky points.

Oh shit.

Luke doesn't have a car, he has *wheels*. Unfortunately, only two wheels, attached to a motorbike. He stands next to it, proud as a member of the Pony Club with her prize-winning mount.

'No *way*,' I say.

'He's never had a single accident, Joanna. And there's a spare helmet in the top-box,' Frisky says, in a vain attempt to reassure me.

'He could have a spare set of limbs and I still wouldn't get on that thing.' The more I look, the scarier it seems: like an insect's endoskeleton in black and chrome, a proper macho Hell's Angels bike. Funny, Luke doesn't look the sort to sacrifice virgins or bite the heads off bats.

'Are you coming or not?' Luke calls over from the other side of the road.

'Sorry, but it's not really my sort of thing.' I stop myself adding, *because bikes are the biggest death-traps known to man and only someone with suicidal tendencies would go on one*. I might want more excitement in my life, but there are limits.

Luke tuts loudly, then trudges back towards the house, pausing to scowl at Frisky, then at the front garden, then back at Frisky. 'Bloody cats have been at it again. Shitting everywhere.' He waves vaguely at the flower-beds, and I see something very strange: he has a scar, exactly like his grandfather's, on the palm of his right hand.

I realise I've been staring, so I smile and say, 'You'd think they'd be more grateful, the local cats, given all you do for them.'

He stares at me as though I am quite, quite mad, then his expression changes to one of sympathy. He thinks I have lost my marbles. 'Yeah. Right. Got to go. Stuff to do.'

And he disappears back through the splendid stucco doorway. 'I think my grandson's small talk needs a bit more work, eh, Joanna? In the meantime, let's see whether we can rustle you up a taxi.'

My plan was to go to bed as soon as I got home. I could imagine the squidgy vanilla smell, the same way Luke smelled when he passed me.

But when I arrive back in Salzburg Avenue, there are several obstacles in the way of my deepest desire.

A huge bunch of stinky chrysanthemums. A case of wine. And my mother.

She's waiting by the window, an anxious hand covering her mouth, and when I walk into the living-room I'm convinced she's about to faint. 'Thank God you're back,' she says, as though I've been trekking through the Sahara rather than sitting in a conservatory eating olives.

'But you met Frisk . . . Roger, Mum. He's hardly the type to keep me imprisoned as his sex slave, is he?'

Mum sniffs. 'He seemed very charming. Too charming, perhaps. If he's not planning any funny business, why exactly is he getting you drunk?'

'Drunk?' Bugger. I meant to chew gum in the cab.

'I can smell alcohol on your breath.'

'Grapes,' I lie. 'They were a bit ripe. They just smell like wine.'

She gives me a look. 'Talking of wine, these were delivered for you today. Six bottles of Rioja. From a timeshare company in Spain?'

'How bizarre,' I say, deciding it might be better not to mention the chat I had with a lovely guy called Miguel last week.

'And the flowers have come from MoneyCard as a thank you for signing up for their Premier card. Jo, what's going on? I'm worried about you. About people taking advantage.'

I'm too tired to get crotchety with her. 'Mum, I've no intention of spending any money on the card. The timeshare thing is a mistake. And Fris . . . Roger is harmless. I enjoyed myself this afternoon. I haven't had fun in such a long time.'

'That's all very nice, but will fun make you feel better? Because I can't help thinking that getting better ought to be your priority right now.'

I want to explain that I've been wondering about the point of getting better if all it means is more of the same. That Frisky has made me feel normal for a few short hours. That fun seems a pretty worthwhile objective to me.

But then expecting my mother to embrace the concept of fun would be like expecting an Eskimo to see the point of a bikini. 'You're probably right,' I say. 'And the doctor said my priority is sleep, so if you don't mind, I've an appointment with the land of Nod.' I use the childhood phrase deliberately, hoping it'll make her back off.

She smiles at me but I'm sure the brightness in her eyes is caused by tears. 'Oh, Jo. Things were so much simpler when you were a little girl, weren't they?'

I could tell her that, if anything, things seem simpler now. Remind her about neutron bombs and new Ice Ages, and the Yorkshire Ripper, and a million other retro anxieties.

Instead I kiss her gently on both cheeks, drag myself into the bedroom, and climb into bed fully clothed.

As I pull the duvet over my head, the air is stale and smells so powerfully of sleep that I feel that familiar dizziness, dragging me down, a long way from Salzburg Avenue . . .

Chapter 14
Frigophobia – Fear of Cold Things

'Look who's here to see you!'

My little brother opens his left eye, then closes it wearily. 'Big deal.'

My parents' bedroom smells of sleep and sick and Nivea face cream. It's three in the afternoon, but the thick curtains are still closed, trapping the heat of the day inside. It only takes a few seconds before I feel faint; no wonder Timmy looks ill.

I'd like to leave, as he doesn't want me here, but I know I'd get a telling off, so I force my face into a sympathetic smile. As Dad keeps reminding me, *he's not well at all, Jelly Bean. You should have seen the doctor's face.*

My mother strokes his hair, which is damp with sweat. 'Poor Timmy,' she whispers, 'my poor baby boy.' She's lying next to him in bed, Kermit the Frog sandwiched between them. Mum's face is as pink as her lacy nightie, and a single vertical furrow runs between her eyes. It appeared after Timmy's marathon nosebleed yesterday and makes her look old for the first time.

'Can I get anything for the patient?' Dad asks. 'Ice cream? Jammy Dodgers? Cheese on toast?'

My stomach rumbles. I haven't eaten since the Weetabix I shared with Misty in the kitchen before anyone else got up.

Mum scowls in the direction of my stomach. How dare it rumble in the sick-room? 'Go on, Timmy,' she says, 'before Greedy Guts Jo eats everything.' And Timmy giggles.

I stare out of the window. I've taught myself not to cry when she says things like that. Dad tells me she doesn't mean it, 'It's the tablets that help her sleep, they make her say strange things.'

It's not even fair. Most of the girls in my class are fatter than me. But the blessed Timmy doesn't get hungry the way normal people do, and uses his lack of appetite to wrap Mum round his little finger. No wonder he never seems to get any taller.

'Why don't we go and make some lunch for both of you, Jo?' Dad says, and I follow him willingly. As we leave the room, I glance back at Timmy's face.

Smug.

I don't hate my mum. But flipping heck, I do hate my brother.

In the kitchen, Dad slices cheese into perfect rectangles while I take care of the ice cream. He's no chef, but his cheese on toast is OK, when he doesn't wander off and leave it to catch fire under the grill.

'Sorry we forgot lunch, Bean,' he says. He always calls me Bean when he feels bad about something. Originally it was Jo Jelly Bean. Then Jelly Bean. Now Bean, to save time. It might be odd but it's nicer than Greedy Guts.

'It's OK,' I say, though it isn't, not really. His tongue sticks out slightly as he concentrates on cutting even wedges off the block of Cheddar. My mouth waters. 'I'll get the ice cream.'

Our chest freezer – the biggest in the street, naturally – is in the garage, through a door that always sticks. Must get Dad to fit it. Otherwise, there could be a disaster when the four-minute warning sounds.

Last night, after the long wait in casualty, I couldn't sleep so I read my library books with a torch under my quilt. And after that I wondered if I'd ever sleep again. The news for number 17 Greenham Lane couldn't have been worse. Mum and Dad bought it brand-new when I was two years old; it has huge windows and an open-plan living-room, completely different from the gloomy terrace where all my baby photos were taken.

But the gloomy terrace would have offered a much higher chance of surviving Armageddon. According to the shelter guidebook, the ideal space is a cellar or a room without outside walls. But our only room without outside walls is the under-stairs toilet and there's barely enough room for the dog in there. We need enough space for four of us so that means either the hall or the garage. But the hall leads to the glass front door (danger of flying debris). At least the garage has no windows, and I know the brickwork's strong because Mum drove into it the second time she borrowed Dad's brand-new company Ford Sierra (I was quite pleased: it is the most horrible car in the world, like a big green jelly mould).

Actually, the book wasn't guaranteeing that anything above ground would withstand an atomic explosion, but persuading my parents to move to a house with a deep cellar (or, preferably anywhere in north Wales) is my medium-term plan. In the meantime, beggars can't be choosers.

I lift the freezer lid, and peer inside. Lumpy snow sculptures sparkle back at me under the fluorescent bulb. Chicken wings and stray peas are stuck fast in the ice that lines the edges, as though they've been there since the dawn of time. The catering-size pack of Walls Neapolitan comes out easily enough – it never lasts long. Ice cream is the one thing Timmy and I agree on. In the shelter we'll finish it in the first hour. Which I suppose is just as well. It'll be quite hot after the bomb drops.

'You OK in there, Bean?' Dad pokes his head through the door. 'I'll pop this up to the patient.' The cheese on toast is cut into fingers, arranged like a lattice in my Peter Rabbit baby bowl (I'm sure Timmy only pretends to like it because it's mine).

'Right.' The cheese smells wonderful and my mouth waters.

He frowns. 'I'll make you some in a minute. Timmy needs a bit of encouragement to eat anything at the moment and until the test results come back, we all need to give him extra treats. You do understand, don't you?'

'Yes, Daddy.'

He grins, and his eyes crinkle at the sides, like Paul Newman's. My father is handsome, like the man in the gravy ad on ITV: the one where the wife comes in and sees he's making her dinner and she's so surprised that she loops her arm around his back and kisses him.

Sometimes I think Dad's waiting for Mum to do the same, but she never does.

He disappears up the stairs.

'Don't forget pudding,' I hear him call from the landing.

I pull the lid off the ice cream carton: it's two-thirds full, three thick stripes of strawberry, vanilla and chocolate, like a frozen flag. I take two bowls and the ladle we use to serve up soup, and begin to scrape away at the surface. Still rock hard. Time never goes more slowly than when I am waiting for ice cream to thaw.

I ram my finger into the chocolatey stripe, and the cold spreads through my skin, before my body temperature melts a thin layer of ice cream on to my finger, which I lick clean. I do it again, and again, hooking my finger a little more each time so that more of the chilly mixture settles on to the tip . . .

'Jo-ooo . . .' my father's voice drifts down to me from upstairs. 'Any sign of pudding for the patient?'

I stare down at the carton. There's a fist-shaped gap where the brown stripe was, only the pastel pink and creamy vanilla are left. I've eaten every drop of the chocolate.

Chocolate is Timmy's favourite stripe.

'Coming up,' I shout. I feel sick, and not because of the ice cream. I scoop some vanilla into his bowl and wonder if I have time to run to the shop, but then I remember Sainsbury's isn't open on a Sunday. Then I have a brainwave. I open the cupboard where we keep the sauces. HP, Heinz ketchup, mustard . . . I look in vain for chocolate topping but then remember that I finished the last of it yesterday evening, when no one was looking.

I head for the bin: it hasn't been emptied, and fortunately the bottle is near the top, coated in crumbs and marmalade. It feels worryingly hollow when I pick it out but it's worth a try. I turn it upside down, bash the bottom end and pray there's enough in there . . .

A first drop of sauce dribbles out into the bowl, landing on the white ice cream like a paw-mark in snow. A second joins it, and a third, smaller each time and then I take a teaspoon and mix furiously, trying to blend it with the vanilla to produce an authentic chocolatey shade.

There's no more left now and the colour's not quite right, but then it's dark in the bedroom, and Timmy's unwell so maybe . . .

The dog shuffles in from the living-room, and cocks her head to one side, bemused. 'Wish me luck, Misty.'

I take a deep breath and, grasping the bowl, run up the stairs. My family look up as I enter the room, and I feel – not for the first time – like an intruder, someone who's stumbled into the wrong bedroom. The wrong house.

'Timmy's finished his toast already,' Mum says proudly, pointing at the plate in his lap. 'Except the crusts, but we'll let him off today. I bet you can fit in a little bit of ice cream, can't you, darling?'

She reaches out for the bowl, and to my delight, takes it without looking and loads the spoon with ice cream. She holds it to my brother's lips and he takes his time before opening them.

I wait now. His eyes are closed and I'm beginning to believe I've got away with it when they snap open like a puppet's, and lock on to me.

'She's done something to it,' Timmy hisses.

They're all looking at me now, accusation on every face, and though I know I *am* guilty, I resent the way my parents automatically assume I'm in the wrong.

'Jo?' My father's voice is a warning. My mother tastes the ice cream and pulls a face.

'There wasn't . . . any chocolate left. Only strawberry and vanilla,' I begin. 'And I know how much Timmy likes chocolate so I tried to make some. With chocolate sauce.' It isn't a lie. It's just not quite the whole truth.

'You ate it,' Timmy shouts, forgetting his invalid act for a minute. 'You ate the chocolate bit because you didn't want *me* to have it.'

'Is that true, Jo?' Dad asks.

I'm about to answer, to tell them it was an accident, to wait for the inevitable speech about how disappointed they are with me, when Timmy picks up my Peter Rabbit bowl, still criss-crossed with the tiny crusts of bread that he was too delicate to chew. His face is neutral, but his eyes are mocking as he lifts the bowl above his head and then hurls it, crusts and all, across the room at the wall.

It shatters into quarters but I don't seem to hear the smash for several seconds.

'My bowl,' I whisper. My baby bowl, a present from my dead godmother, the oldest thing I own, lies in pieces on the deep creamy carpet.

My mother looks from me, to the floor, to Timmy, and back to me. Making her mind up. It doesn't take her long. 'Jo. Go to your bedroom. Now.'

'But . . . '

'You know how ill your brother is and yet you put yourself first.'

'But my bowl –'

'It's a *thing*, Jo. Your brother can't be mended.'

I try to catch Dad's eye but he stares at the floor. I wonder whether I can get away with picking up the pieces and sneaking the crusts into my bedroom, because I'm still hungry and I know I won't be allowed out till much, much later.

'I'm waiting.'

I hear the steel in my mother's voice and decide against

foraging for bread. I look at Timmy and his face is surprisingly sulky. He got his way, didn't he? I'm in disgrace.

But then it occurs to me: when I'm in trouble, he's no longer the centre of attention. I fight the urge to stick my tongue out at him. It's a novelty to win, for once.

And as I leave the room, I know one day the tables will be turned again. The day the Bomb drops, I'll be the favourite. Because I'll be the one who's saved our lives.

Chapter 15
Ergophobia – Fear of Work

The incident with the double-glazing salesman, coming as it did after the free case of Rioja and the complimentary chrysanthemums, finally persuaded my well-meaning gaolers that I might need a little more freedom. It wasn't my fault that the salesman was still there when Dennis got home: we'd long-since stopped discussing thermal insulation, and were talking instead about his wayward teenage daughter. So it was out of order of Dennis to accuse the man of 'preying on vulnerable members of society'.

I don't know who was more insulted, the salesman or me.

So, as part of my rehabilitation, I am going back into the office today, for the first time in two months. Or I am, if I can pluck up the courage to open the door. I've now been standing here for fifteen minutes, trying to stop my hands shaking.

I know there's nothing to be afraid of. No, really, there isn't. This has to be the safest workplace in Wiltshire. The flooring is anti-slip. The edges of our desks are rounded and we have an ioniser, and fully lumbar-friendly adjustable office chairs, and mesh screen-covers to protect our eyes from glare. Our council was the first in the country to insist the cleaners use only eco-friendly detergents. Even the calendars and pictures Sellotaped to the metal dividers between work-stations conform to strict equal opps guidelines so no one takes offence.

Come *on*, Jo. It's not as if I'm going back to work properly. This is a re-familiarisation experience, otherwise known as having a cup of tea with your old colleagues. All part of my readjustment to normal life. And let's face it, anything has to be better than playing the Elizabeth Barrett Browning of Salzburg Avenue. My life is so uneventful that some days I have to pinch myself to check I'm not still in a coma.

So, yet again, tea is the test of normality. *If* I pass this one, then I have weeks of meetings with the council Occupational Health department to look forward to, before I am allowed to return to the cut and thrust of civil protection.

My so-called career. As a teenager, I was desperate to do something worthwhile, like be a doctor or a dentist. Though it was less to do with vocation and more to do with wanting a guaranteed place in a nuclear fall-out shelter. I suppose that began around the time when Timmy got ill, though before my flashbacks, I couldn't have pinpointed it so accurately.

But when I fainted during a dissection of a sheep's eye in biology, I had to revise my plans. After watching a contraband copy *Threads*, I decided my next best chance of a bunk in the bunker was to work in civil protection itself (even though the officials in that TV show died in their shelter, buried alive). I didn't quite know what it'd involve, except that when the four-minute warning came, I'd be able to say 'open sesame' or whatever the password was, and join the others who'd rule the world, post-nuclear holocaust. I wasn't that interested in ruling the world, thanks, but I imagined myself with clipboard and an austere haircut straight out of a 1940s' war movie, relaying information about casualties and fall-out with an air of tragic dignity.

By the time I graduated, the Berliners had demolished their wall, and the whole idea of bunkers and hiding from the Bomb under your kitchen table seemed laughable. Maybe to most people, it always had. But I was already on my unstoppable path towards civil protection.

So I don't have my name down for a place in one of the 'secret' shelters that dot the countryside round here (these days they're used mainly by horny adolescents looking for privacy). But before my accident I did have a perfectly pleasant existence running computer programs predicting the possible consequences of super-rats invading Courtbridge Courtyard, our main shopping centre, and answering calls from the public about everything from rabies to radon.

I'm pretty lucky. One of my monthly bulletins was about workplace injury and even the safest seeming jobs have their downside – bakers are ninety times more likely to get asthma from their work than the rest of us, typists get more back trouble, and teachers get more depressed. Rock stars risk guitar nipple. And twenty-six popes have been assassinated in office.

But still I can't go into our danger-free office. My palms are sweating now. When I wipe them on my blue silk skirt, they leave child-like handprints behind.

What am I trying to prove? I can do this some other day. No rush. That's what everyone keeps telling me. All I need to do is sneak away, no one will ever know I was here . . .

'Jo!'

Oh shit. *Mikey*. So much for making a sharp exit.

'Bloody hell. I'd hoped for a dirty great scar at least,' he says, running towards me. I want a hug, but the wooden tea-tray he's holding is in the way, so we kiss cheeks over the top of the pile of paper bags: I catch a whiff of a familiar citrus scent.

'Lemon drizzle cake,' I say.

'Yup. Cooked to order by the lovely ladies of the kitchen, specially for you. But I didn't think you'd want to brave the canteen today so I got you a takeaway.'

My hands are still shaking, but now my mouth's watering in anticipation of my favourite cake. 'Actually, I'm not sure I want to brave the office either.'

'We've been looking forward to seeing you, Jo. Hasn't been

the same without you – and we're lost without your safety bulletins.'

'I'm not quite sure . . . ' But he's already elbowing me towards the door marked 'Accident Prevention, Public Protection and Civil Defence (APPPCD)'. When you're an invalid, people seem to think it's OK to push you around.

It's odd to see the office as an outsider would. Sharon, our admin lady, is restocking the stationery cupboard, counting everything twice to make sure no one's playing fast and loose with the Post-Its. Burt, our balding techie, is on the disaster simulation software, calculating the effects of a plague of locusts on Courtbridge Garden Centre, maybe, or an accident involving a golden syrup lorry on the bypass. New Age Donna's got her back to me and she's filling in an online quiz about her Hollywood soul mate. She'd no doubt insist this is legitimate research for her role as publications manager, which involves writing the leaflets we distribute on open days (e.g. *If You're 'APPy and you know it: a Guide to the APPPCD Department. Staying Safe in Courtbridge*).

In that instant, I wonder whether I actually *want* to come back.

'She's HERE!' Mikey announces, and they all turn to face me. Sharon abandons her padded envelopes to envelop me in a huge, unwelcome hug. She smells of chip fat and Opium perfume. I try not to breathe through my nose: ever since my conversation with Frisky, I'm convinced he's right, that smells trigger my flashbacks. I don't remember any bad experiences with chips and Opium but you can't be too careful.

'Jo! Great to see you! You look so well!' she says, clinging on for so long that I'm scared I'll faint from holding my breath.

Eventually I wriggle away: Donna and Burt are lined up to take their turn, as if I am a minor royal. Donna smells of henna and Burt of Lynx deodorant but at least his hug is brief and embarrassed. Our emotional reunions over with, we stand back in awkward silence.

When someone comes in with their new baby, there's something to coo over. Perhaps I should invite them to inspect my bald patch.

There's a cough from the corner. *My* corner.

It's taken me years to earn the best desk, shifting places every time someone left, like a chess grand master. My desk has a window ledge for postcards and mugs, a view of the smokers' courtyard, plus the biggest benefit of all: a wall behind me, so no one can ever sneak up on me while I'm emailing Lorraine.

My desk is my salvation.

Except . . . my desk has an interloper. I only catch a quick glance before the girl ducks back behind her screen.

Mikey gives me a nervous look. 'Oh, you won't have met Ruth? She's in charge of keeping your seat warm until you come back.'

Ruth's mousy head appears above the monitor, an inch at a time, as if she's scared of snipers. She gives me a babyish wave (she only looks sixteen). 'Hello, Joanna,' she squeaks. 'It's been terribly easy taking over from you.'

'Really?' I say, through gritted teeth. 'Nice to know my absence hasn't caused anyone any inconvenience.' Who does she think she is?

'N-n-no, its been easy because your filing system is so wonderful,' she fawns. 'And I've been watering your African violet. It's doing so well.'

For a moment, I am speechless. These, then, are my achievements in life. A corner desk. A thriving houseplant. And a filing system so easy a child can use it. My irritation at Ruth disappears as I realise I only have myself to blame. I've avoided responsibility all my professional life, so why on earth should I resent being instantly replaceable?

Even Mikey doesn't know what to say now. Finally he remembers the cake. 'Lemon drizzle! Come and get it! While stocks last.'

'I'll put the kettle on,' says Sharon.

'I'll help,' says Donna, perhaps terrified her chakra is going to be thrown off course by my quiet fuming. Burt merely takes a slice of cake and returns to his computer. And I don't think Ruth's taking any chances: she's staying put.

Mikey hands me the largest slice of lemon drizzle. 'Good to have you back,' he says, then adds, in a whisper, 'Ruth is a temporary measure. They only got her in to prove your job was indispensable. Otherwise they might have tried to cut numbers in the department.'

'Indispensable? In what way exactly? Because I'm the only one who understands the photocopier's collate function?'

'No need to get narky with me, miss!' he says. 'It's not me that got knocked over by a push-bike. The powers that be have had to work bloody hard to contain the scandal. Doesn't exactly enhance our image as safety gurus.'

His teasing takes the wind out of my sails. 'Sorry, Mikey. I suppose you're right. I've dedicated my life to accident prevention, so if *I* can't manage to stay safe then what hope is there for any of us ...' I decide not to dwell on this depressing act. 'Wish someone had warned me about the mini-me, though.'

'I thought Dennis would have mentioned it.'

'God, no. He wouldn't dare do anything that might interfere with my equililbrium.'

'How boring. Well, you get your ass back in here and you'll get no mercy from me. Just the way you like it, *girlfriend.*'

I feel myself blushing. 'Is that what you say to the luscious Councillor Fothergill?'

'Only when she's *very* naughty!' And he winks at me. 'So when do you think you might be back?'

I shrug my shoulders. 'Dunno. I suppose it might be different if I thought I'd be making a difference.'

He pulls a face. 'One bang on the head and now you want to change the world?'

'No.' I think of Frisky, fighting for his country, or Dr Williams, fighting for my life. 'But I can't think of a single thing I've ever done that I'm proud of.'

'Blimey. Well, neither can I. Problem you've got, Jo, is too much time to think. Sooner you're back here the better.' And he punches me lightly on the arm. 'And at least you're more decorative than mousy little Ruthie.'

'Maybe.' I look down at the cake and see that I've crushed it with my hand. 'Listen, Mikey. Do you think the others would be horribly offended if I disappeared? The slightest thing tires me out these days.'

He looks at me more seriously. 'I'm sure we'll cope. But will you cope? Are you coping, Jo?'

I cram the bag of cake into my handbag. 'Do I have a choice?'

Mikey grabs my hand. 'Oh, there's always a choice, Jo. You just need to learn to work out what it is.'

From: Joanna Morgan
[mailto:scaredycat@headbangers.net]
Sent: Wednesday 12 April
To: Dennis Diffley
CC: Courtbridge Accident Prevention, Public Protection and Civil Defence Team
BCC: LusciousLorraine@tramp.net
Subject: Easter Safety Bulletin: Death by Chocolate

Dear colleagues,
I'm back! Yes, Deputy Diffley has given me special dispensation to work on the Safety Bulletins from home before my brain goes permanently absent without leave. So, with Lent nearly over and the Easter bunnies running for cover, here are some scary food and drink statistics.

- Countries where people eat the most chocolate have higher suicide rates, but fewer murders.
- One eighth of admissions to UK hospitals are gastric in cause.
- Seventy-eight per cent of children eat the ears off a chocolate bunny first. And a million Britons have an eating disorder.
- But take comfort from the fact that you're 100 times more likely to die in a flood than of food poisoning.
- Chip stealing is the number one cause of rows in restaurants.
- Excessive alcohol shrinks the left-hand side of your brain, and champagne corks are the second commonest cause of eye injuries (after squash balls).
- 493 injuries a year are attributable to cakes and scones.

So . . . surely it's only a matter of time before Dennis launches 'Courtbridge Against Cakes', the nation's first campaign against baked-goods related accidents. You know it makes sense!

Keep safe, everyone, and just say NO to second helpings,
Jo 'The Scaredy-cat' Morgan

Chapter 16
Ichthyophobia – Fear of Fish

Dennis's response to my little joke wasn't quite what I'd have hoped.

'I knew I shouldn't have let you do that bulletin.' He came home two hours early, specifically to tell me off.

'Come on, no one takes it seriously.'

'*I* take it seriously. I can't believe you've been so disloyal. I'm a laughing stock. As if I'd ever take on something as trivial as cakes.' He was pulling so hard at that kiss-curl that he risked ending up with a bald patch to match mine.

'Well, exactly, Dennis. It's daft. Silly. A joke. I had quite a few emails back saying it made people giggle,' I told him. I didn't mention that Mikey had sent me a side-splitting account of Dennis's reaction when the message pinged into everyone's inbox. 'You should take life less seriously.'

He stared at me as if he didn't recognise me. 'No. You should be taking it *more* seriously. After all you've been through.'

'But . . . ' He was beginning to get on my nerves. I'd never really minded Dennis's underdeveloped sense of humour, after a childhood on the receiving end of my brother's stupid 'jokes'. Perhaps the ability to laugh at yourself only becomes essential when the going gets tough.

'But nothing. This is exactly what's worrying me about

you, Jo. Unpredictable behaviour. Sending off for endless junk mail. Treating salesmen as your new best friends. And now this. Sometimes I wonder whether that doctor of yours knows what he's doing, frankly.'

'What, you think I should be booked in for a lobotomy? Or doped up on something? You know how I feel about mind-altering drugs, after the effect they had on Mum.'

His face softened and he sat down on the corner of the sofa. 'No, that's not what I mean. But, well, the devil makes work for idle hands and the accident seems to have affected your judgement.'

He took off his tie and sighed. I joined him on the sofa: his eyes were bloodshot and hooded, and I noticed for the first time that the hair on his temples had gone completely grey. My anger turned instantly to guilt. I was turning Dennis into an old man. 'I know you're worried. But rather than let the devil find me work, why not give me more to do? You always say I have great ideas. I could, I don't know, write some reports for you. Or plan the talk you're meant to be giving to the St John's Ambulance Brigade next week.'

His face took on the James Herriot-about-to-euthanise-a-heifer expression. 'Hmm. Not sure we can risk letting you loose on my speeches yet. No, I'm thinking more of wholesome pursuits. More fresh air, or something practical. Watercolours are meant to be very therapeutic and would do wonders for your co-ordination.'

I gave up then, before I told him where to stick his paintbrush. But in the week since that email, my parents have launched a full-on programme of activities to keep me busy. Mum's day trips now start earlier, finish later and involve physical exertion or art 'therapy'. There can't be a visitor attraction, gallery, or 'paint your own pottery' café in a thirty-mile radius that we haven't visited.

Dad let slip that the Maine Coons are feeling neglected. Their protests include hiding mortally wounded mice under the sofa until they rot, and weeing in my parents' bed.

I can almost understand now why Timmy found it so

impossible to give up his status as the One Who Needs Attention. I've never had so many organic Easter eggs or been taken on so many magical mystery tours.

The one place I haven't been is the Monday Club. I can't face the unrelenting cheeriness of Dr Williams. I've got enough busybodies in my life and anyway, my mother, busybody-in-chief, is deeply suspicious of Frisky. She's just left after a wet afternoon at some wildlife park alongside the motorway. 'Animals can be so healing to watch, don't you think, Jo? The way they simply exist?'

I couldn't feel much healing going on as we stood in a barn, watching a group of depressed-looking ostriches pecking at their food troughs. The 'park' was really a commerical ostrich-meat farm with a few rabbits and guinea pigs crammed into an outbuilding named 'Petting Paradise', which sounded seedier than they probably intended. My expectations were as low as they could be but I still felt disappointed.

Mum was so wet by the time we got home that she abandoned me at the front door. 'I've got to dash, darling, or I'll miss *Deal or No Deal.*' During the long dark nights of the eighties, Mum only had eyes for Timmy and Noel Edmunds.

I didn't protest too much and now I'm safely inside, I draw the curtains to stop the neighbours seeing in. It's another deathly afternoon on Salzburg Avenue, though tongues are no doubt wagging at the newly abandoned maroon Mini on the corner. It *must* have been a joyrider as no Salzburg Avenue resident would drive a wreck like that.

My shoes make a sucking noise when I pull them off, and I can't be bothered to change my damp socks. I fill the kettle but then don't see the point in switching it on, as there's nothing I fancy drinking. My mother's stocked the cupboards with Ovaltine and camomile tea and organic hot chocolate powder; every beverage has additional benefits.

Really I'd like some booze – Frisky reignited my taste for it – but it's not even 5 p.m.

My stomach rumbles so I go in search of food. Brain boost multi-seed millet mix? Tofu and alfafa casserole? Mum's used stealth tactics to turn our kitchen into a branch of Holland and Barrett. No wonder I sometimes catch a whiff of illicit chips on Dennis's breath when he gets in. Yet another thing he doesn't get at home.

I'm excavating the freezer in the hope there might be something with E numbers lurking at the back, when the doorbell goes. Perhaps it's that bloody librarian again, the books she left must be overdue by now.

I ignore it, but then the chimes are accompanied by dull thumps on the door, like a large bear in search of porridge.

I don't know why I don't feel at all frightened when I go to answer it. Apathy, perhaps. If someone really wants to break in, ransack the house, abduct me for a life of degradation and exploitation, good luck to 'em. Got to be an improvement on a life of day trips.

But it isn't a burglar.

It's Frisky's grandson.

Luke looks all wrong on the doorstep, shifting from foot to foot, his neck slightly bent so he doesn't hit his head on the rain canopy.

'Oh. It's you. Hello,' I say, before something important occurs to me. 'How do you know where I live?'

'Frisky ordered that taxi-cab for you, remember?' His voice is brusque, but I catch that hint of an American accent again.

I try to work out why on earth Frisky might want to contact me. 'Oh God. He's not ill, or . . . '

'Gramps is fine,' growls Luke, saying the childish nickname with real venom. 'Well, as fine as he ever is.' He stares at his feet, which are in those filthy trainers again. He badly needs a makeover. With a long bath, a decent suit and a chirpier demeanour, he'd be what Lorraine calls 'top totty'. Mind you, I can talk. I spotted the first hairs growing on my bald patch this morning, a soft fuzz, like hamster fur. *Irresistible*.

'Right . . . and so the reason you're here is?' I smile politely.

'He sent me to fetch you. He wants to take you out.'

'Eh?' My brain isn't working fast enough to process this.

'But how did he know I'd be in? Hang on. Have you been watching me?'

Two perfect crimson circles appear on Luke's cheeks. 'No. Just waiting for you.'

I feel like I'm in an episode of *Twin Peaks*. 'I'm finding this all a bit odd, Luke, to be honest. It's very sweet of Frisky, but I've had a tiring day. Perhaps you'd be kind enough to tell him I'm . . . indisposed.' Oh God, now I'm talking like a Jane Austen heroine.

Luke folds his arms. 'It's easier to let him have his way, really, he always wins and it's a waste of energy to try to resist Frisky's dark powers.'

It's the longest sentence I've heard him speak. His face is deadpan, so I can't tell for sure if he's joking. 'You make him sound sinister.'

He sneers, revealing brilliant white teeth, startling in that dark face. 'No, not sinister. A charmer. But charm can be kinda dangerous.'

'What an extraordinary thing to say about your grandfather.'

Luke shrugs. 'You don't know him yet. So you ready? Or I'll wait.' He sounds determined.

'But . . . but . . . ' I'm floundering. I don't doubt he will wait, and if he's still here when Dennis gets back, I'll have yet more explaining to do. 'No way am I getting on a motorbike.'

He smiles properly, for the first time. God, he should *so* be in the movies. 'No need,' he says and points outside, at the beaten-up maroon Mini. 'Gramps has gone and bought us some wheels.'

Half an hour later, I'm in this red peril of a car with Frisky and Luke, still not quite understanding why I'm there.

'I'm keeping up with the Joneses,' Frisky says, as we speed away. 'Everyone else has wheels, so I've gone one better. I've got wheels *and* a chauffeur. Vintage, too.'

Luke grunts. 'You mean, prehistoric.' The way he drives

surprises me, confident but careful, as if he has a transplant patient or a priceless statue in the back of the car.

'So where have you been in it so far?' I ask.

'Do you know what, Joanna, we haven't actually been *anywhere* yet? Saved it for you. This is our maiden voyage! Ha ha. Let's hope we bowl the maiden over, eh, Luke?' And Frisky chortles away happily for several minutes.

When we picked him up from the villa, he clambered straight into the back of the car, and when I tried to climb into the passenger seat – it seemed rude to leave Luke on his own, like a glorified cabbie – Frisky shouted from inside, 'Oh no, no, come and sit with me, Joanna. We can have a catch-up.'

He immediately told me off for missing the Monday Club. 'Our lovely young doctor Nathan's been quite bereft, looking at that little pocket-watch of his and sighing,' Frisky said, extra loud, casting glances at his grandson in the rear-view mirror. He then treated me to his opinions on rap music and global warming. 'I like to keep up, Joanna, nothing worse than an old boy who still lives in the 1940s.'

But he refused to elaborate on his plans for the outing. 'I just had a feeling you might need a treat.'

I'm beginning to realise that Frisky lives in a different world from most of us, with so much time on his hands yet so little left. Perhaps he has a God complex. Or maybe he's lonely. Either way, his enthusiasm is so infectious that saying no to him would be like telling my mother that cats don't have souls.

'Nearly there,' says Frisky, sounding more like an excited child than a megalomaniac.

We're on the outskirts of Courtbridge now, the area known as New Town. There's an ugly trading estate of buildings built entirely from rusting corrugated iron. Then there's the Courtbridge Shopping Experience, with its DIY store and furniture warehouse and gargantuan new pet store (what on earth do they sell there – genetically modified gerbils?). And finally there's the Courtbridge Leisure Experience, which holds experiences I'd rather avoid: wave machines, multi-gyms and saunas.

'Hang on, Frisky. We're not going *swimming*, are we?' I say. I cringe at the thought of the chlorine stinging my eyes, of wading through a soup of kiddie wee and lost beige plasters. 'Only I don't have my cossie . . . ' It occurs to me then that he could buy me one, so I add, 'And I've got a very bad bout of athlete's foot.'

'Calm down, my dear. I don't wish to know the status of your fungal infections and anyway, who said anything about swimming?'

But Luke is driving into the car park, executing a driving-test perfect reverse into a tight spot.

'Well, I don't think I should be doing weight training either.'

'Golly, we are worked up. Don't you like surprises?' Frisky rubs his hands together.

I try to smile. 'No, I don't. Actually. I prefer a bit of advance warning.'

He shakes his head sadly. 'Yawn. But don't worry, I'm not going to make you jump through any hoops. Or perform any physical jerks whatsoever.' He climbs out of the car, and I do the same.

'So what *are* we doing here?'

He turns away from the shed that constitutes the Leisure Experience towards the recreation ground. 'You really do need to learn to be a touch more observant, Jo.'

It's only now that I notice the tip of an orange and pink tower poking over the tall hedge. And hear a blast of distorted dance music.

Frisky pulls back his shoulders and stands up straight as if he's headed for the parade ground. 'Hold on to your hat, dear child. We're going to the fair!'

We squeeze through a gap in the hedge, Frisky leading, then

me, with Luke behind us like a grumpy bodyguard. The ground is muddy but at least it's finally stopped raining.

Fairgrounds look creepy in daylight, the colours too bright and the punters too shifty. Half the rides aren't working yet; men are emerging from trailers with miserable eyes and roll-ups between their lips. One pulls a masive khaki tarpaulin off the kiosk leading to the Crazee Caterpillar: a sheet of rain crashes to the floor and some of the water hits us as we pass.

'Watch out!' I grumble. The man scowls back.

Frisky gives me an odd look. 'It's only water. Dear me, the youth of today.'

When I was a teenager, funfairs were full of men your mum warned you about: the kind Lorraine loved. Craggy boys with tattoos and strong lager and wandering hands. We went to the fair in Newbury every spring and autumn, stalking rides until we found someone Lorraine liked the look of ... first the waltzer ('his acne would make me *puke*!'), the ghost train ('he's a vampire'), then the dodgems ('broken nose, and not in a good way') and the octopus ('now *he's* more like it ... '). Then we'd ride over and over until the guy noticed her, at which point I'd finally be allowed to disembark, with wobbly legs and vertigo, while Lorraine went round the back with Octopus Man. Whichever ride they came from, they all had octopus hands according to Lorraine and that suited her just fine.

Once, someone chatted *me* up: his name was Terry, and he had a gentle face and a huge tiger tattooed on his skinny upper arm. He worked on the little blue kids' train that went nowhere slowly. Lorraine and I crammed ourselves into the wooden seats, and she rang the bell with such ferocity that I thought the rope would come off in her hands. She went crazy when she worked out that he fancied me, then swore she'd never been interested in the first place.

He bought me candy floss and lukewarm Fanta Orange but I backed off before he had chance to try a kiss. I spent the next two months wondering what might have happened if I'd stayed, drawing pictures in my diary and imagining our floss-coated lips meeting in the glow of a thousand green and purple lightbulbs. No one tried to kiss me for four years after that.

'Right, Joanna. When was the last time a gentleman attempted to win you a goldfish?' Frisky interrupts my nostalgia trip.

We've reached an old-fashioned coconut shy, where hairy brown shells are stacked on top of each other. Luke still hangs back, looking bored.

'I hope there aren't goldfish here. Courtbridge Council doesn't allow the use of live animals as prizes,' I say.

Frisky sighs. 'Well, aren't you the life and soul of the party? If you're going to behave like this, then we might as well take you home.'

I open my mouth to snap back, *I never asked to come here*, but stop myself. Putting the emancipation of goldfish to one side, is there anything worse than a killjoy? When exactly did I turn from a bit of a wimp into a total wet blanket?

I try to pinpoint that moment. Maybe it was after Timmy got ill, or when I joined the council. But I was always willing to laugh at my own paranoia, and never tried to pour water on other people's ideas.

Nope. I freeze as I remember exactly when I crossed the line. My hard-liner fundamentalist super safety consciousness began in the weeks after I moved in with Dennis, as I added dozens of new precautionary measures to the ones I already followed. Nothing could be left to chance.

Frisky looks worried. 'Not having one of your turns, are you, Joanna?'

'No, no. You're right, I am being stupid. I promise I'll try to be less of a misery guts.'

'Oh, don't fret. Anyhow, I can't see any fish, so your conscience is clear.' He hands over a two-pound coin to the thin girl who's running the stall. She gives him three balls without looking: she's too busy gawping at Luke, flicking her black hair out of her eyes and pouting. He stares resolutely at the ground.

Frisky takes aim at the display. The first time he misses so badly that even the girl notices, moving swiftly out of the danger zone. 'Just getting my bearings,' he assures us before throwing again . . .

The hard ball smashes into the bottom row of coconuts, a direct hit that should bring the whole display crashing down. But all it does is wobble slightly and Luke seems to wake up. He glares at the girl, and then reaches over to take the final ball from Frisky.

He squares up to the coconuts, so tall and determined that the girl jumps out of range. He stretches his arm back like a cricket fast bowler, testing the movement twice before he's ready. Then he performs a throw of such force that the sound of the ball smashing against the shells seems to reverberate around the fairground.

But the column of coconuts is still intact.

'What the hell is this?' Luke growls. That American accent is unmistakable now. 'Those shells are nailed down, aren't they?'

The girl cowers.

'Cat got your tongue? I want my grandfather's money back *and* a prize for the lady.' He folds his arms across his chest.

'But . . . it's my dad's stall. He'll kill me if I give prizes away.'

Luke doesn't move. 'Well, let me deal with your father then.'

She seems to be weighing up who scares her more – Luke or her dad – and eventually fishes in her money-belt to retrieve the two-pound coin. Then she rummages around beneath the counter before handing me a small furry goldfish, with non EU-compliant plastic fins.

'Not that one,' Luke says and points up at the display. '*That* one.'

'It's OK, Luke,' I say, 'I don't mind.'

But he takes the small fish from me and holds it out to the girl, who swaps it for a plush deluxe version in multiple shades of orange and yellow. It's the size of a Labrador.

'Um. Thanks very much.'

Frisky is trying very hard not to laugh as I wrestle the fish into the most comfortable position; holding it in front of me means I can barely see, so I settle for squashing the well-stuffed body under my arm.

'I just hope they don't try to charge us extra to take the fish on the rides,' Frisky says. 'Now which one shall we try first?'

Chapter 17

Potamophobia – Fear of Rivers or Running Water

Frisky and I are crammed together in a purple fibreglass gondola, waiting for the sweaty ride-owner to press 'go' on 'Around the World in Eight Magical Minutes'. I refused to go on anything involving unpredictable movements, which ruled out pretty much everything else.

'So are we still feeling grumpy, Miss Morgan?' Frisky asks me as the boat finally jolts forward. Sweaty Bloke has given up waiting for any other customers, so as the gondola pushes its way through the double rubber doors into the darkness, we're on our own. Luke is waiting outside, guarding the mutant goldfish.

Tinkly Chinese music plays from a speaker to our left, and as we creak along at a snail's pace, a spotlight illuminates a cluster of miniature pavilions, with a family of cross-looking Chinese puppets standing guard on top of a pile of rice. 'Not quite as grumpy, Frisky. Sorry. Like I said before, I'm not good with surprises.'

'But they're one of the pleasures of life, my dear. You need to *embrace* new experiences.'

'Frisky, why are you doing this for me?'

'That's rather a direct question. I suppose a direct answer is in order. I can't bear to see people waste their lives, Joanna. I've seen it at the Monday Club, people's horizons becoming so limited that they almost cease to exist. Even my own grandson . . . ' he hesitates. 'But that's a different story. All I know is, I don't want it to happen to you. So when you didn't turn up at the club, I decided on direct action. But if you're coping on your own, feel free to tell me to, what would Luke say, butt out!'

The gondola has moved at least five feet when the music stops and the light goes out on the Chinese family. There's a sloshing sound through the speakers and in the dark, I try to imagine we're sailing through a Venetian lagoon, rather than clunking our way through a fibreglass tunnel on Courtbridge recreation ground.

'I wouldn't say I'm coping, exactly.' On the right, Moscow appears under the glow of a red bulb: the Kremlin with its towers like Christmas tree baubles, ornate tear-drops stacked on top of each other. A dozen Russian dolls stand in a semicircle on a Red Square covered in fake snow. The largest doll wears a child-size traditional fur hat, the front half-covering her painted eyes. 'In fact, sometimes life feels pretty unreal.'

The music changes to a polka, as Frisky takes my hand and strokes it, softly. It's a comforting gesture. 'You know, we all have times like this, Joanna. Times when we're pushed by . . . circumstances into working out who we really are. Strange as it seems, this will be the making of you.'

I shake my head. 'But it's making me worse, not better. I know I've been given a second chance. Beaten the odds. But I can't seem to shake off all my stupid fears. I want to go outside, but it makes me nervous. I want to try new things, but when I get the chance, I complain. Pathetic. Someone *else* . . . no, *anyone* else would have deserved a second chance more than me.' My voice sounds bitter in the empty space.

'You know, Joanna, a man died in *my* plane. The one I crashed, that they then patched up. He had twin girls, three days old when he died. He never got to see them. Did he deserve to live more than I did?'

'Well . . . that's a question you can't ever answer.'

'Exactly. Did you ever wonder why in war, people talk

about bombs and bullets having their name on them? It's the only way to make sense of something so senseless.'

'So maybe that bike had *my* name on it?'

'You'll never know.'

The gondola runs along a particularly squeaky rail, as we pass a display of threadbare polar bears. 'I don't feel like I'm making a very good job of starting over. Shouldn't I be off looking at real polar bears in the Arctic? Or is it the Antarctic? See, I don't even know that.'

'Well, find out. From what I can tell, there's nothing stopping you going to either pole. Or both in fact.'

'Nothing except . . . being scared of flying. Um, and of falling through ice. Of losing the tip of my nose to exposure. Not at all convinced about penguins either. In fact, I'm not at all sure about anything with wings, including ducks, moths and aeroplanes.'

Frisky chuckles; I'm aware of his body trembling. 'Anything else you're scared of, Joanna?'

'Where do I begin? Explosions, dirty bombs, normal bombs, heights, nuclear missiles, fire, criminals with guns, policemen with guns . . . ' It comes flooding out, much easier because we're in the dark. 'Deadly diseases, anaphylactic shock, takeaways teeming with unfriendly bacteria, pizza delivery boys on unlicensed mopeds, anyone who drives too fast.'

'That it?'

'Oh, and ladders. That's it.'

'Not spiders?' I can hear suppressed laughter in Frisky's voice.

'No, strangely enough. If I found a tarantula in a bunch of bananas from the supermarket, I'd probably keep it as a pet.'

As if on cue, our gondola takes us into a lush plastic rainforest, fronds of fern brushing against our faces from both sides. The taped cicadas are so loud, their first chirrup makes me jump. Maybe the man who runs the ride hides in the fake bushes and sprays air freshener at the passengers because I get a distinct waft of exotic flowers.

As we float by, a plastic parrot shrieks, 'Pieces of eight, pieces of eight,' through its closed beak.

'I wonder, Joanna, do you trust me?'

I think about it as we leave the rainforest and head into the American West, where a Spanish straw donkey is masquerading as a cowboy's horse. I'd usually weigh up the evidence logically and thoroughly before knowing the answer to a question like that, but I know instantly that I do trust him. Despite Luke's warnings about his grandfather's eccentricities, there's something fundamentally *good* about Frisky, the way daisies and rainbows are good. 'Yes.'

'Excellent. When I first met you, I sensed that I could help you. And now I realise why. You're living half a life. Fear does that to people. And it won't get better on its own accord. Flight is a perfectly good survival strategy but there are times when *fight* is the better approach.'

As Doris Day sings 'Deadwood Stage', I realise he's right. I started out with an everyday childhood fear of the dark, and my fears have simply multiplied, like bacteria, ever since. 'So what's the magic cure, then?'

'I think it's to tackle fears head on. Confront them. Cut 'em down to size.'

As if it's that easy, I want to snap back. But instead I take a deep breath before answering. 'Might work with spiders, Frisky. But where am I going to find an atom bomb?'

'Ah, you'd be surprised what I can do, my dear. Frisky has friends in high places.' And he laughs again. 'OK. I'll admit a ten-megaton warhead might be a problem, but sometimes all it takes is a little imagination.'

I shudder, remembering Mr Blake's Hiroshima movie and the dreams that haunt me still. 'I think imagination is the one thing I've got too much of.'

'Let me do the imagining, Joanna. Plus I need a project to occupy me.'

'A *project*?'

'Oh golly, I've said the wrong thing again, haven't I?'

I think we're approaching the end of the ride, back on

home turf: there's a model of Big Ben, and a beefeater Paddington Bear. I haven't been to London for years, for fear of carbon dioxide and terrorism and mugging. If I don't do something about my phobias, this might be the nearest I'll ever get. 'No, it's not that, Frisky. I just think you're flogging a dead horse.'

'It's a little early to write yourself off, isn't it?'

'I've been this way for as long as I can remember.'

'And don't you wonder what life would be like if you were reborn, scared of nothing?'

Without thinking about it, I crane my neck to look behind me at the world: I've seen more in this ride than I ever will in reality at this rate. I could have died two months ago without seeing the poles or the Pyramids. I feel a lump in my throat. 'This . . . project. You'd be with me?'

'Every step, Joanna. And I wouldn't do anything that would put you at risk. You have my word.'

Louis Armstrong's 'What a Wonderful World' – the one song guaranteed to make me sob, especially at weddings or funerals – is playing as the gondola approaches the exit. I peek back a final time, and the whole 'world' is lit up with the multi-coloured bulbs. It's corny and cheap yet, in that moment, it's also painfully beautiful.

'All right, Frisky. You've got a deal.'

'Oh, *smashing*. You won't regret it, my dear.'

The front of the gondola pushes through the rubber doors and we both blink as we emerge into the dusk. And then I remember something. 'Frisky. There was no Venice. We were in a gondola, but we never saw the Grand Canal or St Mark's Square or Harry's Bar.'

'Perfect.' He gives me one of those smiles that lifts his entire face from jowls to eyebrows. 'Something to work towards. And where Venice is concerned, there's nothing like the real thing. Now,' he clambers out of the gondola, then holds out his hand to help me, 'I think it's time you chose a more daring ride, to show willing. Don't you?'

*

While Frisky 'answers a call of nature', Luke and I circle the fairground, looking for a ride I can pluck up the courage to go on. Being brave is something I want to begin *tomorrow*. But I know I have to start today.

I try to distract myself by talking to Luke, but he's impossible. If I even attempt a smile, he looks down. Though that moody pout of his looks a lot less convincing now he's clutching my overgrown goldfish.

'I thought that was great, earlier,' I say, gesturing vaguely at the toy. 'What you did.'

'I'm sorry?' He stares at me as though he'd forgotten I was there.

'Sticking up for your grandfather like that.'

Still he stares. Finally he flicks his hand dismissively. 'That wasn't sticking up for Frisky. He doesn't need anyone to fight his battles for him.'

I feel riled. 'So what was that about then?'

'Call it natural justice,' he says. 'I hate cheats.' And then he turns away.

'But you clearly don't hate bad manners,' I say, fed up with his rudeness. His mouth twists, but I can't tell whether it's with contempt or anger. Before he can say anything, he suddenly lurches forward and only just misses falling face down in the mud. It takes me a moment to realise he's been pushed.

'Oi! Are you the fucking bully who's been shouting at my sister?'

The teenager who pushed Luke is short but wide, seemingly free of tattoos but chock-full of menace.

'Hear what I said, fucker?' Behind the Menace is a second youth, who is taller but still built like the proverbial brick shithouse. 'You've had it, mate. All for the sake of a fucking fish for your fucking girlfriend.'

Luke can't deny it was him. There's no one else in the vicinity holding a three-foot orange fish. Instead he says, 'She's not my girlfriend.'

As if that makes any difference. The yobs move closer. The

menacing one has a ring of spit around his fleshy mouth, dribbling in anticipation of the fight. I look round for Frisky, knowing we can't stick around. Yes, there's a tiny part of me feeling relieved that I now won't have to brave the dodgems. But that bit's outweighed by terror at exactly how much damage the gruesome twosome are planning to inflict on Luke. Or me.

'She's not? Why, you a queer? That why you can't pick on someone your own fucking size? Eh?'

'We need to get out of here,' I whisper.

Luke doesn't move. He holds out his palms in a calming gesture. Well, as calming as it can be when you're holding a giant cuddly toy. 'I don't think the discussion I had with the girl on the stall counts as picking on anyone. We would have won this, fair and square, if the entire sideshow wasn't weighted against the player.'

The confidence in his voice throws the boys for a moment. Then the Menace recovers and takes a step closer. 'Fair and square. Fair and square.' He mimics Luke's transatlantic accent, and the sidekick giggles.

I spot Frisky walking towards us, in no hurry, like everything's right with the world.

The Menace lurches forward, jabs his stubby finger against Luke's chest. 'Fair and fucking square, eh, mate? So how's this for square?'

Luke must know it's coming – bloody hell, even I know the Menace is about to do something nasty and I'm usually slow on the uptake – but he doesn't flinch. Just as the thug's fist launches itself towards that distinctively square Freeman Van Belle jaw, Luke intercepts it, effortlessly, by raising the goldfish in self-defence and trapping the thug's hand under its fin. And as the Menace's other fist snaps up in a reflex, Luke grips it and digs his fingers into the putty flesh of his attacker's wrist.

'I hope we can stay *civilised*,' Luke says, looking over the Menace's shoulder at me. 'Jo, why don't you go and take my grandfather back to the car? I wouldn't want us to outstay our welcome.'

'But . . . ' I feel torn between steering Frisky away from trouble – something tells me he would relish fisticuffs, but isn't nearly as strong as he thinks – and not leaving Luke outnumbered *and* hampered by a fish. So I reach down to unburden him of the fish.

It is, I immediately realise, the wrong thing to do. I release the fish and with it the Menace's right hand, which launches itself in a straight line towards Luke's nose. Luke moves an inch so that the fist strikes him on the side of the face, rather than the nose, but I still hear the crack and it makes me want to throw up.

There's a moment of silence that seems to last minutes, as the three men consider their next options.

Luke finally breaks the impasse.

'RUN,' he instructs. So I do . . . my feet splashing muddy water up my trousers, then sinking into boggy quicksands, like running in a nightmare.

I spot Frisky pondering the snack menu hanging from the burger van. 'Frisky. We're off!'

He turns towards my voice and, for a split second, his bewildered look reflects his age. Then he takes in the situation: my trousers blackened from my knees to my ankles; and his grandson running in our direction, pursued by the fat gits, who keep on catching up until Luke lashes out, like a character in a computer game.

'Righto, Jo,' he says and takes my hand (the one that isn't clutching the goldfish) and we run together, trying to work out the least boggy route to the gap in the fence. Frisky's breathing heavily, and for the first time I suddenly understand that, for all his bluster and energy and strength of character, he's still eighty-five. I clutch his hand hard, feeling the strange smooth texture of his palms.

Only when we reach the fence do I dare to look back and there is Luke, surprisingly close, with an elegant trickle of blood bisecting his face from cheekbone to chin. The thugs are way behind: both absolutely covered in mud. Their clothes, faces and hair are caked.

'You OK?' he asks me, without breaking his stride.

'Yes,' I pant back. 'Terminally unfit, though.'

'I hope it's not *actually* terminal. That would be a shame,' he says, and grants me a fleeting glimpse of that dazzling smile. He's incredibly calm for someone who's just been punched and chased by two men who want to do him serious damage.

We're by the Red Peril now, and somehow I force myself into the Mini's cramped back seat, while Frisky deigns to get in the front. But the faffing has cost us seconds. The men are closing in on the car. 'Sitting comfortably?' Luke turns the ignition key.

The car splutters and fails.

'Oh, golly,' Frisky says, sounding excited rather than frightened. 'And the man we bought it from swore it always started first time.'

'Have you all locked your doors?' Luke asks, almost casually. 'Might be a good idea.'

I do as I'm told while Luke tries the ignition again. It sounds a touch more sprightly this time, but still refuses to go all the way. I feel as though I might explode from the tension. The waltzer would be child's play compared to this.

I catch Luke's eye in the mirror and he mouths, 'It's OK.' And at that point, third time lucky, the engine fires.

Luke reverses ferociously out of his space, no longer the cautious Sunday driver. I look through the back window and see the men shaking their fists, cartoon style, as we leave them behind.

Only once we're safely on the ring road does Frisky speak again. 'Well, bloody hell. What a hoot. Haven't had that much fun in years.'

'Are you quite bonkers, Frisky?' I say, my breathing ragged.

'Well, yes I am, but that's not the point. You must be feeling the buzz.'

I shake my head. 'Don't be silly.' It's true that the fear is fading now and, OK, in its place, there is, yes, all right, a slight tingle in my fingers and toes, but that's purely a physical reaction to extreme exertion.

We cross the roundabout, and I notice the daffodils, thousands of them, as if someone has dropped a vat of emulsion from a helicopter, splashing bright yellow paint everywhere. How strange that spring has arrived and I hadn't realised.

'What I can't get over,' Luke says, deadpan, 'is that we ended up in all that trouble over a three-foot goldfish.'

'Yup,' says Frisky. It's the first time they've agreed on anything. 'I think the goldfish should be our new mascot. And a mascot has to have a name, after all. Jo? I think that's down to you.'

'Any suggestions?'

'Let me think, my dear. It should be symbolic, don't you think? Freddy the Fearless Fish? Or . . . Goldie the Valiant?'

But then it occurs to me. There's only one thing my fish can be called. 'No, I've worked it out. I hereby name this fish . . . Lucky!'

It starts as a giggle, but within seconds, the car is shaking as the three of us laugh harder than I've heard anyone laugh for years.

Chapter 18

Cenophobia – Fear of New Things or Ideas

I seem to have taken up permanent residence in the doghouse.

The night of the fairground episode, Luke dropped me off on the main road, and as I walked up Salzburg Avenue, I noticed that the bungalow was all lit up like Santa's grotto. I realised this was unlikely to be good news.

OK, so I had stopped for a little ouzo back at Frisky's house, but I wasn't drunk. I was just excitable after our great escape. And I know Mum said . . . well, shrieked . . . that they were about to call the police, but the cops would have told them to stop panicking and wait twenty-four hours.

It's not as if I didn't leave a note. Which I pointed out to them, when they finally stopped shouting.

Dennis waved it at me. '"Gone out, back soon"? Is it any wonder we wanted to send out a search party?'

'But it's true,' I said, weakly. 'I had gone out. And I was back . . . ' I paused as I noticed that the clock on the mantelpiece really *did* say half past nine. No wonder it was dark. ' . . . well, if not soon, that at least before it got too late. And there was no need to worry Mum and Dad.'

'I think there was. Where the hell were you?'

'With Frisky,' I said, forgetting that I hadn't actually told the Love of My Life about the New Man in My Life. 'Don't look like that, Dennis. Frisky's a patient at the clinic. Mum's met him. It's no big deal, he's eighty-five years old.'

Mum nodded. 'I should have mentioned it, Dennis, sorry. I sort of thought Jo wouldn't see him again. I'm not at all sure he's a good influence.'

Dennis shook his head in disbelief. 'You're socialising with a *patient* in his *eighties*? Imagine what could have happened. Are you right in the head?'

I stared back. 'In case you haven't noticed, no, I'm not, actually.'

He frowned and bunched his fists. 'Jo, you know I didn't mean it like that.'

'I'm not a child, Dennis, so please stop treating me like one.' At that moment, I was relieved I'd left Lucky in the Mini by accident; clutching a three-foot goldfish might have undermined my argument.

'I'll stop treating you like a child when you start behaving like an adult. Obviously.'

My father coughed then, and Dennis swore under his breath, as if he'd forgotten my parents were there. I looked at each member of the welcoming committee in turn: Mum with her hand-wringing, thirty-years-of-practice doomsday demeanour; Dad and his 'I'm not listening' ostrich approach to anything uncomfortable; and Dennis, reliable righteous Dennis, with his inescapable certainty that so easily slips over into dogma.

And then I wondered what they were seeing: this unpredictable creature with a bald patch, in place of the scaredy-cat they knew and loved. I don't know whether I was buoyed up by what Frisky said, or by the ouzo, but I wanted to tell them how I felt. 'I know I'm different now,' I began. 'But different doesn't mean mad, does it? The accident was a turning point for me. A reality check, making me re-examine whether I'm happy with the status quo.'

Dennis's eyes had narrowed, but his voice was controlled. 'And are you?'

Oh shit. I should have seen that coming. The big

question . . . if I answered yes then I'd lose my chance to make changes. But if I answered no, then all hell would break loose. I played for time. 'Oh, it's nothing *major*. More a state of mind thing. Taking a few more risks. Being a bit braver.'

'You didn't answer my question,' Dennis said, displaying the pedantry that got him where he is today. 'Are you happy? A yes or no will do.'

He didn't have to do that, did he? I mean, he could have let me off the hook. Surely the rule of thumb for Mr Cautious should be never ask a question unless you're prepared to hear the answer?

'No. I'm not.' It was like waiting for the bomb to drop after the four-minute warning. My mother's lips did that cat's bottom, pursing thing and I had to fight the instinct to qualify it, backtrack, tell her it wasn't her fault; but now I'd said it, I had to stick to my guns. Dad fiddled with his Aston Martin cufflinks. And Dennis . . .

Dennis looked at me until I had to look away. Then he said, 'Lynda, Ted. Thanks for coming over, but I think it's time for bed. We could all do with some sleep.'

And since then, he's only spoken to me if there's no alternative. It's his way of showing that my behaviour on Wednesday night was *not* acceptable. As if I hadn't already got the message.

Unfortunately, this is also the weekend he's booked a romantic mini-break to a mystery destination. There isn't much laughter in the car with Dennis at the best of times, but today the stillness is oppressive. And if he can see the contradiction involved in giving me a treat *and* punishing me at the same time, he's not letting on.

So, sitting in the car, speeding up the M40 (is this Britain's dullest motorway?), I know that I've neither been forgiven or forgotten. But instead of feeling contrite, I feel irritated: am I meant to apologise for wanting life to be more exciting? I open my mouth to talk to him about it but he turns up the volume on *Any Answers* where some vicar from Weybridge is having a rant about litter.

Dennis . . . ' I try again.

His beige-brogued foot nudges the accelerator up by two or three extra miles per hour. This is as close as he'll ever get to displaying his irritation. After all, what's Dennis's temporary annoyance compared to the threat global warming poses to the planet? Even with a scary trucker behind him, full beam blazing, Dennis refuses to go beyond an optimally fuel-efficient 56mph.

So I too focus on the road ahead, on the chevrons that mark the distance between us and the next car, trying to ignore the distance between me and my soul mate. This is a *temporary* thing, caused by my head injury. Normal service will be resumed shortly, and I will remember what it is about him that I love, and he'll realise that me getting out more isn't a threat to our relationship. We will all live happily ever after.

If I can only get to Sunday night without blowing my top, it'll be fine. And the fact that he's sent me to Coventry might be my best hope of keeping the peace.

'You've brought me to *Coventry* on a romantic weekend?'

Dennis looks at the hotel, then at me, then back at the hotel again. 'But it's called the *Warwickshire* Plaza Hotel. Warwick. You know, castles and cobbled streets and Shakespeare and swans . . . ' His voice fades away.

'As opposed to Coventry, with ring roads and The Specials and empty car factories?' I say.

Dennis's shoulders are slumped and if I didn't know him better, I'd swear that the stuck-out bottom lip means he's trying not to cry. His best-laid plans *never* fail. 'I can't believe it.'

We've spent the last forty-five minutes driving round the ring road, while Dennis refused to let me look at the print-out with the directions on it. I couldn't tell whether this was male navigational arrogance, or a reluctance to spoil my surprise.

Either way, it was pretty clear that we weren't headed for anywhere that could have inspired a sonnet.

'Well, we're here now. I suppose we ought to make the best of it,' I try to sound jolly. He looks so crushed.

'Are you sure?'

'Yep. After all, if you're with the right person, anywhere can be fun.' After the Trappist journey we've just had, my words sound oddly hollow to me. But they seem to satisfy Dennis, who perks up immediately as he carries our bags towards the glass-and-marble entrance to the Plaza. I envy him that ability to switch moods in an instant: since the accident, my resentments linger like the smell of spilled milk on car upholstery.

The hotel is glossy in a *Dynasty* way, all polished brass and shoulder-pads. It must have been *the* place to be seen in Coventry twenty years ago. Perhaps it still is. The receptionist is so skinny that I'm surprised the overactive air conditioning doesn't blow her over. She hands us his 'n' hers plastic keycards and calls the porter, who is desperate to load our pitiful weekend bags onto his huge roller-trolley, but Dennis snatched them back and we take the lift to our floor on our own. He's too tight to tip.

'There's a leisure club,' Dennis says, pointing at a colour photograph of two women in bikinis who should be on Page 3, but instead are posing next to a very small swimming pool. Judging from their flicked hair, the picture was taken around the time of the 1981 Royal Wedding. One of them either has a twitch, or she's winking provocatively as she stands next to a sign reading 'Genuine Swedish Unisex Sauna'.

'Dennis. You don't think this is some sort of naturist venue, do you?'

I swear his eyes light up for a second, but then he frowns. 'Give me some credit, Jo. I checked this out very carefully on the internet.'

Though not carefully enough to discover that it was miles from Shakespeare Country. We walk along the gloomy corridor and unlock the door to our room, which is heavy on orange and yellow wallpaper but clean enough. I walk straight to the window: thoughtfully, there's a net curtain to obscure the view of the ring road. 'They didn't have any rooms overlooking the cathedral left when I booked,' Dennis says, which seems strange, as ours was the only car in the car park. And, weirder still, when we were meant to be in Warwick.

The heavy fire door slams behind us and we stand there. Before the accident, Dennis would have been tearing at my clothes by this point, telling me in every detail what he planned to do to me. I catch his eye and he looks away, then begins to unpack, every movement exaggerated, like a mime artist performing a sketch.

I do the same. Arranging my toiletries in the burgundy bathroom takes me five minutes, as I experiment with different layouts, finally settling for a smallest-to-largest line-up, like the Russian dolls in the fairground ride. Back in the room, I spend ages positioning my clothes perfectly on the hangers. I place my socks in one drawer, and my knickers in another.

And when I run out of things to hang, I pick up the complimentary *Coventry Evening Telegraph* and immerse myself in stories about sewage leaks and school reunions.

'I might go exploring,' Dennis says, after a while. 'Do you want to come?'

'I know it sounds a bit pathetic, but the journey's really tired me out.'

He hesitates, then smiles tightly. 'I understand. Why don't I go and suss out the sights for an hour or two?'

'Good idea. I'll be much better after a little nap.'

He nods, and leaves the room. I think he's pretending too.

The thought makes me feel hot, and I go back to the window, but I can't open it. The cars race past four storeys below, paintwork shining in the spring sunshine, on their way to Saturday things: children's birthday parties with conjurors and goody bags, trips to the DIY shop to pick dream-home paint colours, long lazy lunches in the pub with football on the big screen.

Frisky pops into my mind from nowhere. I wonder what he's doing with his Saturday afternoon. Is he sipping wine in the garden, while Luke takes his motorbike for a spin? Or maybe Luke is shirtless and, I don't know, regrouting tiles or . . . well, to be honest, I'm too preoccupied with the shirtless bit to care about the details of the renovations.

I shake my head to banish the image. Dennis. I must focus on Dennis. He is a good man. He's worried about me. He's booked a luxurious hotel, so we can spend time together, work on our relationship. Because they do need work, relationships, don't they? That's what everyone says. Lorraine, the Prime Minister, all those magazine agony aunts. It's all part of the natural cycle of things, ebbing and flowing, ups and downs.

I'm lucky, aren't I? Dennis has stuck by me, despite the bald patch and the salesmen and the rest . . .

I grab my handbag and head for the door. Dennis has made an effort this weekend, so it's only fair that I should do the same.

I haven't been able to face shopping in ages, but having a makeover mission makes it easier. Coventry has all the same cloned chain stores as Courtbridge, so I manage to spend £150 without breaking a sweat. I'm just considering whether to head back to the hotel, when I bump into Dennis in the street.

'I thought you were tired,' he says, then spots the shopping bags and chuckles. 'Now, that's always a reliable sign that a woman's on the mend. So it was a good idea of mine to come here then?'

'Yes. Though I don't know that I would have chosen *Coventry* for a mini-break. It feels a bit *nothingy*,' I say.

'Don't judge a book by its cover, Jo. Look at these,' and he waves towards hoardings displaying a temporary photographic exhibition, 'Phoenix from the Ashes'. 'You know the city was wiped out in 1940?' He leads me over to one of the boards, which shows the spot where we're standing, before and then immediately after the worst night of bombing. The first image is a postcard, the clock stopped at 12.30, the scene busy with purposeful people, a smart suited man striding across the cobbles, two women in pencil skirts running towards the edge of the frame, late for lunch perhaps. A pre-war car with bug-eyed headlamps is parked in the centre, and the shops are all pristine, their stripy awnings advertising tobacco.

The second is barely recognisable as the same place, except for the shell of a three-storey building in the background, and the clock, miraculously still attached to its metal telegraph pole. The women and the awnings have gone: in their place are men in dusty overalls, hands on hips, inspecting the damage. Rubble seems the wrong word for the piles of girders and masonry, defocused by clouds of dust and smoke. I imagine the smell of bonfires and rotting.

'It's so sad.' I look around me, wondering how it felt to have to pick up the pieces.

'I've been giving myself a guided tour,' Dennis says, 'shall I show you?'

And I follow him around, dodging determined shoppers, looking beyond the Gap posters and the traffic signs. He shows me the ruined cathedral, its bombed-out framework retained in memory of the city's losses.

'Bloody hell. Imagine you'd been fighting abroad the whole war and you came back to a city you didn't recognise.' I think of Frisky and wonder what was waiting for him when he arrived home.

'Nothing stays the same, Jo,' Dennis says.

'No.'

We carry on walking, up Spon Street. 'They moved some of the oldest buildings from the rest of Coventry here after the war,' he says, back on to safe ground.

'What a weird thing to do. Like creating a mini theme park.'

'But it looks good, doesn't it?'

The street is almost *too* preserved, like a film set. 'What would it do to the *souls* of the building, though, moving them from one bit of the city to another?'

He laughs. 'Do you really think buildings have souls? And ghosts, maybe? I thought you were more rational than that, Jo.'

'Ah but that was before ... ' and I stop, wondering whether now's the time to tell him about my flashbacks. Or the fact that my overactive memory can't seem to recall any moments that involve both Dennis *and* me having fun. But I don't want to spoil things. ' ... before the accident, and now of course I believe in Father Christmas and the Abominable Snowman.'

'But you are getting back to normal, Jo, aren't you?' He says this hopefully, like a child wanting reassurance that a trip to the dentist will be filling-free.

'It's slower than I thought.'

'You can't hurry these things,' he pronounces, back in expert mode, though quite what makes him an authority on recovery from head injury I don't know. 'And you mustn't put pressure on yourself to rush back to work, especially after the incident with that silly bulletin. I mean, it's not exactly going to bring the council to its knees if you miss a few issues.'

I stop walking. After my day in the office I decided against tackling Dennis on the recruitment of the Girl who's Stolen my Desk, but his comment irritates me. 'What, is the new girl more decorative?'

He tuts. 'Don't be silly. She's only there to stop your workload building up. As soon as you're ready to return, she'll be out on her ear.'

'What if I'm never ready to return?' Or don't want to.

'Oh, *Jo*,' he says, the voice of compassion, 'you mustn't worry. There'll always be a job for you *somewhere*. I mean, it might not be possible to work at the same level, but the important thing is not to feel stressed. Sometimes a change is as good as a rest ... '

'That's something to look forward to then,' I mumble.

If he hears my sarcasm, he decides not to comment. Instead, he's warming to his theme, adding grand hand gestures like a TV history presenter. 'Change is nothing to be afraid of. Look at Coventry! Risen from the ashes. OK, not as picturesque as it once was, but a vibrant place that focuses on its future, not its past.'

'Are you saying I'm not as picturesque as I was before?'

'Ha ha, don't be daft, Jo. You're lovely.' He plants a cursory peck on my cheek, before turning back to the buildings. 'But this place has such energy, can't you feel it?'

'Hmmm. Maybe.'

He closes his eye and takes a deep gulp of Coventry air. 'I can.'

I wait. People look at him curiously, as he absorbs the energising aura. Eventually I nudge him. 'Dennis? I'm getting a bit cold, maybe we could go back to the hotel?'

He opens his eyes. 'Oh, all right then. But you are pleased you came, aren't you, Jo?' His voice is pleading now.

'Of course I am. It's great. Exactly what we needed.' I wonder what Frisky's going to say when I tell him about my romantic weekend in Coventry.

And then I curse myself for my disloyalty.

Dennis dresses for dinner, occupying the shell-themed bathroom (there's a steam-wrinkled print of *The Birth of Venus* above the scallop-edged burgundy bath) while I change in the bedroom. This embarrassment about our bodies is new.

But, after all, *nothing stays the same, Jo.*

As soon as I hear the shower running, I try on my new clothes. I've never before owned a purple polyester bra and knickers set, and the colour makes my skin look cadaverous. But the underwired cups form a handy shelf, offering my boobs up like a pair of violet-iced cup-cakes. Not that Dennis ever fancies a nibble these days . . .

I banish the self-doubt and try on the rest of my shopping. The blue flowery print dress looked fresh on the hanger, but now it's more like the curtain-clothes the Von Trapps wore in

The Sound of Music. Cute on a family of singing Austrians, but not sexy.

I pull the neck down and the shadow of my cleavage appears in the mirror. I stretch fishnet tights across my legs and ignore the goosebumps. Then I sit at the dressing table and apply Magnolia Flower foundation. It was the lightest shade I could find, but it still looks orange on my pale face. My hair is lank, despite the £15.99 Energising Fixing Mist, and I attempt an old man's comb-over across my fuzzy bald spot. Only the shoes look like they belong to a non-head-banger, and though the sky-blue leather straps look soft, they're already digging into my ankles.

The shower stops and I sit on the bed, experimenting with the most appealing position. I could dispense with the curtain-dress and pose like a lingerie model but what if he turns away? Before, I only had to utter a *double entendre*, or lick my lips, and Dennis would respond like one of Pavlov's dogs. Now . . . well, I can't shake the feeling that his reaction on seeing me semi-naked would be to fetch a fluffy dressing gown from the bathroom, 'we can't risk you getting a chill'.

I perch on the end of the bed, both feet on the floor in the best traditions of chaste Hollywood heroines, and reach for a magazine to flick through, so that I don't look posed. I gaze at pictures of posh people's gardens, all stripy lawns and box-hedge mazes and teams of nurserymen. Does their Capability Brown view make them happy I wonder.

Dennis hums on the other side of the door. Is *he* happy? He must miss the sex, but could his role as my protector offer a kind of consolation? There's something about the way he watches me that makes me feel like a bird in an ornate cage, with just enough room to stretch my wings, but never enough to take off.

Now I'm being silly. And anyway, hasn't it always been like that? I used to like feeling protected.

The door handle turns and Dennis emerges, dressed in black trousers and white shirt, his grey tie draped around his neck, ready to be knotted. He blinks at me.

'Is that new?' he says, waving at the curtain-dress.

'Yes. And the shoes. From my shopping spree.'

He looked me up and down, his eyes opening wider when he clocks the fishnet tights. He blushes slightly. 'Very nice.'

I stand up and angle my head so he can kiss me. He hesitates and, finally, leans down and touches his lips against mine fleetingly, a tease of a kiss. But then he darts sideways, so his cheek brushes against mine. It's soft and still cool from the shaving water, and my own skin tingles slightly from his aftershave.

'Very nice,' he says again, before pulling away. As he concentrates on tying his tie, I feel as hollow and empty as one of my mother's organic carob Easter eggs.

Dinner at the Plaza is served in the enormous ballroom. It's full of chubby middle-aged Coventry couples dressed to the nines. A pianist sits at a baby grand and pounds his way through a medley of show tunes.

We're shown to a small table near the door and Dennis scowls. The seats are upholstered in peach velour, the nap worn by thousands of pairs of buttocks, and the tablecloth is the same sickly colour. We're handed enormous parchment menus by an elderly male waiter. My copy has no prices.

'So . . . ' Dennis says.

'So?'

'Here we are.' He stares at the menu. 'Choose exactly what you want, my treat. Of course, fish is good for the brain. Although the latest research on mercury levels is rather alarming. Honestly, it's a full-time job keeping on top of it all. Lucky it is my job, eh?' And he chuckles.

'This afternoon puts it in perspective. All those people wiped out in one night of bombing. Makes mercury seem quite a distant threat.'

'Different times, Jo. Different times. Just because we're not about to be carpet-bombed doesn't mean we shouldn't take precautions.'

I imagine Frisky sitting with us, nudging me under the

table. 'Yes, but look at all the precautions I took. And I still ended up in a coma.'

'Well . . . ' and he seems to be thinking something over, 'if you'd been a good girl and remembered your Green Cross Code, then it wouldn't have happened.'

I freeze for a moment. 'So I brought it on myself?'

'That isn't what I said.'

'No, but it's what you meant, isn't it?'

'Of course not. It was a joke. Could you keep your voice down, Jo?'

I look around the ballroom but can't see anyone looking in our direction. A large group of rowdy diners drowns out our bickering. 'Or what?'

'Oh God,' he says, putting the menu down. 'You're not going to get in one of your *moods*, are you? I hoped we might have seen the last of those.'

I'm about to snap something back when the waiter arrives. I haven't even looked at the menu. 'You order for me,' I say and Dennis looks surprised but goes ahead: two melon balls in kirsch marinade ('can we have it without the dressing?'), two salmon fillets with salsa ('salsa on the side, please?'), vegetables of the day ('but no potato'), two glasses of tap water and a half-bottle of French house red.

When the waiter leaves, Dennis asks, 'Is that OK?'

'You know what's best for me, don't you?'

He sighs. 'This weekend wasn't a good idea at all, was it?'

'It's not the weekend . . . ' I pause while the waiter delivers bread rolls, wine and water. Shouldn't I let it go, try to enjoy the evening? We're never going to change, and even soul mates have rough times. 'Listen, Dennis. What I said about not being happy. It's not to do with you. I just get frustrated with my own progress sometimes.' There. Olive branch offered, all he needs to do is say something nice, then we can carry on as before.

He nods. 'It's bound to be difficult. I mean, it's very difficult for me when you're like this, but I have to remember that you're not yourself. I simply keep believing that the old

Jo Morgan is hiding under that rather prickly exterior –' he gives me a long-suffering smile, 'and that she'll soon make a welcome reappearance.'

If the olive branch wasn't metaphorical, I'd snatch it back. Why is it *always* about him? I bite my lip shut, and try to call on the limitless patience possessed by the old Jo Morgan, to fight the overwhelming urge to chuck my tap water in his face. And the bread roll. And even the side plate. Not the wine, though. God knows, I need to keep hold of that.

He lifts his glass, and hands me mine. 'Cheers. Let's drink to a more even-tempered girlfriend!'

I clink my glass so hard against his that I'm amazed it doesn't shatter. 'Whoops. Sorry. Sometimes I don't know my own strength.'

I realise things are different when we take the lift upstairs after dinner. The food was second-rate, but the other guests didn't seem to care. The rowdy table got noisier and more raucous until I was so sure they were a group of swingers that I mentioned it to Dennis. His face took on a wistful air. Then he ordered a full-sized bottle of wine.

No sooner have the lift doors closed on us, then he reaches out to touch my dress. It's an oddly unconfident gesture, like a trainspotter touching a steam engine he's admired for decades. When I don't recoil, he moves closer and strokes the fabric. 'Pretty dress,' he says. 'Pretty Jo.'

'Thanks.'

He moves towards me and his breath smells of wine and red cabbage. 'Are you feeling *completely* better now?'

'Well, yes, I suppose so . . . ' I say, thinking what a peculiar question to ask, until I see his expression alter and understand what's behind it.

He puts his arm around me and nuzzles my neck. There's a gentleness that I'm not used to: less like a horny vampire and more like an affectionate pet. It doesn't feel quite right, but after so long, maybe it's too much to expect that it should.

We let ourselves into the room and he kisses me on the lips.

Is this OK the kiss seem to be asking. Are we still all right? Am I allowed to do this to you?

It's messing with my head, because I know I ought to be grateful he's so considerate, that he's taking an interest in me again.

But my body's not co-operating, the urge to turn away is so strong that I have to fight it. I wish I'd had more to drink, but tonight it was Dennis who was guzzling it down.

He's stroking my hair now and I wonder whether he can feel the sticky coating of Energising Fixing Mist. I turn my head so he won't touch my fuzzy spot. It's *normal*, isn't it, to feel odd? It's like getting back in the driving seat after a crash, profoundly off-putting at first but necessary.

As he guides me on to the bed, I close my eyes. I try to take my mind off what's happening. Think of something nice. A sunny day. A slice of lemon drizzle cake. A bunch of roses.

It's not working . . . I can't ignore what he's doing, the change in his breathing since he discovered my matching underwear.

What would Lorraine, my mentor in all things sexual, do in these circumstances? I remember a conversation we once had about fantasies and she couldn't believe I'd never imagined I was in bed with Pierce Brosnan or Robbie Williams or, basically, anyone other than the person I was with at the time.

'But I don't see why I would,' I told her. Suddenly, the reasons are crystal clear.

I attempt to summon up a movie star to serve as Dennis's body-double in my imagination. But my casting couch is empty as Dennis divests me of my purple pants, I focus. Harrison Ford (too old) . . . Tom Cruise (too short) . . .

Nathan pops into my head, suddenly, and I let him linger there as sincerely gentle fingers run up and down my thighs. I try to imagine the heavy breaths in my ear are accented in Welsh, that those hands are the ones that cradled my injured skull.

It's all wrong.

I open my eyes and there is Dennis, his own eyelids

clamped shut as he concentrates. This is wrong too: I don't want him to concentrate, to treat me like a piece of antique lace that might tear at any moment.

Who else? Who ELSE?

And then, there he is, and it seems so obvious.

Luke.

With my eyes closed again, I see his sulky pout and his black hair, then a tanned, defined chest, washboard stomach . . . I feel too prudish to imagine the next bit, skipping straight to chunky thighs, honed calves and then the feet under the loathsome trainers. Outdoor feet, brown, with surprisingly white, square toenails.

I feel my cheeks flushing, embarrassed at my stupid fantasy and weirdly convinced that Dennis might be able to read my mind. But, no, he continues with his elaborate foreplay, while all I want is for it to be over, like losing my virginity all over again, a rite of passage to be endured.

I can smell his sweat, and I turn my face towards the pillow and the sweat is replaced by a scent of laundry starch, powdery and ticklish in my nose. It reminds me of Sunday afternoons: the hiss of the Robin spray starch aerosol and the metallic clunk of the iron against the ironing-board, as Mum pressed an endless pile of shirts and sheets.

I stop myself. It's ten days since my last flashback and I'm tempting fate.

Dennis is hitting all the right spots in his painstaking way, but I feel nothing. I hope he can't tell. What could be worse than *both* of us going through the motions?

Suddenly I can't bear the feeling of his body on mine. I want to push him away, grab his hair, tell him to stop, but I can't hurt him. I'd like to think it'd be over quickly, but Dennis has complete self-control in bed and judging from his efforts so far, we could be in for a command performance.

I turn my head back to the laundry smell again. Dennis is moaning softly now. Sex is meant to bring you closer, but right now he seems a million miles away, lost somewhere I'll never reach him.

I press my nose right into the pillow, breathing in that smell of scorched detergent.

'Is it OK if we . . . ?' Dennis whispers.

I nod, keeping my eyes closed. I feel so alone I want to cry, so I bury my head in the pillow, as if I'm in ecstasy. It makes me want to sneeze, the itch travelling up my nose and just at the point when I think I am actually going to sneeze, it feels as if the bed is falling away and I recognise the feeling and welcome it, floating in mid-air and then . . .

Chapter 19
Radiophobia – Fear of Radiation

Of all the jobs Mum makes me do, I hate this one the most. The naked duvet sits motionless on my bed, its cream fabric stained from sleep and orange juice spills. Harmless.

But the moment I try to contain it with my Snoopy cover, it'll be like wrestling a giant ball of dough. Sometimes Dad helps me, and we make a game of it, but I knew today there was no point in asking.

I unfold the cover, catching a whiff of starch. It smells so *normal*, the just washed smell of a Sunday afternoon in every other house in Newbury. Not the smell of laundry in a house where a child has a *serious disease*.

I approach the duvet slowly, as though I can take it by surprise. The press-studs on the bottom of the cover are undone, and I hold open the flap, before grasping the narrow end of the duvet with the other hand and stuffing it into the fabric envelope. It flops in OK at first and I wonder whether I might be lucky today.

'What have we done to deserve this luck, Ted?' That's what Mum keeps saying, over and over. As if luck is something you earn, like pocket money. Even I know it doesn't work like that.

Leukaemia. It sounds like a heroine from a Shakespeare

play, a spirited girl who dresses up as a boy, in one of those comedies that Mr Blake can't convince me are funny.

'Get in there!' I tell the duvet. It flops over the side, droopily defiant. I cram more of it into the cover, but now it's going wrong, a lousy big lump of padding that makes Snoopy look deformed.

I looked it up in the school library. *A cancer affecting the blood and bone marrow, causing cells to multiply in an uncontrolled way and crowd the marrow, eventually spilling out and travelling round the body via the bloodstream.*

But it can't be cancer because people die of cancer. It killed Mum's mum, and the father of a girl at school. Cancer is a lump they chop off or out.

I stand on the bed now and lift the top of the duvet up above my head, shaking and shaking, but all that happens is the padding gathers at the bottom.

I slump on to the bed, with the duvet on top of me, and punch the mattress. It feels so good that I do it again, pummelling away. The relief makes me feel like giggling until I realise my face is wet with tears.

'What are you *doing*?'

I poke my head up from under the duvet. My little brother stands in the doorway, sneering.

'How long have you been there?'

'*Ages*,' he says, stepping into the room.

'Get out!'

He moves closer. 'What are you going to do? Report me to Mummy?' And he grins, knowing that if I do, *I'll* be the one who ends up in the wrong.

I dab at my eyes with the corner of the duvet. 'What do you want, Timmy?'

'Why are you crying?'

'Will you *stop doing that*?'

'Doing what?'

I groan. 'Asking me flipping questions instead of answering mine.'

'You swore!' He sits next to me and I spot three plasters

layered like pancakes on the inside of his elbow. Mum says they took so many samples for the laboratory that she thought he was going to run out of blood. I wonder what his blood looked like under the microscope. Were the bad bits obvious, like villains in a pantomime?

'Flipping doesn't count as swearing, Timmy. Shows what a little kid you are.'

'At least I'm not fat. Or a spaz!'

I turn to shout at him. The sun's shining through the window and falls on to his back, so the edges of his head and body are surrounded by light. Like an angel.

'What are you staring at, wally?'

'Are you feeling very poorly?' I am the oldest, after all. It's up to me to show an example, to be caring.

'Of course I am, stupid,' he says. 'I got leukaemia and my blood isn't working right so they have to take it out and put medicine in me instead. They wouldn't do that if I wasn't poorly, would they?'

Chemotherapy. The use of specific, selectively toxic chemical agents or drugs to target malignant cells. Medication may be toxic to ordinary cells as well as cancer cells. Side-effects include: fatigue, nausea and vomiting; pain, hair loss, anaemia, central nervous system problems, infection; mouth, gum and throat problems; diarrhoea, constipation, nerve and muscle effects; flu-like symptoms and fluid retention.

'No. Of course they wouldn't.'

He holds his hands up to the window, and the sun shines through them so his fingers glow pinky-orange and don't seem to contain any bones. 'I wonder if the medicine will make my skin change colour? If it was green, I might look like *The Incredible Hulk*.'

I hate my brother and I love him too. I don't understand how I can feel both things at the same time, but I do and I also prefer him the colour he is. 'I don't think they'll replace your blood altogether, Timmy.'

He pulls at his eyes with his fingers, and crosses them. 'Yes they will and I will be a *monster*.'

'You are already.'

He pokes his tongue out, then lies back on the bed, his head resting against my feet. 'It won't hurt, will it, Jo?'

'I . . . ' I can't remember him ever asking me a serious question before. 'I suppose the needle might be a bit sore.'

He nods. 'Mummy bought me chocolate cigarettes to stop it hurting when they took out my blood and put the ginormous needle in my back.'

I feel sick. 'And did it work?'

He closes his eyes, weighing it up. 'Nearly. The chocolate was nice. But the needle still hurt.'

The book said nothing about needles in the back. What else can they do to him? Will Timmy end up like that boy in the bubble in America, touching Mum's hand through a layer of plastic? 'But it'll be worth it. You'll feel wide awake again.'

'Not straight away. They said I am likely to be awfully tired. And then when they've given me medicine, they might put me on the radio.'

'Eh?'

'On the radio. I'd lie on a bed and then they'd put me on the radio. Or the radio on me. Or something.'

Radiotherapy: the use of high energy X-rays and similar rays (such as electrons) to treat disease and destroy cancer cells.

I sit up straight, and he leans into my lap, his eyes still shut. 'This is important, Timmy. What exactly did they tell you?'

He opens one eye: it looks lighter blue than usual. Could it be the illness? 'They told Mum and Dad that depending on how naughty my blood is, they could give me a tiny amount of radio activities. They didn't think I was listening and then I asked them if I got to be a disc jockey like Mike Read and they all laughed.'

Cancer cells will be destroyed but normal cells may also be affected. Immediate side-effects can include the appearance of 'sunburn' on skin: longer-term effects can be noticeable as time goes by. Radiation to the brain can have important effects on growth and development.

'Oh God, Timmy!' I can't help myself. 'They mean

radioactivity. The same stuff you get when an atom bomb explodes.'

He opens the other eye. 'A bomb?'

'A *big* bomb,' I say. 'Like the ones they want to keep at Greenham Common. Bombs like a thousand suns. And after they explode, that's when the radioactivity comes down, like rain that isn't wet. Fall-out, it's called, because it makes everything fall out. Your hair. Your teeth. Your insides.'

'But . . . ' He blinks. 'But why would doctors do something that would make my teeth fall out?'

This stops me in my tracks. Why *would* they? Maybe because adults are so used to living with the risk of death that they don't see it any more. Mum and Dad and President Brezhnev and Margaret Thatcher and Ronald Reagan: they're the ones with the power, and kids have to like it or lump it. Even if it might kill us. It's like the emperor's new clothes: it took a child to see what the adults wouldn't admit to . . .

But I can't say this to Timmy. Instead I try to reassure him, 'Maybe the medicine will make you better on its own and you won't need the fall-out.'

He looks doubtful. 'I might not let them do it.'

I sigh. 'You're just a kid, Timmy. No one will take any notice.'

He stares at me, and for one moment, it feels like me and my brother are on the same side.

Then I hear a pop. I look down and he's pressed shut one of the plastic studs on the duvet cover. As I watch, he does another.

'Timmy!'

'What?' he asks, closing the final stud.

'I *do* that. The studs. It's the only good bit of making the bed,' I shout at him, on the edge of tears.

'Big deal!' He pulls the studs apart and presses them back together again. 'You can do it all over again.'

I snatch that part of the duvet back from him. 'No, that's not right. You can't do it twice. Something bad could happen. Get out!'

He stands up and sways, left, right, then left again before he tumbles to the floor.

'TIMMY!'

He lies on the carpet with his eyes closed and I scramble up to go to fetch Dad but then he opens one eye. 'Fooled you!' Then he reaches a hand under my bed and pulls out a tin of beans. 'What's this doing here?'

Oh *no*. He reaches further back and retrieves more cans: pineapple rings, fruit cocktail, pilchards in tomato sauce. As he stacks up my precious tins like alphabet bricks, I consider my options: lie, and risk him telling tales to Mum, or scare him so much he won't dare say a thing.

'You have to be very grown-up, Timmy, because we're in terrible danger,' I begin, knowing the effect this awful knowledge has had on me. 'The big bombs I mentioned before, well, they're coming, Timmy. Nothing we can do to stop them. But we can get ready, so that when they fall, we've got enough food. Because there won't be any shops any more. Or hospitals.'

His face brightens. 'I'd like no more hospitals. Because there'd be no more injections . . . ' Then he frowns, a grown-up line appearing on that perfect forehead. 'But won't Mummy and Daddy look after us?'

Now what do I say? 'Um . . . yes, of course, they will. It's just, well, I thought I'd help them out because you know Dad's always busy at the bank and Mummy's a bit forgetful. Yes, that's it. Mummy's so forgetful that if we've nothing for tea, she might use our *special* food instead of going to the shop. That's why you mustn't tell her about it. Or Daddy.'

My brother stares at me as if he doesn't believe what he's hearing, which I suppose is fair enough. 'You're frightening me, Jo Bean.'

'It *is* frightening, Timmy. But at least we're ready, not like all the other boys and girls. That's why you have to promise me that you won't tell anyone.'

He begins to push himself up from the floor, kicking the tin tower over as he scrambles towards the door. 'You're loopy,' he says as he leaves the room, holding his finger up to the side of his head and twisting it, in case I don't get the message. 'My loopy sister.'

When he leaves, I listen for his feet on the landing, to hear his squeaky voice telling on me, and then my father's heavy tread as he comes back up to investigate. It's all over.

But nothing happens. I wait one . . . two minutes and then I poke my head out of the door and all I can hear is my brother whimpering behind the door marked 'Timmy's Room, No Entry Without Top Secret Password'.

I bury my face in the clean duvet, sniffing the laundry smell, and wondering whether I'm crying for my brother or myself.

I'm sorry, Timmy, I'm sorry . . .

Chapter 20
Atychiphobia – Fear of Failure

'I'm sorry, Jo ... sorry ... '

Dennis's face is directly above mine and he's panting. It takes me a moment to make sense of the scene. Satin sheets. Air conditioning. Coventry.

'Really, Jo, I am. I can't believe ... '

I don't know what Dennis is sorry for. It wouldn't take Miss Marple to work out that the apology must relate to sex, but what exactly has he done?

'It's all right, Dennis, really.'

He rolls off me, sighing. 'But after all that's happened ... '

'Really, it's no problem.' I carry out a surreptitious check below the sheets. No split condom leaking heat-seeking sperm. No apparent physical damage. So what could it be? Did he cry out the name of Councillor Fothergill at the worst possible moment? Suffer a bout of hair-trigger trouble after such a long gap without sex?

My flashback was chilling; I'd forgotten how it felt to be convinced Timmy might die, though at least now I know he made it. But it was almost worth it to escape from the unpleasantness of the here and now ...

He's almost in tears. 'It's never happened to me before.'

Now we're getting warmer ... surely Dennis, Courtbridge

Council's secret super-stud, can't have suffered a performance problem?

'It's not the end of the world.'

But the expression on his face suggests it is. He lies back in the bed, frown lines criss-crossing his forehead, eyes closed in despair. He breathes so deeply that I wonder if he's fallen asleep. I'm just edging to the side of the bed for a quick sortie to the 'complimentary tea and coffee facility' (otherwise known as a travel kettle) for the sachet of hot chocolate I spotted earlier, when he says, 'Of course, if I hadn't been so worried about what sex might do to you, then there wouldn't have been a problem.'

I stop. 'What did you say?'

He opens his eyes. 'Well . . . since your accident, I haven't exactly felt like coming anywhere near you. Which has proved something of a strain.'

'Hang on. So, according to you, I should have been pulling on the stockings and suspenders the minute I was discharged from the hospital? Or, I don't know, nicking a nurse's uniform to get you in the mood?'

'That's not what I meant at all. I'm simply saying it's hardly surprising that my concern about your health, not to mention your erratic behaviour, has had . . . um . . . unwelcome, *temporary* consequences.' He nods at the end of the sentence, as if he's convinced himself that it'll all be OK.

'In other words, it's my fault you couldn't keep it up?'

His nostrils flare. 'Jo! There's no need to talk like that.'

This sudden coyness, from the man whose sweet nothings used to be so blue they'd shock Lorraine, hurts me. 'I don't think it's fair to blame me for your impotence.'

He recoils at the last word. 'I didn't say that. You're being ridiculous.' Then he stands up and heads for the bathroom. 'I need a shower.'

'It's past midnight, Dennis. And you only had one before dinner.'

'Yes. Well, I'm feeling rather grubby now,' he says, slamming the door behind him.

I sit in bed for a while, before deciding I do still fancy that hot chocolate. I can't get in the bathroom so I decant the water from our complimentary bottle of still water. ('What a terrible waste!' I imagine Dennis saying. 'Tap water is every bit as good and has far less environmental impact.')

As the water bubbles in the kettle, I hear him splashing aggressively on the other side of the door. Before the accident, it felt sometimes as if we were one person, with the same fears and the same thoughts. The only person I've ever known who understands.

Could it be my fault, this most pride-sapping performance issue? Maybe my strange moods and unpredictable behaviour has affected him more than I realised.

And yet . . . did I ask to be mown down by a reckless cyclist? I'd never have chosen this nightmare, but I can't help what happened, or the way it's opened my eyes to the limitations of my current existence. Going back to the old Jo isn't an option.

The Von Trapp dress lies crumpled on the floor, an accident waiting to happen. When Dennis has calmed down enough, he'll pick it up, tutting, and place it back on the hanger. Blaming me again, no doubt.

The kettle clicks off and I stir powdery cocoa into the boiling water. The drink burns my tongue and my throat on its way down. But it doesn't begin to melt the chilly certainty that grips me as I understand that even if Dennis loved the old me, he may never be able to love the me I've become.

Chapter 21
Tachophobia – Fear of Speed

My bald patch is growing back white. I caught a glimpse of myself in the foyer as we checked out of the Plaza and it looked like a pigeon had pooed on my head. I know this is meant to be lucky, but I'm unconvinced.

The Coventry dawn made Dennis's *problem*, and my agonising, seem completely out of proportion, darkness magnifying our argument, like a shadow in candlelight. We were excessively courteous to each other over breakfast, and by the time we checked out, the row was reduced to its proper size.

During the drive home, I was distracted by the snowy fuzz on my scalp. I inspected it in the pull-down mirror, tilting my head to see whether it was the first thing a stranger would notice.

'What are you doing?' Dennis asked, irritated.

'I can't believe you didn't tell me this bit had gone white.'

He shook his head. 'Which bit? I hadn't noticed.'

At that point, something clicked in my head: not a misplaced bit of skull slotting itself into place, but the realisation that it was no wonder Dennis hadn't been able to grasp that I'd turned into a different person, when I looked exactly the same.

Which is why I'm now standing in my bathroom, stinking

of noxious chemicals, with a bright red tidemark around my hairline as if I am rusting from the scalp outwards. The plan is to cover my white blob *and* provide a semi-permanent visual reminder to Dennis that I have changed, killing two birds with one pack of Scarlet Woman dye. I might end up killing myself into the bargain (I discovered on the internet that 576,000 Britons are allergic to hair colourant), though at least DIY dyeing means I'm safe from Beauty Parlour Syndrome, which causes mini-strokes if heads are forced back too violently during hair-washing. Brings a whole new meaning to the phrase 'wash and go'.

I've already got a dollop in my eye, the bathroom floor looks like the aftermath of the *Texas Chainsaw Massacre*, and the state of my blood-red fingernails would instantly put me in the frame. Luckily, Mum and Dad are at the West Berkshire Cat Fancy, so I've got the place to myself.

Time's up, so I step into the shower and let the water run down my shoulders, washing away the chemicals. I've never coloured my hair before in case it went bright green, or caused cancer or multiple organ failure.

My current resemblance to a badger made me reconsider. I wrap my hair in a towel, resisting the temptation to take a look while it's wet. Instead, I begin the clear-up operation, so when Dennis notices the colour (*if* he notices the colour), I can lie and tell him it's a new 100 per cent natural organic shine-reflecting shampoo. I must remember to hide the packaging.

I nearly bought my natural shade (mud-brown) to help the fuzz blend with the rest of my hair, but the woman in the picture on the Scarlet Woman box seemed to be challenging me from her shelf in the chemist's, all flame-haired sassiness. I wanted to be *her*, but that would take plastic surgery, so I thought having her hair colour would be the next best thing.

Back in the bedroom, I dig my old hairdryer out of a suitcase, and the air smells of burned hair when I switch it on and point it at my head, eyes closed again. I run my fingers through the strands: does it *feel* red? It certainly feels thicker but the colour might be appalling. Finally I grit my teeth, turn off the dryer and prepare to face the consequences of my misguided experiment . . .

It's fantastic. The shade makes me look much more alive and the badger spot has disappeared, with a patch of soft red velvet in its place.

Goodbye, dowdy brunette scaredy-cat. Hello feisty auburn-haired vixen.

The only downside is that if Dennis believes the change is down to shampoo, he'll need his eyes *and* his brain tested.

But Dennis isn't the first person to see my transformation. Instead it's strong, silent Luke, picking me up for my latest 'experience'. Not that my parents would approve, but then they're too busy admiring pampered Maine Coons to find out.

Luke toots the horn on the Red Peril and I race out to the car. As I open the door, he does a cartoon double-take.

'Good hair,' he says when I get into my seat, and I feel ridiculously pleased with myself, as if I'd won the Nobel Peace Prize, rather than managed a half-competent dye job.

'Do you think so?' I ask, craving more compliments.

'Yeah, I said so, didn't I?' he says, and puts the Mini into gear, revving the engine before pulling away. Well, that little burst of sociability didn't last.

As he turns out of Salzburg Avenue, I catch a flash of orange out of the corner of my eyes. I turn towards the back seat. 'Oh no. Not the goldfish.'

'Frisky insisted we bring Lucky along.'

The creature's bulging plastic eyes glint triumphantly. 'I can't help feeling it's asking for trouble. He's hardly brought us much luck so far.'

Luke shrugs. 'Like I said before, there's no arguing with Frisky.' I'd love to ask why, and while I'm at it, find out what an American is doing in Courtbridge. But I sense that asking the man of mystery any of this would cross some invisible line.

He begins driving towards the equally mysterious destination. I'm wearing old clothes, because Frisky warned me 'they might take a bit of battering'. I wanted to cancel when he told me that, but now I'm a redhead, I should start acting like one. He's *promised* never to put me in any danger. If you can't trust an octogenarian ex-fighter pilot, who can you trust?

The Peril's engine sounds ugly, like a football rattle, but at least it means neither Luke nor I feel obliged to talk. Eventually he manoeuvres the car into a space round the back of a large warehouse. He reaches behind him to grab Lucky. 'Come on, then,' he says and I'm not sure if he's talking to me or the goldfish.

The building looks menacing, but I can't work out why . . . then I realise. It has no windows. Whatever goes on inside, they don't want anyone to see. Luke turns round. 'One thing, Jo. He's very persuasive, sure. But remember, if there's something you *really* don't want to do, you can say no.'

I stare at him. 'Right. Thanks.' If he's trying to reassure me, it's backfired. He gestures with the fish towards a set of metal steps leading to a fire door.

'Why are we coming in this way?' I ask.

'Frisky insisted. To maintain the element of surprise, is what he said. I guess it's a tactic from the war.' And I think Luke is smiling, though it's too dark to be sure.

I clang up the steps and through the door, waiting for my eyes to adjust to the windowless gloom. But before that happens, I get a big, scary clue: the stench of petrol.

'Where is that smell coming from?'

'Aha,' says a plummy voice to my left. 'The joyous Joanna. Welcome.'

I turn and Frisky comes into focus, a fluorescent orange shape topped by a tuft of white. 'Why are you wearing a boiler suit, Frisky?'

'Oh, smashing!' he says, ignoring my question. 'So young Luke managed to keep the secret? And you haven't guessed.' He shakes his fists like an excited toddler. 'Close your eyes.'

'What? No way.'

'Now you did say you trusted me, didn't you, Joanna? You know that we head-bangers look out for one another.'

I sigh, feeling simultaneously guilty and stitched up. 'All right.' I close my eyes, trying not to remember the hundreds of times I've fallen for my brother's 'little surprises' which always turned out to involve something: a) prickly, b) slimy, c) alive, or once, when he surpassed himself, all three.

Frisky takes my hand, and I feel calmer. The floor seems rubbery beneath my feet and the smell is getting stronger. He stops and guides my hand on to a metal rail at waist height.

'Now you can open your eyes.'

I hesitate, afraid of what happens next. If I don't want to do what Frisky has arranged, will he stop being my friend?

I open them. Then shut them again. 'Oh no, Frisky. No.'

'Now, now, Joanna, my dear. It's *perfectly* safe. Go on, open your eyes again, there's a good girl.'

I bristle, but do as I'm told. Second time round it doesn't look any less terrifying. We're standing on a large balcony and below us is a race track. 'You cannot be serious.'

'When did you turn into John McEnroe?'

'It's not funny, Frisky. I couldn't possibly race a car.'

'They're not cars. They're go-karts.' It's only now that I notice the crash helmet he's holding in his right hand. 'And you'll be fully protected.'

'I can't take control of a vehicle. In my condition!'

'Shhhh,' he says, putting his finger to his lips. 'Don't *tell* them. A three-year-old couldn't hurt himself down there. Look at all the tyres round the edge. Any trouble with steering and you just bounce on and off them like a rubber ball.'

'And that's supposed to be reassuring?' My hands are sweating against the metal rail.

Frisky looks slightly irritated. 'No one says you have to go fast, Joanna. But if you're not going to try at all, then I think we need to review our arrangement.'

'So are we ready to get you all tooled up?' I turn to see a rodent-faced teenager with 'CREW' emblazoned across his chest holding a folded orange jumpsuit and helmet. 'You can change in the girls' bog if you're feeling shy.'

The jumpsuit swamps me; the orange clashes with my new hair. I feel niggled that Frisky didn't notice, but then it was as dark as hell in that viewing gallery.

I must try to connect with my inner redhead, or perhaps with miracle coma girl. Maybe all it takes is a leap of faith. I could have an undiscovered gift for go-karting, go on to represent Courtbridge, Wiltshire, even England.

I pull on the helmet, which makes my scalp sweat, and as I leave the toilet, my reflection in the mirror reminds me of something deeply unpleasant that I can't quite place.

'Now, don't you look the part!' Frisky pronounces.

Luke stares at me, for longer than is polite. Then he mumbles, 'Yes, if the part is a prisoner at Guantanamo Bay.'

That's what my reflection reminded me of. I smile, despite the volcanic bubbling in my stomach. Frisky doesn't seem to have heard his grandson and is already heading down the steps towards the carts. Luke squeezes Lucky between the railings, as if a stuffed toy needs a ringside seat.

'But I haven't given you your safety briefing,' Rat-boy says. 'For the insurance.'

'Dear boy, I used to fly Spitfires. My grandson took a motorbike around the world, Afghanistan to Zanzibar and everywhere in between. And this young lady is the former south-east karting champion. I hardly think we need a *safety* briefing.'

The lie is effortless. I whisper to Luke, 'Did you really take a motorbike around the world?'

He shrugs. 'I was young and stupid.'

An image of Luke on his bike, the wind ruffling his hair like a latter-day Che Guevara, distracts me momentarily from the present danger. I feel rather hot. Must be the jumpsuit.

Rat-boy seems to have realised that Frisky is stronger willed than he is. He thrusts a clipboard at us. 'It's a waiver. You need to sign it to show you know you're not insured.'

Frisky reaches out, and signs it. 'Insurance is for bores. The best insurance is confidence that you're safe!'

'Hang on, Frisky . . . ' I say, but he's already racing down the steps. I follow him: the smell of petrol is so strong now that it's all I can do not to throw up. A row of karts is lined up against the wall, like a regiment of giant insects.

'Ladies first,' he says, and Rat-boy points towards one of the karts.

I approach it, unable to shake the sense that I'm in a trance. Or a nightmare. If I really concentrate, surely I can wake myself up. 'How . . . ?' I can't see how you're meant to climb into the thing.

Rat-boy scowls at me, then sniggers. 'You're south-east champion, are you?'

'*Women's* champion,' Frisky says, and winks, as if that explains everything. 'Allow me, Joanna.' He grips my hand and manoeuvres me into the hard moulded seat, taking each of my legs and placing them gently into position. 'There!'

The machine is so flimsy: a few bent tubes of metal around an ancient-looking engine, with four boy-racer wide wheels. The average tricycle is more robust. Rat-boy manages to stop guffawing long enough to check my body is in the right position, then bends across me and presses a button.

Grrrrr . . . the engine splutters into life, then settles into a thunderous noisy roar. Rat-boy points at the wheel and the pedals but I can't hear what he's saying because of the engine and the crash helmet; the helmet seems to be shrinking, putting pressure on my poor brain.

'Did you know,' Frisky shouts at Rat-boy moves over to start his engine, 'that many go-karts are powered by modified lawnmower engines?'

I peer down at the vibrating motor. It's not the most heartening news I've heard recently.

'And apparently,' he drones on, as Luke's engine springs into rumbling life, adding to the cacophony, 'they were invented by American air force chaps twiddling their thumbs after the war. You see, it's boredom, not necessity, that's really the mother of invention.'

Rat-boy gives us a final, scathing glance before running back up on to the balcony. After a few moments, the opening chords of the *Grand Prix* theme music rise above the rumble of the go-karts. Frisky gives me the thumbs-up and I grip the steering wheel.

'PRACTISE LAPS FIRST!' Frisky shouts across at me and waves for me to pull out, like a polite motorist letting an old lady out into the traffic. I hesitate for a moment, until he revs his engine at me, and then I know I have no choice: I tap the pedal with my foot and the kart doesn't move. A second tap, with a little more force, jerks me forward so violently that I almost hit my helmeted chin on the wheel.

I try again, and the same thing happens, but I keep my nerve and the leap forward is less dramatic. 'Kangaroo petrol', that's what Dad called my first attempts at driving. Timmy, of course, had the smooth moves of a rally champ. Maybe Frisky would have let me off if I'd told him I failed my test five times for undue hesitancy before the examiner took pity on me and nodded me through. 'After all, love,' he said, 'never going above third gear isn't actually a crime. But don't tell anyone I said that.'

On the go-kart, there are no gears and no reverse, and the only way is forward. I edge along, trying to keep the same pressure on the pedal, but the machine's vibrations keep knocking my foot away. My bones feel like they'll crumble to dust but, far more scary, my head is definitely being squeezed by the crash helmet.

It feels like it did when I woke up from my coma.

'We haven't got all day, you know, young lady.'

Frisky draws up alongside me as I creep forward. 'I'm not *really* enjoying this, Frisky,' I say, my voice wobbly from the intense shaking.

'What?'

'I said I'M NOT REALLY ENJOYING THIS!'

We take a bend, the first on the track, and I slow down as

he surges forward then reins himself back again. 'Sorry, my dear. Never could resist going full throttle. Hangover from the days when going too slowly meant falling out of the sky! Now, what was that you said?'

I sigh so hard my breath mists up the visor. 'This isn't my sort of thing at all, Frisky. I'll finish the lap but –'

'You can't . . . ' his voice keeps being lost under the music, ' . . . rest of your life . . . in the sand like an ostrich . . . in your comfort zone. The whole point . . . you take risks . . . today's session is meant . . . speed is fun . . . '

I steer my car towards the side of the track and stop, my orange fireproof arms folded across my chest and my bottom lip sticking out, though my majestic pout is wasted behind the helmet. So much for miracle coma girl.

Frisky pulls over and climbs out of the kart. 'Are we in a sulk now, Joanna? Because I warn you, I can probably outsulk you. Especially when I've gone to so much trouble to organise today.'

I look up to the balcony, to try to stop my eyes filling with tears. Lucky the goldfish stares down at me, unblinking.

Luke has stopped behind us, and is untangling his long legs from the impossibly narrow framework. I feel hot *and* faint now, and begin to tug at the crash helmet, but the plastic lining and my own damp, dyed hair are stuck, like a cream cracker on the roof of your mouth. The more I push, the more panicky I become. I can't faint here. Not in front of Luke.

Though I'm not sure why that of all things matters so much.

'The point is, Joanna,' Frisky continues, determined to finish his speech, 'you're stuck in a rut, doing only what you've done before. We agreed that I would help you out of the rut. But that won't happen if you lose your nerve at the first hurdle like some silly colt.'

'Frisky, I know. I've tried. And failed. I don't think I'm quite . . . ' I lean my leg against the tyre wall ' . . . up to it. Not so much a thoroughbred, as a lame duck.'

'We didn't win two wars with defeatist talk like that.'

I'm struggling to stay upright, never mind form any kind of sensible response.

'But we did win wars through bullying, I guess?' It's Luke, his voice lighter than his words.

Frisky shakes his head. 'As usual, Luke, you don't know what you're talking about. In those circumstances, if I were you, I would butt out. But of course, that American part of you can't help wanting to intervene in matters that don't concern you.'

I wait, almost hoping Luke might take the bait and reveal the tiniest glimpse of who he is. Not because I care, really. Just that I hate unanswered questions.

But Luke isn't riled. Instead he speaks very slowly, 'You never learn, do you, Frisky? I'd have thought you'd have realised by now, with all those decades of wisdom, that you don't always know what's best? That sometimes you can do more harm than good?'

Frisky's face is ninety per cent covered by the helmet, but his eyes suddenly seem so sad and empty that I have to look away.

'But Joanna agreed,' he says finally.

'It doesn't give you ownership of her soul, does it? Are you all right, Jo?' Luke asks, and my name sounds different when he says it. I feel even more faint.

'I'd like to . . . get this off,' I point helplessly at my head. 'Ideally.'

Luke moves towards me and tugs gently at the helmet. 'Relax,' he whispers. Well, it sounds like a whisper, but it must be louder, or I wouldn't be able to hear him over the twanging guitar music.

He touches the back of my neck as he tries to break the vacuum. Finally, the helmet pops away and he pulls it off in one movement. I feel literally light-headed, but suddenly self-conscious about my sweat-soaked hair. I only hope the dye hasn't run.

'All right?' he asks.

'Yep, right as rain,' I say. Then I look past him to Frisky. He still hasn't taken his own helmet off, but everything about his posture – the slump of his shoulders, the hang of his hands, the half-hearted way he's kicking at the wheel of his kart – suggests resignation. And, for the only second time since I met him, he looks his age. Last time it was the fault of the yobs at the fair. This time, it's *my* fault.

'Time to go, then?' Luke says.

'OK,' I say. I take a step towards Frisky. 'I'm sorry I couldn't go through with it, Frisky. Thanks for trying.'

He holds up a hand. 'None of it matters, my dear. I'm only a silly old fool with mad ideas. I'll stay here a while, perhaps take this beast on a lap or two.'

I try to think of something else to say, and fail completely. I follow Luke back up the steps. Rat-boy is waiting at the top. 'Early bath?' he sneers.

'Something like that,' Luke says, grabbing the goldfish.

'You won't get a refund, you know that?' Rat-boy's smirking at the prospect of an afternoon off.

'It doesn't matter,' Luke says, sounding less patient this time. 'Jo, I'll drop you home once you're changed.'

I nod, then turn a final time. Frisky is back in his go-kart, and I wait for him to start the engine and give the kart a run for its money. But he doesn't move. I watch him for one . . . two minutes and he does nothing.

'But what about him?' I ask Luke. I'm responsible for knocking the stuffing out of Frisky. He's more vulnerable than I'd ever imagined.

Luke smiles. 'I guess Frisky's Dunkirk spirit will pull him through.'

The journey back home is silent – even the Red Peril's engine sounds subdued – but it's a strangely comforting silence. Luke grips my hand to help me out of the car once we're back in Salzburg Avenue and I have this mad urge to cling on, because it feels like he's transferring some of that strength to me.

'Bye then.' I try to pack regret, sadness, a little embarrassment into those two words, because I'm pretty sure I won't see him again. In return, he gives me a final squeeze of the hand, then looks away.

I go straight to bed, exhausted and defeated by the day and my own failure. But I can't sleep. Was it really so hard to go round a circuit a few times, for Frisky's sake? I'm a lost cause. What made me think I could ever change?

I toss and turn for two hours, but my mind's too full for sleep. When I get up, red dye has run all over my pillow. It's time to settle back into my old life, build bridges with the people I rely on, starting with Dennis. I decide to cook his favourite ethically caught tuna steaks as a treat, though I hate tuna.

But as I put on my shoes for the walk to the organic shop, I notice something by the front porch. I open the door, and pick up a small parcel, wrapped in pages from today's *Daily Mail*.

I take it inside, tearing through the pages, until I reach a final layer of tissue paper. It occurs to me that it might not even be for me – could Dennis have a secret admirer? Is this a love token from Councillor Fothergill? – but I'm too curious to stop now.

Inside the tissue paper is a carving of a fish, smaller than my palm and almost weightless. The creature is plump and round, rather than long and thin like a goldfish, and the wood it's made from is palest brown, with the scent of soap. When I shake it, there's a rattle and I notice another tiny fish inside the hollowed-out belly.

A note has been folded up and poked through the gap between the scales. I tease it out and open it. 'Not fishing for compliments, but asking for forgiveness,' it says, in the curliest of handwriting. 'A boor is a bore, however old. Next time, I will listen. And I do sincerely hope there will be a next time. There's a braver Joanna fighting to get out, I know it. Next time I promise I'll help, not hector. Your fishy friend, Frisky.'

A warmth passes through me, as if this tiny fish has magic powers.

I am still under Frisky's wing. And however much of a coward I am, the view of the world is so much better from there . . .

Chapter 22
Syngenesophobia – Fear of Relatives

When you're a head-banger, you lose track of public holidays. So when I woke up this morning and Dennis was still snoring next to me, I jumped to the obvious conclusion.

'Dennis, you've overslept! Get up!'

I say the obvious conclusion, but actually it was troubling. Dennis, I'd bet my life on it, has never overslept in his life. Or been overdrawn or exceeded the speed limit or used milk a moment after midnight if the sell-by date's passed. *Rules are there for a reason, Jo.*

His eyes opened, the pupils shrunken in panic and he snapped up to a sitting position. Then he sank back into the pillow. 'Mayday!'

'What? Are you poorly, Dennis?' I asked, my heart sinking. Dennis is the worst patient in the world. Still, he'd cared for me, so perhaps it was my turn as Florence Nightingale. 'Shall I call in sick for you?'

Still with his eyes closed, he said, 'I didn't mean Mayday as in SOS. I meant May Day as in the bank holiday.' He lay there, chuckling gently. 'I can't believe you didn't realise.'

I couldn't believe it, either. Ten weeks since the accident. Plenty of time to have regained my equilibrium, yet the irrational irritation I felt towards my chuckling bed-mate suggested I had some way to go.

Dennis chuckled through breakfast, then, when he noticed it was winding me up, disappeared in the car. 'It might be an idea if you got dressed, Jo,' was his parting shot.

So of course I'm still in my nightie. And I've been seized by the urge to do a spot of gardening. It's a little nippy out here, but imagining Dennis's face when he gets back from the shops makes me giggle and warms me up nicely.

First I top up the seed trays I've started leaving out for the squirrels and birds. This is in direct contravention of the rules that Dennis explained to me when I moved in, 'I don't agree with feeding wild animals. The only difference between rats and squirrels is the bushy tail, and anyway, leaving out food interferes with natural selection.'

At the time, I was too lovestruck to disagree, and my counter-argument – 'but they're furry' – wasn't exactly a clincher. But after spotting playful squirrels in Frisky's garden, I think the species deserves a few pumpkin seeds for pure entertainment value.

I haven't turned into a total soft touch: I use all my strength on the weeds, which have the cheek to fight back. Those dandelions in particular don't seem to recognise that I have suffered a head injury and therefore should be given an easy ride – but I have weapons at my disposal. I fetch a hoe from the shed and drive it into the moist earth with my slipper. Slipper! I didn't even own a slipper before February.

All my frustration is suddenly focused on that bloody slipper, the burgundy velour size five embodiment of what's frustrating about my life. Comfy, middle-class, prematurely middle-aged, non-slip.

I push the left slipper off my foot and pull the hoe out of the ground. Then I bring the hoe down on my slipper, striking it on the fluffy upper and grinding at the fabric.

'This isn't what I want,' I hiss at the slipper, swinging the hoe back up in the air and down again. The slipper is now coated in mud, but the man-made fibres are holding up well.

Too well. I try to slice through the fabric, holding it in place with my right foot. Eventually, it tears slightly and, though it's only a minor victory, I remove the other slipper and prepare to take my revenge on this one too.

'Err . . . Jo?'

I turn, the hoe poised high in the air, like a golf club. It's my mother . . . and my father . . . and Dennis . . . and Lorraine. Their mouths hang open, each expression subtly different, like a set of masks. My mother's is Horror, my father's is Shock, Dennis's is definitely Disgust, and Lorraine's is hovering somewhere between Comedy, Tragedy and Hilarity.

'Hi,' I say, waving with the hand that isn't clutching the hoe.

'Aren't you *cold*, Jo?' Dennis asks icily.

'Not 'specially,' I reply. I'm not totally sure what to do at this point. A gust of wind propels my nightdress into the air, revealing my pale legs and grey knickers. Dad looks away. 'But I might nip in and get . . . changed, now you're here. Wasn't expecting visitors.'

'I think we gathered that much,' Lorraine says as I scuttle past.

I give Dennis a *look* and he frowns. 'It was meant to be a surprise, to celebrate your fantastic recovery. Oh, and another landmark date . . . '

'What?' I rack my brain. I'm sure it's no one's birthday.

He tuts. 'It's exactly two years since we became cohabitees. Happy anniversary, Jo!'

I disappear to our bedroom to find something more suitable to wear. Admittedly, a full Pierrot outfit would be more suitable than my current one. I rummage through my quarter of the built-in wardrobe, feeling increasingly irritated. Dennis has a system for clothes, which are always arranged in strict rainbow order, red, orange, yellow, green, blue, indigo, violet. It was a good job he explained it when I moved in, because it wasn't immediately apparent from his section, which ran the full gamut of colours from charcoal grey to slate. It's taken perseverance to get him to experiment with pastel shirts.

I pick a purple cord skirt and a clashing orange top, a protest against the 'surprise'. I find them all in the kitchen, huddled together. They spring apart as soon as they sense my presence and I realise there's some kind of family conference going on.

'So are the men in white coats stuck in traffic?' I ask.

They manage tight, awkward smiles and I look past them to the breakfast bar. My two ex-slippers are lying there, muddied and mortally wounded. *Je ne regrette rien.*

After a long pause, Dennis claps his hands together. 'Right. Is everyone hungry? I have all the ingredients for a top-notch surprise barbecue brunch going begging.'

'A barbecue?' This doesn't sound like *my* Dennis. 'But what about the health risks posed by undercooked meat? As I'm sure you remember from last summer's safety bulletin, there are 4000 extra food poisoning cases for every degree Celsius rise in temperature. And 1400 people are injured by barbecue equipment.'

He raises his eyebrows. 'Well, when I said barbecue, I wasn't actually suggesting direct contact with unhygienic hydrocarbons.'

'Nor, I'm sure, exposure to the potential carcinogens produced by burning food,' I say, feeling strangely giggly.

He looks at me suspiciously. 'Yes. Quite right. So who fancies giving me a hand?' He reaches into a large carrier bag and pulls out steak and chicken.

'I will,' Mum says, eager to help.

Dad is eyeing up the carrier bags. 'Got any wine?'

'We don't really keep it in the house any more, not since, well, you know ... ' Dennis says. 'But if you really feel the need ... '

'I definitely feel the need. I'll go and fetch some,' Dad says, disappearing out of the door.

Lorraine nudges me. 'Shall we go and lay the table on the patio?'

I follow her out, not bothering to pick up placemats or cutlery. We settle ourselves round the side of the garage, out of sight. Lorraine's the only nice bit of my surprise, and the fact Dennis thinks it's now safe to let me see her must mean I'm on the mend.

She looks knackered, black shadows under those big green eyes and an inch of dark regrowth next to her honey-blonde highlights. But tiredness has always looked sexy on Lorraine, which is a good job as she works insane hours as a midwife, plus having a social life twice as active as the average undergraduate.

'Like the hair,' she says eventually. 'Very Sarah Ferguson.'

I flinch: I'm sure the colour's more chestnut than ginger.

'Thanks. I think. Dennis thinks it makes me look fiery.'

She lights a cigarette. 'So. Are you really mad, or are you only pretending?'

'What kind of a question is that?'

'A perfectly reasonable one. Don't I have a right to know whether my mate has turned into a loon?'

'S'pose so.' I think it over. 'I'm not sure I'm any more or less of a loon than I was before. But I might be a loon in a different way, now?'

'Yeah. I mean, you always were weird. I still remember the time you thought the fire drill was Armageddon.' She takes one deep drag from the cigarette, then grinds it out under her kitten heel. In her mind, the one-drag policy qualifies her as a non-smoker.

'I feel like I'm changing, though, Lorrie.' I'm thinking aloud now. 'I've always been too afraid to do anything out of the ordinary.'

'And now? I haven't exactly seen you heading for Everest.'

Her casual contempt irritates me. 'Um, well, you haven't exactly seen me at all, have you? Not so much as a bunch of sodding flowers.'

She shrugs. 'I was told not to over-excite you.'

'And since when did you obey rules?'

'Yeah. Fair enough. I guess, if I am totally honest, I was

worried what I'd find. And your behaviour today hasn't exactly put my mind at rest. Gardening in your knickers isn't normal behaviour. Nor is murdering slippers.'

'They bloody deserved it.' I giggle.

'Yeah. Too right,' she agrees.

'It's not just the slippers, Lorrie. I'm not very good at censoring myself any more. So it doesn't really matter whether it's an inanimate object or a person that's getting on my nerves. I don't hold back. Doesn't matter who it is. Dad. Mum. Dennis.'

'Well, you can be as rude as you like to your parents, but try not to alienate Dennis. Most blokes are rubbish with sick women. You're lucky he's not spent the last few months drowning his sorrows in the pub.'

I nod. I certainly can't think of a single one of Lorraine's exes who'd have looked after *her*, even though most of them are doctors. Indiscriminate flirting hasn't attracted the kind of man who sticks around. 'Yes, I know he's a good one. But he's so over-protective. He watches me like he's my body-guard and . . . ' I hesitate, 'well, I almost wonder if he doesn't quite like having a sickly girlfriend at home.'

She stares at me. 'And why on earth would he like that?'

'I don't know.' It does sound rather silly, now I've said it out loud. 'Because I won't run away, maybe? I mean, you know how his mother behaved, doing a runner to Spain before he even left school . . . '

Lorraine tuts now. I'm sure it's the same tut she uses when women scream too much in labour, or make unreasonable demands for epidurals or aromatherapy oils. 'That's ridiculous. Dennis isn't the type to get hung up about his childhood, and you're getting your knickers in a twist for no reason at all. Sounds to me like you need to pull yourself together, Joey, or people will run out of patience.'

Now it's my turn to stare. After all the pussyfooting around from everyone else, it's a shock to hear someone tell me what they really think. 'Right. So now I know.'

Her expression softens. 'I don't want to upset you, but

Dennis isn't a saint. All men need attention or they'll look for it elsewhere.'

I think about her constant advice when I first got together with Dennis. It feels like someone else's life. 'I suppose I should be back in the basque and stilettos as well?'

'Or whatever else turns him on.'

'Well, that'll be precisely nothing at the moment.'

She looks up, suddenly a bit *too* interested. I wish I could take it back, but it's too late. 'Things not good on the bedroom front, then?'

'I'm sure it's a temporary thing,' I say, though I'm not sure at all.

She lights another cigarette, leans back against the pebble-dash, coming over all Rizzo from *Grease*. 'Temporary things in sex can soon become permanent if you don't put in the effort.'

'Mmmm.'

She looks at the red burning tip of the cigarette, trying to choose the optimal moment for her single, precious drag. 'Mmmm? So what's going wrong then?'

I consider whether Lorraine might have some pearl of wisdom to impart, some amazing technique tip that will transform my love life. But I can't shake the suspicion that she'll get more out of any confessions than I will. 'Like I say, it's temporary. I don't want to talk about it.'

She opens her mouth, as if she's going to insist on the details, but instead she takes her drag, then sighs the smoke out slowly. 'Time to set the table then, I guess. What a way to spend a bank holiday.'

The sky is grey and the food is bland but we're all trying very hard to pretend to enjoy ourselves.

Mum and Dad sit at opposite ends of the melamine-topped table, ignoring each other. Dennis is next to me (when he isn't fetching second and third helpings of more GM-free, taste-free food) and we ignore each other. Lorraine sits on the patio steps and checks her watch every couple of minutes, wondering how soon she can escape.

At least she can.

The kitchen timer beeps through the open window, and Dennis jumps up to attend to whatever now needs basting or flipping or disrobing from its tinfoil flak jacket.

There is a smoky smell of barbecuing in the air, drifting from someone else's garden, one where the occupants aren't too fussy about salmonella or campylobacter. In contrast, the dishes in front of us contain ghostly chicken with faint marks from the griddle, and a coleslaw of shredded cabbage and onion that's whiter than Dennis's exposed knees. The cheese slices have melted against the plastic wrapping.

I think of Frisky's scary cheese: gooey and germ-filled and almost unbearably delicious. The salty olives, the pine-scented wine, the chewy bread. Is he sitting in his conservatory, while Luke prowls the neighbourhood in search of cat-nappers?

'God, I wish I was there.'

Oops. I said it out loud. Lorraine raises an over-plucked eyebrow and Mum, sensing trouble, inspects a pallid chicken wing.

'Where?' Trust Dad to ask the question.

'Oh, I must have been day-dreaming,' I say, buying myself time to think of somewhere suitable.

'About where?' Lorraine says, and I scowl at her, *cheers mate.*

'Um.' I ponder acceptable locations. Frisky's conservatory isn't going to cut it. Back at work? No, too insulting to suggest I'd rather be at my desk than with my family. Then I remember the fairground and have a brainwave. 'Venice! Yes. That's where I wish I was.'

Mum and Dad nod: I've got away with it. Lorraine looks incredulous – she knows I hate travelling any further than Swindon.

'Ah yes,' I continue. 'The Grand Canal. St Mark's Square. A gondola steered by a gorgeous Italian with a massive pole.'

Lorraine sniggers and – ugh – Dad winks in her direction.

Mum sighs with longing. 'I've always fancied going to one of those masked balls they have there in the winter. The costumes are beautiful. I saw it on TV, it looked so romantic.'

'The masks are nothing but a bloody great excuse for a brief encounter with someone else's other half,' Dad says. '"Oh, sorry, sweetheart. Thought you were the wife with that mask on." Ha ha. Wonder if it'd catch on at the Rotary Christmas dance?'

Mum looks stricken until she exerts the supreme effort needed to pull her pursed lips back into shape. It's not as if Dad has ever needed an *excuse* to cop off with someone else's wife.

Dennis appears, bearing steak. There's no charring, no dangerous pink insides. Our steaks resemble one of Dennis's slippers: evenly browned, overcooked slabs of leather.

'So what's the joke?' he asks.

'Jo fancies going to Venice for a romantic weekend,' Lorraine says.

He frowns. 'But Venice means flying, silly! I prefer somewhere like ... Coventry, for example. Birmingham's only a few miles up the road. Did you know, Birmingham has more canals than Venice?'

Lorraine helps herself to a piece of steak. 'You reckon the West Midlands beats Venice?'

Dennis blushes. 'I was most impressed with Coventry, that's all. Modern cities are not always the prettiest, but there's an energy about them you don't find in places like Courtbridge.'

'Really,' Lorraine says, sounding dubious. 'Are you getting paid by them to do PR or something?'

Dennis laughs a little too heartily. 'Now, who else fancies some of this steak? One hundred per cent organically reared, and guaranteed BSE free!'

The afternoon passes slowly. By six, all the food has been thoroughly chewed and sits in glutinous layers in our stomachs. Lorraine is giving my father a 'therapeutic' neck rub and his eyelids flutter in ecstasy. She's loosened his shirt so she can manoeuvre her healing hands down his shoulders and he emits the occasional deep orgasmic sigh.

Dennis is preparing the decaff. Mum stands by the ornamental water-free wishing well, staring into space.

'Penny for them?'

'Eh?' She seems startled.

'I just wondered what you were thinking about.'

'Did you? Me?' She smiles shyly, astonished that her thoughts should be of any interest. 'I was thinking about the cats, actually. I bet they're asleep in a big ball. Smelling like biscuits.'

I don't quite know how to respond to that, though I suspect she'd rather not know that cats can carry the plague, and kill 275 million small birds and rodents in UK gardens every year. So, after a suitable pause, I peer down the well and ask, 'So what would you wish for, Mum?'

She stares into the depths of the well, all six inches of it. 'Oh. Well ... health, wealth and happiness for you and Timmy. Health mainly, of course.'

'Timmy couldn't make it today then?'

'Oh. I rung him but he'd gone to New York. Work. Or was it for a party? Dear me, what a life he leads.'

Timmy is safer conversational ground. 'Yes. Quite a life ... Mum. Do you think he is happy?'

That puzzled look again. 'Well, I should think so. He can have everything he wants. No ties.' Then she smiles. 'Not that I'd have a clue what to do with all that freedom.'

'I think freedom's overrated, Mum,' I say. Lorraine is the 'freest' person I know, from free love with married men, to free time spent exactly as she chooses, accountable to no one. Yet she's never seemed happy to me.

Mum opens her eyes wide. They were always bloodshot when I was little, from the crying and the pills. Now I notice they're the same ice blue as Timmy's. 'Yes, that's right, Jo. People today make themselves so unhappy expecting everything to be wonderful, all the time,' she says. Then her head shakes slightly, as if she's disagreeing with herself. 'I might be wrong about that, though,' she adds.

'No, you might be right.' I suddenly feel desperate to understand my mother better. 'I mean, we expect to get it 100 per cent right in our jobs, our homes, our social lives, our relationships.' I look back at the bungalow. 'Especially about relationships.'

The words linger between us. She turns her head slightly, towards my father. He is telling a joke: we can't hear his words, but his posture is unmistakable, the way he's leaning over Lorraine and – oh God, now he's going for the punch-line – and as she laughs dutifully, he reaches out a hairy hand to squeeze her thigh.

'I always knew what he was like, you know, Jo.' Her voice is a whisper. 'Before.'

'Before what?' I match her low tone, like an animal trainer trying not to frighten off a nervous stray.

'Before I married him ... he had quite a reputation in Newbury, you know.' And her face is wistful. 'The *Alfie* of West Berkshire, a different woman in every pub. But not many people realised that was only part of him. He wanted to settle down, too. He was a bank manager, after all. You know where you are with a bank manager.'

Dad has sensed that he's being talked about, and removes his hand from Lorraine's leg. 'But ... you must have loved him, Mum?'

'Yes,' she says vaguely. 'He had all the lines, you know, Jo. No one had ever told me I was their perfect woman before. And he did want to be a good husband, but I knew all along that marriage wouldn't make him a new person, though maybe I didn't realise quite how hard it would be at times ... ' She hesitates, and her wary expression convinces me she's talking about her zombie phase. 'Anyway, it's all in the past. But just remember, Jo. People don't change. Can't change. Refusing to accept that is responsible for so much misery in the world.'

Dad's eyes meet mine across the garden and he grins. I've

always thought of Mum as the victim – she plays the part so well – but her words make me wonder. All he did was live down to her expectations. She makes it sound more like an arranged marriage than a love match. Maybe she never loved him at all, but he was a safe bet. And maybe he knew that all along . . .

'And he did his best, as a father,' she adds. 'He was a good provider.'

Before the accident, I'd have disagreed: my stock memories of my childhood almost all involve Dad letting me down. But in my flashbacks, he's no cartoon villain, he's just a man who loves to be centre-stage, but isn't equipped for the supporting role of fatherhood. I'd almost feel sorry for him if it wasn't for that final betrayal.

Dennis appears, bearing a tray laden with his decaff brew and his stoneware unbleached mugs and no-sugar sweetener. Is Dennis my safe bet? Am I his? I have a vision of us in this same garden in twenty-five years, clutching the same unbreakable mud-brown mugs. ('Why would we need new ones, Jo? These have years left in them. Made to last.') And all the time wondering whether life might have been different if I'd been allowed to drink from bone china.

'There's another thing,' Mum says, an unfamiliar urgency in her voice.

'Yes?'

Dennis is bearing down on us, so I turn my back on him, desperate to hear my mother's wisdom.

'Humans pretend to be unselfish, but in the end, it's every man for himself. You know, like that song in *The Italian Job*. Self-preservation is what it's all about. Whereas cats don't bother to pretend. That's why I prefer them. You know where you are with a cat.'

I stare at her for several seconds before I notice that her pinched mouth has softened and curled up at the edges. Then I realise. My mother has actually made a joke.

There's a first time for everything.

Chapter 23
Melophobia – Fear of Music

Dr Williams is not all that interested in my fascinating conversation with my mother, or in Dennis's safe barbecuing techniques. He's more concerned about my extra-curricular activities.

'You went go-karting? As in, racing round a track in an open-sided, high-risk motor vehicle? Whose bloody bright idea was that?'

'Mine?' I try to lie, but my intonation gives me away. 'OK. OK, it was Frisky's idea. But actually I chickened out on the first lap, I'm such a scaredy-cat.' In one short minute, I've revealed myself to be an idiot, a wimp and a tell-tale tit.

'Frisky. I should have known. Go-karting and funfairs don't exactly sound up your street.' He taps his fingers on the desk, like a headmaster trying to think up a punishment.

'He was only trying to help.'

'Oh he was, was he? You know, at medical school we were warned that a little knowledge is a dangerous thing.' Mild-mannered Nathan is nowhere to be seen: he's definitely in consultant mode now, bordering on arrogant.

'Frisky doesn't mean any harm. I'm sort of . . . his *project*.'

'Well, I don't want a tug of war, but you're *my* patient. I can't have amateurs messing about with your head.'

I'm desperate to redeem Frisky. 'But he's got a brilliant theory about the flashbacks.'

'What does Professor Freeman Van Belle have to say, with his extensive background in neurology?'

But when I tell him Frisky's theory, the cynicism vanishes.

'Proust.' He grabs a notebook and began to scribble.

'Eh?'

'Proust wrote about it. In *À la recherche du temps perdu*. The smell of a Madeleine cake dipped in tea transported him back to his childhood. Lots of us have experienced that on a small scale, of course, but Proust expressed it better than most.'

'But why smells?'

He draws me a diagram on his pad, like a child's drawing of a fluffy sheep. 'OK. Each part of the brain has a different name and a different function. So this bit . . . ' he points at his diagram, 'is the limbic area, which processes smell *and* deals with emotions and memories. And when the chemical molecules make their way up your nose, they send messages which bounce around different parts – hippocampus, hypothalamus, olfactory cortex and the amygdala – and seem to make those memories triggered by smell much stronger and more *convincing*, somehow, than ones triggered by a name or a photograph. That's why big money is so interested, everyone from perfume companies to supermarkets.'

'But there's a big difference between what's happening to me and, I don't know, shops using the smell of bread to make you hang around and buy more stuff.'

'Yes, there is, but your visions could be crucial in helping us understand the process. Just think, Jo, you could improve our understanding of the limbic area.' His eyes are glossy with excitement.

'What, by donating my brain to medical science?'

'No, you can do it while you're alive. I was thinking of a little piece in the *Lancet*, say? You could be at the vanguard of a new sensory world.'

I feel an itch of irritation: I didn't really take Frisky's daft comments about Nathan fancying me seriously, but all the same it's a shock to realise that I'm simply Exhibit A in his marvellous career. 'Hmm. I know this sounds selfish, but I don't know if I have the energy for anything that isn't going to help me directly, to solve my problem.'

'From my professional point of view, Jo, there's only one person in the world who can stop it happening.'

I sigh. 'And I suppose he's some top neurologist over in California, with a waiting list as long as the Golden Gate Bridge.'

He puts his pen down. 'Actually, the expert I have in mind is rather closer to home. In this room, in fact.'

I lose my patience. 'Yeah, because you've really got the answers.'

Nathan flinches. 'Not me ... ' he says, in the extra slow voice he must reserve for his worst head-bangers. 'You.'

'Oh. Well, I'm not exactly making much progress so far.'

'Then stop trying too hard. In my experience, the answers tend to have a way of making themselves known. Like women and a good wine, you can't hurry them along.' He smiles like a cheeky schoolboy, and I remember why all the nurses rave about him. 'Please think about the research, though. Maybe we could name a syndrome after you.'

'What, go down in history, like Mr Alzheimer and Mr Tourette? No thanks.'

'What about Scaredy-cat Syndrome?' Nathan lifts up his notebook. Next to the brain, he's drawn a cartoon cat, its tail and fur standing on end and its eyes wide open.

He tears off the page and I take it. Every detail is rendered carefully in blue biro, from the whiskers to the two sharp teeth pointing out of the cat's jaw. And when I look more closely, I understand: 'That actually *is* me, isn't it?'

'Yup. Cute, isn't she?'

I blush. 'I reckon I've lost eight of my nine lives this year. Can I keep this?'

'Sure.' He tidies away his Biro in an ancient Power Rangers

pencil case, then calls after me as I get to the door. 'Oh, and Jo?'

'Yes?'

'Go easy on the go-karting. You want to hang on to that ninth life, if you can.'

What I neglected to mention to Nathan was that Frisky has already set up our next 'date' – for tonight. And by the time I get home, Frisky's on the phone. He's had to promise that he won't make me do anything involving alcohol, aviation, animals, anti-social behaviour, aquatic sports or air-sea rescue. 'And that was just the "A"s, Joanna. Honestly. Gave me an entire alphabetical list. Luckily tonight's event is entirely risk-free, but our young doctor doesn't want to lose a hair from your head,' Frisky tells me. 'It's definitely more than a professional interest. He's not for you, though. Too grey. You want someone darker. Someone at home with nature . . .'

If it wasn't so ridiculous, I'd swear that Frisky's trying to fix me up with dark, nature-friendly Luke. But maybe Frisky *is* right about the good doctor. That cartoon has freaked me out, and his comments do sometimes border on the inappropriate. I guess the only other people he meets are patients, and the ones at Fright Club were mainly hairy blokes.

The trouble is, even if I wasn't attached, I can't imagine being with Nathan. He's a bright boy, but he's seen me at my worst. He needs someone sharper, sassier.

'Where is it?' Lorraine asks. She's reluctantly giving me a lift to Frisky's house for tonight's mystery activity. In return for the lift – and an alibi, as Dennis would never shut up if he knew where I was going – I get a lecture about living dangerously, which is a bit rich. I've been her alibi often enough, but she's gone all pouty because she doesn't like the tables being turned. She's the one who has adventures and I'm the delighted audience, clapping my hands in excitement as she takes her bow, after blow-by-blow accounts of oral, alfresco or adulterous sex.

Lorraine! Of course. *Doctors and nurses.* 'Not far now. Listen, Lorraine?'

'Yep?' She's monosyllabic, punishing me for the misdemeanours I'm about to commit.

'If I said I had the perfect man for you, what would you say?'

'Um, let me think. What about, don't talk shit? Is it down here?' She indicates towards Frisky's neighbourhood, the poshest part of Courtbridge.

'Yes, it is. Right and right again, then over on the left by the lamppost. But I really think this one could be for you. Bright. Witty. Sexy Welsh accent.'

She frowns. 'You haven't mentioned what he looks like yet, so he must be minging.'

'No, he's . . . ' I try to think of his selling points. How would my brother advertise Nathan to this most discerning of customers? Then I remember the shoes on the desk. 'He's got terribly big feet.'

'Huh, as if that means anything. It's a myth about feet and dicks, I've done the hands-on research, remember.'

'He's tall as well. You told me that's a more reliable indicator. And he has gorgeous brown eyes.'

She turns down Frisky's road. 'Trouble is, Jo, the only men you've been meeting lately are either patients or doctors, so this bloke must fall into one of those categories.'

I sigh. 'It's down here. The tatty house.'

'I'm right, aren't I? So which is it?'

'Doctor. But not all doctors are the same.'

'All the ones I've met are.'

I've heard her rant about male medics a million times before. Doctors, apparently, are never motivated by generosity of spirit and a desire to help people: instead it's greed, power and a desire to fondle women with impunity. 'Ah, but Lorraine, you've never been out with a brain specialist.'

'What, the kind of bloke who was good at woodwork at school and now wants to take his junior hacksaw to your skull?'

I've never thought of Nathan drilling holes in people's heads before, but I suppose it's all in a day's work. The scene from *Indiana Jones* where they're forced to eat monkey brains enters my mind and won't go away. 'He's very nice,' I say, knowing how weak that sounds.

'And since when have I ever fancied nice? Thanks but no thanks.' Lorraine pulls up outside the house. 'Right. So you'll call me when your outing is over.'

'If that's OK? I do appreciate this, Lorrie.' I try to win her over with the nickname I used back in the days when we used to prowl fairgrounds together.

'As long as you know what you're doing. And what you've got to lose.'

'But . . . ' I want to challenge her, ask her why she's so keen I stay with Dennis, when for the last three years she's been slagging him off as a bloody boring bastard. What's changed? Then it occurs to me. *Now I'm a head-banger, she thinks he's the best I can do.*

'What?' she says.

'Nothing. I'll call you later, so long as I'm still in one piece.'

Frisky greets me in a burgundy quilted dressing gown, Courtbridge's answer to Oscar Wilde.

'I'm not early, am I?' It's past six, and Frisky's body-clock usually runs to Greenwich Mean Time, so his state of undress surprises me.

'Oh no, just need to finish my ablutions, my dear. Why don't you join Luke in the garden?' And he disappears without another word.

The house is still a work-in-progress, though in fact I struggle to see any progress at all. I walk through the conservatory into the garden, which is dazzlingly green. The bluebells have died back, the oaks are covered in wiggly leaves and the last pink blossom clings stubbornly to a row of fruit trees next to the caravan.

Finally I spot Luke. He has his back to me, and his frayed grey T-shirt is damp with sweat that clings to his shoulder-blades, so they look like sprouting wings. I say nothing for a moment, watching his jerky movements.

He stops, then turns warily. I think I catch a hint of a smile when he realises it's me, but maybe he's grimacing against the light. 'I didn't think you'd be back, after what happened with the go-karts.'

'But it must have been you who delivered the little fish, surely?' Frisky's wooden fish is hidden in my underwear drawer; every time I take out fresh knickers, I get a whiff of spice. It's taken me a whole week to work out why it seemed so familiar, then I remembered: it's sandalwood, like my father's favourite aftershave. But so far, so good. No flashbacks.

'Oh, *that's* what it was. He was very mysterious about that package.'

'Well, I thought I ought to give him a second chance.'

'Really?' Luke scowls like James Dean.

There's a pause and I try to think of something to say, to break the silence. I look down at his hands, holding secateurs. I spot the pink scar on his palm. 'Pruning? Is this the right time of year?'

He shrugs. 'I don't know. The gardening season's different here. Back home, I could plant any time of year and it'd grow, no matter. . . . ' He cuts the sentence short, as if he's annoyed at himself for giving anything away.

'Back home?' I repeat, casually.

'San Francisco,' he mumbles. 'Guess this is home now, though.' He peers around him and his face turns mellow.

'You don't like England?' I say, then feel stupid. How could the miniaturised Court Bridge compete with the Golden Gate? 'Not so many earthquakes, at least.'

'No, no earthquakes at all.' He flicks the clip on the secateurs, snapping the blades back together. 'I better put this away. You'll need a chauffeur.' I hear America in the elongated 'firrr' of the last word and I wonder why he's here and if he'll ever go back.

He walks towards the caravan and I sense Frisky behind

me, in the open doorway of the conservatory. He's changed into smart black trousers, a lilac shirt and a darker purple cravat. 'Impossibly shy, that boy, but he'd be devastated if he knew it makes him seem rude and surly. Such a shame no one will persevere.'

'Maybe he doesn't want anyone to persevere.'

Frisky laughs. 'Everybody needs somebody, as the Blues Brothers had it.'

I stand back and look at the huge villa, four storeys of it, and wonder who Frisky's somebody is – or was. I think of these two men, rattling about, avoiding each other, with that inexplicable gulf keeping them apart. 'Yes,' I say, softly. 'Now, about where we're going tonight. Can I have a clue?'

Frisky taps the side of his nose. 'Not yet, Joanna. But don't fret, you'll find out soon enough.'

Frisky insists we sit together in the back seat of the Red Peril again, and now Luke won't look at me at all.

We leave Courtbridge and as we take the ring road, Frisky begins to hum tunelessly, which seems to be driving Luke mad. Every now and then I see him reflected in the rear-view mirror, glaring at his grandfather. Of course, when Frisky realises, he ups the volume, winking at me.

'Will you can it, please?' Luke snarls.

'Temper, temper,' Frisky says. 'I'm only doing it to disguise the rattle of that bloody engine. Can't you drive less noisily?' And he winks at me, trying to recruit me to his side of the argument.

I turn away and watch Courtbridge whiz by. This is my favourite time of year: just after nature has woken up, but before Wimbledon and the hay fever season. We pass row after row of red-bricked semis, sporting hanging baskets with yellow and blue primroses, the last line of defence against the grey tarmac of the dual carriageway.

I wonder what Luke makes of summer here? Don't all the girls in San Francisco wear flowers in their hair? My blurry mental image includes women like the ones in the old Timotei adverts, wearing linen smocks and hempseed kaftans. They're hanging out in the street, jazz and blues notes spilling out from cafés. Though, isn't that New Orleans? In San Francisco, flamboyant gay men lean out of open-topped trams, flirting with the conductors as they head up and down the steep streets. Staring death by earthquake in the face, living for the moment.

Anyway, whatever it's like in San Francisco, even the prettiest Wiltshire spring must be a let-down. So what *is* he doing here? Why move halfway round the world to a place you don't like, living with a relative you clearly loathe?

Luke stops the car outside a row of shops in a seventies' breezeblock arcade; there's a tanning centre, a modern blond-wood and chrome caring-sharing pawnbroker, a Chinese herbalist offering help with insomnia and impotence (I wonder how Dennis would react if I bought him ginseng teabags to keep his pecker up) and an off-licence. The place is deserted, except for a small cluster of kids kicking an empty Coke can around.

'That's what I like to see,' Frisky says as he scrambles out of the car, 'young people involved in traditional country pursuits, rather than surfing the infernal internet.'

He leads the way towards a shop I hadn't noticed before. It's not really a shop at all. A third of the width of the other frontages, with indecipherable writing above the door. Japanese? Chinese?

Frisky pushes open the reinforced metal door – we're not in Kansas any more, Toto – and walks down a narrow corridor. Everything's scuffed: the rubber floor, the beige walls, all the way up to the pine-clad ceiling. There's a smell of damp and it feels as if we're going underground.

'Mr Clint!' Frisky spots a thin boy in the distance, at the end of this never-ending corridor.

The boy turns and he isn't a boy at all. His body *is* boyish, slim arms poking from a grey short-sleeved shirt that hangs off a narrow chest. But his face is much older, with ground-in lines on his forehead. 'Sir Roger,' he says, bowing his head briefly.

Frisky raises his eyebrows at me, whispers from the corner of his mouth. 'He got the wrong end of the stick when we first met and now it's too embarrassing to explain. But it does mean I get a discount on the sake,' he whispers, then turns to the man. 'This is Joanna, a friend of mine.'

Grey-shirt man nods. 'Friend. A very beautiful *friend*, Sir Roger.'

Oh God. He thinks I'm Frisky's girlfriend.

'And this is my grandson.'

Luke greets the man in what sounds suspiciously like Japanese. Curiouser and curiouser.

Mr Clint looks at Luke, then me. 'Ah, grandson and grandson's friend.' He seems relieved.

'No, not his friend, *my* friend,' Frisky begins, then shakes his head. 'Oh, it doesn't matter. I'm sure it's less embarrassing for you, Joanna, if he thinks you're Luke's girlfriend.'

I consider this as Mr Clint leads us off to the left, down another corridor. I imagine Luke taking me on a city tour of San Francisco, introducing me to his cool friends in their cool apartments, telling them all about me and . . . and this is where I blush like I used to whenever Lorraine sussed out my latest crush on some impossibly with-it boy at school. Because what could Luke, with his motorbike and his studied surliness and his mysterious past, possibly tell his mates about me? 'Here's Jo, she works in local government and has given up her glamorous life in a Wiltshire bungalow to be with me.' Or, 'Meet Jo, she survived a life-threatening encounter with a push-bike and now divides her time between hiding from the mad woman who runs the mobile library, and feeding the ducks with her mother.'

Fortunately the room we're shown into is dark, so no one can see my flushed cheeks. It's a tiny space, not much bigger than an average bathroom, with no windows. As my eyes adjust I see plastic chairs dotted around the walls, a smoked-glass coffee table in the centre of the floor, and a TV monitor with an electronic box beneath it. Mr Clint fiddles with a remote control, cursing in his own language, before the screen pings into life, revealing a group of happy-looking Japanese teenagers holding . . . oh God. Holding *microphones*.

'Frisky?'

In the blue glow from the screen, his skin resembles a dinosaur's. 'I racked my brains, Joanna. Something edgy, but not risky. Something fun but challenging. Not involving wildlife or speed or combustible materials.'

'But . . . '

He rests his hand on my arm. 'Hear me out, Joanna. There is method in my madness. OK, I know you're scared of bombs and armed robberies and implausible diseases but there's more than that. It's my contention that the thing that scares you most is *speaking up*.'

I'm about to reply that actually I'm more bolshie than I ever was before my accident, but then Mr Clint adjusts the volume on the huge speakers that cling to the walls. Plinkety-plonk electronic music fills the room. He nods, satisfied, then backs politely out of the room, without turning his back on us.

'So what's the cure for a girl who doesn't like to be heard?' Frisky continues. 'I couldn't think of one, until I remembered Mr Clint. Big hit in these parts, especially since the Honda factory moved in. Because there's nothing a Japanese car executive thousands of miles from home likes more than a top notch night of karaoke . . . '

'But I can't sing, Frisky.' I feel a wave of nostalgia for the go-kart track.

'Doesn't matter one jot, Joanna. The secret of karaoke isn't the voice of an angel, but the soul of a rock star. It's about letting it all hang out.'

'I've never let it hang out in my life, Frisky. I wouldn't know where to begin.'

'About time you learned, then, my dear. And . . . ' he smiles as Mr Clint reappears, holding a small tray with a porcelain flask and three cups, 'to help you find your voice, there's always sake.'

I turn to see Luke cowering in the corner. 'Not a fan of karaoke?'

'I just don't like sake.'

Frisky tuts. 'How rude, Luke. A sip of sake wouldn't exactly kill you, would it? No bloody cultural awareness, Joanna. Anyone would think he's still hung up about Pearl Harbor.'

Luke seems to shrink several inches and I want to stick up for him, ask him whether he really did speak Japanese back there. And if so, where he learned it.

'Bloody Americans,' Frisky adds, for good measure. 'Now, what should we choose as our opening number?'

There is no escape. I reach out to pick up one of three beakers on the tray, and fill it with liquid from the flask. When I hold it to my nose, it smells of nothing but alcohol, and I down it in one, like medicine. My throat burns, but in a good way.

'That's the spirit, Joanna. We'll have you belting out songs like Shirley Bassey before you can say "Diamonds Are Forever".'

Frisky's confidence in my diva tendencies is ill-founded. In the time it's taken me to finish most of the flask – this sake is surprisingly moreish – I haven't sung a note, but he's spanned a wide musical repertoire, from Cole Porter and ABBA to The Prodigy. Frisky's 'Smack My Bitch Up' lacks a certain street-level conviction, but you can't fault him for effort.

'Where do you know the modern songs from, Frisky?' I ask him as he sits down for a rest after an energetic rendition of 'The Real Slim Shady'.

'Oh, I like to keep up with the latest grooves. One Extra on my digital radio is rather good for hip hop. Whereas young Luke is an old fart, doesn't listen to anything recorded after the millennium, do you?'

Luke glares back but doesn't say a word. I wonder if they're like this at home.

'I'm feeling quite hoarse now, Joanna, don't you think it's time you took the baton? Or rather, the microphone? After all, this session is meant to be for your benefit.'

'In a minute. I'd rather listen to you.'

'Now that I don't believe for a single moment.' He leans over to pour some sake and a few tiny drops fall from the flask. 'Ah. Terribly quaffable, isn't it? So, what's stopping you, my dear?'

I sigh. More pop psychology. 'I'm not much of a singer.'

'Ha! Hasn't stopped me, has it? Let's think about this. You're among friends.' He glances at Luke. 'Not that *he's* helping. But no one's going to laugh.'

'It's not that, Frisky. It's just that . . . ' and then I hesitate. Why *is* this such a big deal for me? My objections to go-karting were reasonable enough, but no one ever died singing karaoke. Yet somehow I can't bring myself to do it. 'The thing is, I'm actually more than capable of speaking up these days. In fact my family have a job shutting me up. So I can't see why belting out a chorus of . . . I dunno, "Rescue Me", is going to turn me into a new woman. No offence.'

Frisky grins. 'None taken. But don't you ever stop analysing, Joanna? Because my other reason for bringing you here is to get you to be more spontaneous. Maybe even have fun. Let that foxy red hair down.'

I take a sip from my tiny beaker. 'I suppose you're right. I do want to, but . . . I can't explain it. It's like I'm looking at the world from the outside. Like that story, the little match girl, who peers into all these cosy sitting-rooms, but is never allowed inside.'

'And what happened to her?'

I smile ruefully. 'She froze to death.'

'Right. Not exactly a role-model, then, is she?'

'No. But that's how it feels. I want to come in from the cold. But it's frightening. Unsettling. I don't know where to start.'

'Hate to sound like a do-gooder, but with a single step? Or a single note?'

I want to say yes. I really do. 'I don't know what makes me so *pathetic*.'

'Oh bugger. What is it with girls, putting themselves down? Trust me to get it wrong, as usual!'

'It's not your fault that I'm stuck in a rut that's lasted decades, Frisky. It's bound to be tricky to climb out of it.' I drain the last of the sake. 'Mind you, this is helping. I know it shouldn't, but it's warming me up a treat.'

'Right,' he says, springing up from the chair. 'Let me go and fetch *more*. Luke? Keep our guest entertained, will you?'

Frisky bounces off down the corridor to see Mr Clint. Luke and I look at each other. 'You're not much of a singer either then?' I ask, eventually.

'I kinda liked it at school,' he says. 'Sang in a band. Rock, you know. That's why he said that about liking *old* music. Just because I hate the dumb rap stuff he *pretends* to like.'

'You were a singer?' It's the last thing I would have expected of grumpy Luke.

'Only in high school, like I said. Isn't every guy in a band?'

I try to imagine Dennis in a band. Pouting at teenage girls. Going without socks. Bumping and grinding with an electric guitar. It makes me giggle. Or maybe that's the sake taking effect. 'No, not every guy. So didn't you want to take it further? Play one of those huge stadiums?'

He shrugs. 'Maybe I day-dreamed a little. The girls, you know.'

'Popular, were you?' It's easier to ask questions when I can barely see him.

'I was the only one whose voice had broken. And the guitar distracted them from my zits.'

The sound of Frisky's laughter drifts from the corridor. He sounds as though he's going to be a while. 'So did you have a good voice?'

'I dunno. OK, I guess. But then I used to listen to the bands I loved – Guns 'n' Roses, Van Halen, you know – and decided as I'd never be that good, there was no point being average.'

I can't reconcile what he's saying, with the way he lives now. Once, he had ambition. Once, he wouldn't settle for anything less than wonderful. Now he lives in a caravan. 'And did you find something you could be the best at?'

He looks away. 'Ah, you wouldn't believe me if I told you.'

'Try me,' I say, emboldened by the dark.

'Geology.'

'Rocks?'

I catch a glimpse of a smile as he says, 'Not any old rocks. Tectonic plates?'

My fuddled brain takes a while to remember what they are. 'Uhhh . . . earthquakes?'

'Yup! Seismology. If you're a boy growing up in California, chances are you're either gonna get into surfing or quakes. And I never did like getting saltwater in my eyes.'

I think back to my silly remark in the garden about Wiltshire having no earthquakes. 'So is that what you did, then? Became a seis-molo-gist?' The word sounds strange, like a snake hissing.

He nods. 'Yeah. Not as exciting as it sounds.' He sounds bored now, like he wants to shut me up.

I strain to hear whether Frisky's on his way with more sake. Nope. It's gone suspiciously quiet in the corridor. Luke is fiddling with his watch: in the gloom, the fluorescent Roman numerals stand out, and the tin dot of radioactivity on the second hand seems to slow down before my eyes.

A jingle-jangle electronic tune leaks from the speakers, like toxic waste. 'Do you know how we turn this off?' I ask.

Luke looks up. 'Don't think you can. It's a force bigger than both of us.' And then I think . . . maybe I'm wrong, it could be a trick of the light . . . he *winks*.

'In that case,' I must be more pissed than I thought because I can't quite believe I'm going to ask this until the words are out of my mouth, 'maybe you'd join me in a song? Just to get

Frisky off my back? He's not going to let me off until I've done one.' There! I *did* say it. Bloody hell.

He turns his head slightly, so I can't see how he's reacting. Oh God, maybe I've gone and done it now. Old Brooding-pants wouldn't lower himself to doing something that might be even remotely embarrassing. And I don't think that was a wink at all. It was a twitch of irritation …

He mumbles something which sounds like 'shit'. Well, that's charming. I'm about to say something I'll regret when he walks across to the ring-binder that Frisky's left on the coffee table, and picks it up. His face is silhouetted against the TV screen. 'So which one?'

'Eh?'

'Which number are we going to murder together?'

'But … ' I hesitate. 'But you said it was *shit*. Which was unnecessarily offensive, really, when you think about it.'

He says patiently. 'No, Jo. I said *sure*. Now help me choose a song before I change my mind.'

Frisky nearly drops his tray when he comes back into the karaoke room. Luke and I are side by side on plastic chairs, hunched together over the songbook, reading through the list. Actually, we've only got to the 'B's – every teen title brings back a rush of memories.

'I used to love Adam Ant,' I say, as I try to work out whether I have the vocal range to carry off 'Stand and Deliver'. Actually, I don't have the vocal range to carry off 'Humpty Dumpty Sat on a Wall' …

'He was a *pussy*,' Luke says. 'Aerosmith on the other hand … '

'Not for me. They must have been bigger in the States than here. It must be weird for you, living here. What is it they say? Two countries divided by a common language. But we're divided by music, and TV and books, too, aren't we?'

'Ah, it's no big deal. And you had *Sesame Street*, didn't you?'

'Yes, but we also had *Blue Pe* … oh, hello, Frisky.'

Luke moves away from me so quickly that his chair nearly topples over.

'My, my. I turn my back for a second, and *look* what happens. A love-in.'

Luke and I pull faces at each other, but there's something else there: it feels like an alliance against Frisky's merciless bossiness. Or maybe it's my imagination. Even so, I realise I've finally relaxed. 'Hardly a love-in. Luke and I were just trying to pick a good song for my karaoke debut. And he's agreed to do the backing vocals.' There! Backing vocals. That sounds so much less intimate than 'duet'.

Frisky frowns. 'Oh. Right.' He puts the tray down with a bang. 'Well, I'm glad you've changed your mind,' he says, sounding the opposite. I think he must be feeling left out. 'So what's it going to be?'

I flick through the book. Already my courage is fading: the microphone seems to glow with menace, though logically I know it's only the LED power indicator showing it's switched on, ready for me to mangle a musical classic.

The most popular titles are in bold. 'Stairway to Heaven'? Too slow. 'Bat Out of Hell'? I reckon Luke might love that one but Nathan would never forgive me for head-banging. 'The Greatest Love of All' is surely kamikaze karaoke – only Whitney and Dolly have the voices to carry that off.

'So much choice,' I say, feebly, flicking backwards and forwards with increasing impatience. 'Like a Virgin'? The thought of doing *sexy* in front of Luke makes me cringe. I plough on. 'Hotel California'? No. 'Billie Jean'. No. 'American Pie'. God forbid. 'Crazy' is way too close to the mark, and 'Love Shack' is worse than 'Like a Virgin' in the inappropriately sexual stakes. 'I Got You Babe' is wrong without a beehive and a facelift, and even a karaoke *ingénue* like me knows that 'Summer Nights' is so over-exposed.

'For Pete's sake, Joanna. You know we pay by the hour in here. It's not life or death.' Frisky takes the book from me. 'Let me choose.'

Before I've finished refilling my beaker with sake, Frisky's on his way to the computer monitor to key in the song he's picked. 'So what is it?'

'Wait and see.' He hands the microphone to me, then finds the second behind the TV and gives it to Luke.

Luke and I face the screen. I hold my breath as the computer locates the tune.

'Get ready!' flashes in front of us, followed by a countdown. 'FIVE, FOUR, THREE, TWO ... '

It starts with piano scales as practised by beginners, up and down the keyboard. But these are different. These are scales that *millions* of people worldwide would recognise in an instant. 'Frisky! I can't believe you chose *this*.'

But he holds out his hands, as if it was beyond his control. 'It's the law. All karaoke sessions must include this record.'

I turn to Luke and he winks. It's definite this time, no trick of the light. I gulp, but that's more about the song than my singing partner.

Honest.

We miss our cue – somehow it doesn't seem right to hear the music stripped of Freddie Mercury's voice – and exchange expressions of embarrassed camaraderie before launching ourselves into the most murderous rendition ever attempted of 'Bohemian Rhapsody'.

Actually, it wasn't that murderous: not even manslaughter. Luke hasn't lost the voice that won him pre-pubescent admirers in high school, and I managed to satisfy Frisky with my enthusiastic backing vocals. Right at the end, Luke stopped singing and spoke those final lines like a poem, as if he meant them. 'Nothing really matters ... '

When the number finished, there was a moment of silence that seemed to last a very long time. Luke looked like he was about to put his arm around me, to say *we did it, kid*, or something similar, but then stopped, his hand caught in mid-air and his lilac-grey eyes widening in panic. Then the plinky-plonky music began again and we pretended it had never happened. It would be so much easier if we were both men; the achievement, minor as it was, definitely called for mutual backslapping or a chummy high five.

Frisky talked me into a few more songs, 'now you're all warmed up', and it got easier and easier, thanks in part to the sake, I am sure. It felt liberating and I began to understand that the point of karaoke isn't how you sound, but how loud you are.

But while I was yowling my way through glam rock and ballads with Frisky, Luke had returned to his seat by the wall. He didn't look at me and after a while, I began to wonder whether I'd imagined that moment of solidarity.

Mid-'My Way', there was a knock at the door and we were booted out of our room by the next group, a bunch of raucous women celebrating 'Mental' Madge's fiftieth birthday. Frisky gave her a big kiss and tried to persuade them to let us stay, until Mr Clint distracted us with fishy-smelling green tea.

And now I'm in the back seat again with Frisky, heading for Courtbridge.

'Now, that was fun, wasn't it? Go on, Joanna, admit it!'

'Yes. I'm hoarse, but happy.' My voice is husky from sake and singing.

'Ah, I know the very thing for that. Luke, stop at that garage! LUKE!'

Luke slams on the brakes and steers sharp left, brave manoeuvres given that the Red Peril is held together with filler and could disintegrate at any moment. He stops in the middle of the forecourt, pulling on the handbrake with an ugly screech. Frisky tuts, then disappears into the little shop.

He emerges holding a bag, the silhouette of a half-bottle showing through the brown paper. Surely not more booze?

'This'll sort you out,' he says as he climbs back in beside me.

'Frisky, I appreciate the thought, but I feel rather drunk already so I think I'll pass.'

He frowns at me, then smiles that Austrian-blind smile, his

face rippling upward in amusement. 'Oh, the Scotch is for me. *These* are for you.' He reaches into the bag. 'Close your eyes.'

I want to protest, but it seems churlish after all the trouble he's taken tonight. The sake bill alone must have been a week's pension. 'OK, then.'

'Now open your mouth,' he says. I hear the ripping of plastic and then rustling. 'Here we go. This'll sort you out.'

He places a hard pellet on my tongue. My tastebuds begin tingling instantly, and the heat spreads to my throat and before long, there's an icy blast of menthol and . . . what is that? . . . eucalyptus, yes, that's it, feeling like it's freezing the hairs inside my nose and . . . oh no. Not here. Not again . . .

Chapter 24

Theatrophobia – Fear of Theatres

'Aa-ah-ah-uh-ah-ah-aaah . . . '

Earth, *please* swallow me up. If there's ever a good time for the four-minute warning to sound, it's now.

'Aa-ah-ah-uh-ah-ah-aaah . . . oh, lovely. A Fisherman's Friend always clears out the passages, eh, Jo?' My father stands dressed only in his Y-fronts, practising his scales. The waves of menthol that waft from his wide open mouth help to mask the sweaty feet smell of the men's changing room.

Actually, Newbury Amateur Operatic Society only has one changing room, but a curtain made from old bedsheets hangs from the ceiling to preserve the modesty of both sexes. The men dress on the window side of the curtain, because no Peeping Tom would want to eye up the male members. Behind Dad, there are two pigeon-chested teenagers who joined because their mums are in the chorus and bullied them into it. Huddled by the radiator are a couple of middle-aged men who only come because they're worried their wives might fall under my father's spell (he has *that* kind of reputation). And the rest of the blokes are Life Honorary Members, all retired, who'll be in the cast until they die. Literally. One had a heart attack in the wings just before curtain-up on the opening night of *Brigadoon*, perhaps because he was so excited about the two lines he'd been allocated. Luckily someone else knew the words; the show must go on.

My father begins to dress. First, he covers those skinny legs with a pair of scratchy-looking brown trousers that are too big for him. Joyce the wardrobe mistress hates male costumes. She prefers creating vast polyester frocks in clashing colours, and never lets fact or historical detail get in the way of her designs: for *South Pacific*, her exotic islanders wore pink and violet 'grass' skirts made from recycled nymph costumes, previously used in *A Midsummer Night's Musical.*

So Joyce always leaves the men's costumes till last, buying them from nasty charity shops in Reading. Dad draws the line at wearing dead men's shirts, especially since the legendary *Oklahoma!* lice outbreak, so he's brought in one of his own from home. He takes a brand-new shirt out of a Burton carrier. 'You get bags more buzz at Burton, eh, Bean?'

Buying a new shirt is the only way to get an uncrumpled one. Nothing in our house has been ironed since The Diagnosis ten weeks ago. I've mastered the washing machine (well, apart from the incident with my green PE knickers and the 60 degree whites cycle). But I won't iron in case I scorch the shirt, or my arms, or forget to switch it off and the house burns down while Mum's at the hospital and I'm in double Geography. I didn't used to worry about stuff like that, but now I know you can't take anything for granted.

'It looks fine, Dad.'

Mum's at the hospital tonight. She always packs a picnic on the days when Timmy has his chemo: Cresta orangeade and cherry drops for his sore mouth, crust-free ham sandwiches cut into tiny triangles and a Fry's Turkish Delight, which is soft enough not to make his mouth ulcers sore. It all goes in a hamper, together with toothbrushes and toothpaste, and a bundle of fresh T-shirts and pants, in case Timmy's *poorly* later. Actually, Timmy's clothes are the only things that still get ironed.

After making the sandwiches, Mum nips to the newsagent for a new set of comics: the *Dandy*, the *Beano* and Timmy's violent favourite, *Warlord*. He's very fussy about the characters he likes: Korky the Cat is 'spaz!' but Bomber Braddock and Roger the Dodger are 'ace'. Sometimes Mum also slips in the latest copy of *She* or *Woman's Own*.

'I don't know why you buy those things,' Dad said this morning, when she came back from the corner shop, 'the stories are always the same.'

'I need to escape, Ted,' she said.

'By reading about . . . ' he picked up an old one, from a pile lying on the telephone table, '"My Bigamist Husband"? Or, hang on, "My Holiday Romance Hell"?'

'It helps to read about people who've had horrible things happen. Makes me feel better, to know some people are worse off than us.'

Dad flinched. 'Except they're not, are they? Worse off than us? How much worse does it get than this, Lynda?'

My mother's eyes narrowed and I wasn't sure whether she was going to break down or lash out. After a few seconds, her shoulders dropped further than normal. 'I suppose you haven't changed your mind. About coming with us to the hospital?'

It was Dad's turn to look away. 'Regional managers' briefing. You know I would if I could.'

'Do I? The regional managers, don't they have kids?'

'Yes, of course they do, but it's not done to mix business and family at the bank. You know what they're like.'

'And I suppose you're still going to the dress rehearsal, too?'

Dad sighed. 'Well, who else is going to play Henry? Cyril, who couldn't hear his cue if it was blasted into his lughole from a megaphone? And if I did come with you, who would look after Jo tonight?'

Mum looked up in surprise, as if she'd forgotten I was there in the kitchen. I pushed my Sugar Smacks around the bowl. Not my Peter Rabbit bowl of course. That was beyond repair after Timmy hurled it across the room. But at least he hasn't told them about the stockpile.

'Using one child to avoid your responsibilities to the other, Ted? I didn't think even you would stoop so low.'

She left the room before she could hear Dad's whisper, 'I learned all I know about that from you.'

So tonight, Mum'll stay over at the hospital, tossing and turning on a put-me-up bed that must have put up hundreds of parents, but never given one a good night's sleep. Even Mum, the world's deepest sleeper, now has insomnia.

'Will you do my make-up for me, Bean?' My father reaches across to a small plastic box, and pulls out a tin of foundation the colour of boot polish. He hands me the tin and a dirty sponge, then moves two wooden chairs so they're facing each other. He wraps a stained peach towel around his neck and pats the chair opposite him. 'Come on then.'

I grind the sponge into the dried-out make-up, while Dad holds his salt-and-peppered fringe off his forehead. When he closes his eyes, little creases appear, running from the outside edges of his eyes to his hairline, but as he relaxes, they melt away. His skin is brown, though it's still May; he only has to go out in the garden for five minutes to catch the sun. Everything about his face is manly, square and solid: perfectly straight eyebrows, a long symmetrical nose, and plump lips. He's a looker, my father.

In the corner of the changing room, three of the old boys are practising their dance routine, humming 'I'm Getting Married in the Morning'. Luckily most of them were changed before I got there. If there's anything worse than Dad in his pants, it'd be them in theirs.

I begin on his cheeks, and as I press the sponge down, it emits a sour, flannel smell. Dad's nose wrinkles, but he doesn't complain. He just takes another lozenge and sucks hard.

I step back to examine my handiwork. He's now as orange as Morph, but the colour hasn't disguised the purplish-grey tiredness under his eyes.

'Plaster it on, Jojo. The footlights will make me look like a dead body unless there's at least half an inch of the stuff on there.'

Dead body. My hand stops halfway to his face.

Timmy's going to die. I know he is. He's so white now, that if we put him on stage, the footlights would shine through him, proving he's nothing but bones and organs linked by veins carrying poisoned blood. *Toxic Timmy the Leukaemia Lad*.

Dad opens his eyes. 'I keep forgetting how hard this is on you,' he says.

'I thought I was quite good at putting it on,' I say, though I know he's not talking about the make-up.

'I'm not talking about the make-up. I know you and Timmy bicker, but it doesn't mean you don't love him. It's bound to be scary. And all the running backwards and forwards to the hospital, means me and your mum don't have much energy left for you.'

And when *did* you have energy for me before? I want to ask, but now I'm twelve, I know that's too babyish a question. 'It's OK, Dad,' I say, reloading the sponge with make-up. He lets go of his fringe and reaches out to touch my hand.

'You know, we do love you every bit as much as we love Timmy, Bean. He needs us more right now, that's all.' He gulps. 'Sorry, that sounded like a line from one of those slushy TV movies your mum likes.'

I want to believe him. I even think that *he* thinks he means it. But I've got eight years of evidence, eight years of them putting my brother first. And what will happen if Timmy does die? Won't they wish it was me?

'Hey ... ' Dad's hand moves up to my cheek, and his thumb wipes away a tear that's welling in my left eye. 'I know you're worried about him. Your mum's wrong when she says you don't seem bothered.'

I can't tell him that the tears are for me, he mustn't know what a selfish daughter he has. Instead, I say, 'Dad? Is Timmy going to be all right?'

He hesitates. 'I think so, Jelly Bean, but I can't promise anything. Nobody knows anything for sure in this life, eh? All we can do is hope for the best and . . . ' He looks away.

In my head, I finish his catchphrase, the one he suddenly realised he couldn't say out loud. *And prepare for the worst.* That's what *I'm* good at, and when the bombs are on their way, and I can finally put my plans into action, that's when they'll be proud of me.

'Hello Ted-eeee?' Charmaine's squeaking door-hinge of a voice could penetrate a lead-lined nuclear bunker, so the curtain is no barrier at all. 'Are you decent?'

She doesn't wait for an answer: she pokes her head through a gap between two sheets, like a pushy child playing peek-a-boo. Her face is covered in stage make-up, her complexion so bright it looks as if all her freckles have joined up to make a giant rusty blob.

'Charm, I'm sure it's bad luck to see me beforehand,' Dad says, all twinkly-eyed.

'No, silly, that's brides and grooms!' She laughs. 'Hello, Joanna, sweetie. How are things?'

I ignore her, focusing on Dad's face. I grind more colour into the shadows under his eyes, but it makes no difference.

'Oh, you can't do it like that, Joanna, you'll rub his face off, hang on. Cover yourselves up, boys, I'm coming round!'

There's a wolf-whistle from Derek, the retired accountant who is playing Colonel Pickering, Dad's musical sidekick. I hear the click-clack of her heels on the parquet floor, and in moments, she's behind me. Her tiny hand darts over my shoulder to grab my sponge. I turn on her. 'I'm doing *fine* thank you, *Mrs* Craig.'

Her costume is very low cut, with a black bodice, full green skirt, and a seal-grey crocheted shawl that makes her eyes look more steely than usual. Her red curls stand up several inches from her scalp, making her head look enormous and her body even smaller. I suppose if you were a man, you might think she was attractive.

'Doesn't look fine from here,' she said. 'It's uneven.'

'Girls, girls,' Dad protests, half-heartedly. 'Much as I love being fought over, it's only the dress rehearsal.'

Charmaine pouts. 'Well, if she's done your foundation, let me finish you off.'

Dad's wonderful eyebrows pop up and then down, as if he has no control over them. I will him to say no, to tell the daft tart that I'm doing OK, that she ought to concentrate on trying to look less freaky for curtain up.

'Bean, would that be all right? You've done a great job, love, but Charmaine has a few years more experience in the make-up department.'

'Oi, Teddy! Not that many years,' Charmaine says, not waiting for my answer and nudging me out of the way.

As she leans in to fluff up his hair, Dad gives me a resigned look and mouths 'sorry'. I watch as she takes a lipstick out of her frilly toilet bag. 'Pucker up,' she says, and then giggles as she applies it to his lips: the brownish colour looks all wrong, as if he's appearing in *It Ain't Half Hot, Mum*. When she's finished, she whispers something in his ear and, before pulling away, brushes her own lips against his cheek.

'Just you wait, Henry Higgins,' she says, when she finally tears herself away. Her lipstick is smudged.

My father waves weakly, as she disappears back behind the curtain. 'How do I look, Bean?'

'You look the part ... Wish Mum could see how hunky you are,' I say, extra loud, so Charmaine gets the message: hands off my dad!

Chapter 25

Dishabiliophobia – Fear of Undressing in Front of Someone

Friends are the new family, according to one of the magazines Mum keeps buying me. This doesn't make me feel any better about my life, as the article also said the average Briton has eighteen friends. I can count mine on the fingers of one hand.

The trouble is, scaredy-cats don't make friends easily. As children, we hide behind our mothers' skirts, frightened that the bolshier kids will decapitate our dolls. Doesn't change much when we reach adulthood.

Despite being my best friend, Lorraine's exactly the kind of girl who would happily dispatch my dolls to toy heaven, then still expect me to plait her hair next day. At parties, she's the one holding court in the corner, while I am putting crisps in bowls and comforting the obligatory weeping guest. I'm not a 'must have' friend; I've lost touch with most of my classmates from Reading University. I lived at home then, so never really bonded, and I sometimes wonder if they're meeting up all the time, peering at the old photos and trying desperately to remember my name. 'Was it Jane? Or Joan? The nervy one? I wonder what happened to her,' they might say, in between trying on wedding dresses and patting each other's baby bumps.

But Lorraine is still here, and we're out to play for the first time since my accident. I'm relieved she didn't force me to go clubbing or pulling. Maybe she thought it wouldn't boost her chances tagging along with 'Loon' (her current nickname of choice: since primary school there've been dozens, including Joey Deacon, Virgin, Hermit, Ostrich, Bungalow Bore and Super-Square – the last one sung rather than spoken, to the tune of *Wonder Woman*).

Instead of a wild night out, she's booked us into a day spa. She picked me up, N'Sync blaring and the sunroof open, to drive to a mock Tudor house built on a ley line near Glastonbury. The sign outside reads 'Earth Customs' with 'We Make Your Baggage Disappear' in smaller letters underneath. We've checked in, completing a hippie-dippy health questionnaire that helps the staff decide whether we should go through the Green Channel ('nothing to declare') or the Red Channel ('where our customs will help you offload your stress, insomnia, irritable bowl, jittery skin and restless legs').

'Have you noticed,' I ask, as we carry our hempseed slippers and unbleached cotton robes to the changing rooms, 'that everyone else here is *pregnant*?'

'Oh terrific! I spend my entire working life with breeders, and I can't get away from them in my time off.'

A woman with a tiny neat bump, as if she's eaten one holistic muffin too many, glares at her.

'Don't they have anything better to do than loaf around looking obscene?' Lorraine continues, as she strips off completely, revealing her perfectly trimmed runway of pubic hair, flat stomach and enhanced breasts. They're quite something, those boobs. I've seen them before, post-op when they were newly stuffed, but now the scars have healed completely and the twins bounce lightly as she moves around. They make me think of that song, 'Like a Puppet on a String'.

'Well, I suppose they don't, really,' I reply, feeling quite shy at showing my pasty body. 'They probably need distractions from the forthcoming bodily Armageddon.'

'They're bloody everywhere,' she says. 'Not just here but on the street, in the supermarket. In the old days, pregnant women used to stay at home and wait.'

Now, Lorraine has never been what you'd call the epitome

of compassion. When she announced her decision to become a midwife, I didn't understand it at all, until she explained that she couldn't stand offices, needed endless excitement but was too thick to be a doctor, too weak to be a fireman and too short to be a policewoman (they've changed the rules now, of course, and I can't help thinking she'd be quite a hit with a truncheon). And she also hated old people and cheeky kids, so training as a general nurse wasn't an option. Which left midwifery, 'Healthy people, lots of drama, plus the kind of view that'll remind me why I'd rather die than hear the patter of tiny feet.'

But this level of vitriol is new. 'Seems a bit harsh,' I say, and she shrugs, sending the boobs up and down, a movement that now reminds me of raised eyebrows.

We immerse ourselves in the overgrown wooden barrel that someone with a very vivid imagination has labelled 'natural swimming pool', and after a few minutes' chit-chat about soap stars, she points at two more pregnant women. One is strapped into a navy blue school-style swimsuit that looks more like a punishment than swimwear; the other is confident enough to wear a bikini, her distended stomach forming a curved ledge for her breasts.

'Twenty-two hours, epidural, no stitches,' she says, nodding towards the woman in the swimsuit. 'And the other one is going to assume she'll sail through it, maybe with a bit of Indian head massage from some right-on *partner*. No chance. Caesarean.'

I stared at her. 'What?'

'Whenever I see a pregnant woman, I can't help predicting her labour.'

'Ri-ight.'

'Oh, don't look at me like that, Jo. It's hardly a major crime. I have a stressful job and if a little harmless speculation stops me taking out my frustration on my delightful patients, then that's a good thing, isn't it?'

'Well . . . I suppose so. But you never used to be like this.'

'Like what?'

I examine my water-wrinkled fingers in close detail, as I try to work out how far I can afford to go without damaging our friendship. 'I suppose you seem a bit . . . angry.' I wait for her to lash out but she doesn't so I plough on. 'And, kind of, *bitter*.'

'Bitter?' The echoey room removes any expression from her voice. 'Yeah. I suppose that's pretty fair.'

'But why, Lorrie?' Even with her hair damp and her eye-shadow smudged by the steam, Lorraine looks better than anyone else in the whole spa. So she's gorgeous. She has a cool car. A small but immaculate flat with a Juliet balcony and a power shower. Endless men at her beck and call. OK, she has a love-hate relationship with her job, but at least as long as babies are being born, she'll never be unemployed. And in the event of worsening international relations, her place in a nuclear fall-out shelter is guaranteed.

She sighs. 'I can't believe it myself but I've realised I want one.'

'One what?'

'A bloody baby.' She looks distraught. 'And not just a baby, but a bloody husband too. Can you believe it? Me?'

I don't know what to say. For as long as I've known her, she's insisted a baby would be 'about as welcome as a sexually transmitted disease, thank you very much. Which, when you think about it, is not a bad definition of pregnancy.'

'So what's changed your mind?'

She shakes her head. 'Not a clue. It's definitely not being a witness to the miracle of birth day after day.'

'No. I bet it's not. So . . . what are you going to do about it?'

'Find myself a man, I suppose.'

I laugh so loud that Bikini Bump woman looks up from her copy of *Baby Makes Glee: Preparing for your Precious Bundle*. 'Well, Lorrie, that's hardly going to be a big challenge for you, is it?'

She frowns. 'It's one thing pulling a man for gratuitous sex. Quite another finding a keeper. I've never shown any talent in that direction.' Unlike her four elder sisters, all married off, with a clutch of little ones. I always wondered whether the reason Lorraine was so loud at school was because no one ever listened to her at home.

'Only because you didn't want security till now. You need to refine your targets.'

'How do you know I haven't been doing that?' she says. 'I might have been out hubby-hunting already for all you know.'

'Have you?'

Lorraine sighs again. 'Let's just say, I wouldn't bother buying your bridesmaid's dress yet.'

'Oh, but Lorrie, you're probably looking in the wrong place. A nightclub isn't exactly ideal territory for keepers.' It's a novelty to be the one offering advice.

'Right. And where is, then? Work, I suppose, like you and Dennis? The only men I meet are fathers-to-be, married hospital porters and married consultant obstetricians. Not prime candidates for Mr Right.' This time there's no mistaking the sourness in her voice.

'But don't you think you'd be bored with a steady bloke? I mean, look at Dennis. As steady as they come. And he'd drive you crazy, wouldn't he?' I try to lighten the rapidly darkening mood.

But she doesn't laugh. Instead she slaps the water, and the way she does it, I have a strong suspicion it's me she really wants to slap. 'I said to you before, you're not being fair to Dennis. He's a perfectly good boyfriend.'

'Perfectly good. Yeah. Perfectly good for a loon, that's what you mean, isn't it?'

'Oh, pur-lease. Turning it round to yourself, again. Because none of us can compete with a coma, can we? You need to get over it, Jo. I dunno, get back to work, do something to distract yourself from being self-obsessed.' She gives me a false smile. 'Or maybe you and Dennis should have a *baby*.'

And she pushes herself out of the pool and slops towards the changing rooms, her swimming costume leaking water and her footsteps leaking irritation. I sit in the pool on my own (it's not big enough for me *plus* a pregnant woman) and try to make sense of it all. A baby? Me? Poor thing would grow up frightened of its own shadow.

But I suppose she has got a point about the self-obsession. Before the flashbacks, I'd have protested like crazy at the idea that I was a spoiled brat, but now I can see that the 'tragedy' of my childhood wasn't parents who ignored me, but my own fixations and inability to relate to the real world. Unless . . .

Unless my crazes were my only way of blocking out reality: Timmy's illness, Dad's constant stream of women, Lorraine's relentless teasing, none of which I had a hope of controlling. In the midst of all that chaos, the twelve-year-old Joanna Morgan only ever seems ahead of the game when she's planning for the nuclear holocaust. It gave me a sense of purpose, however warped.

I shake my head and wet hair slaps my neck. That's crazy. I was just suggestible. Mr Blake has a lot to answer for.

Lorraine and I meet again at lunchtime. We chomp our way through organic bean salads and moon-harvested vegetables without mentioning our spat. We sip tea that promises to restore our equilibrium and chat about our forthcoming treatments. But I know neither of us have forgotten it.

That article of Mum's said that four-fifths of female friendships end due to rivalry or jealousy, and while I'm being inexpertly manicured by a teenage beautician, I wonder if that's what'll happen with Lorrie and me. Friendship depends on the preservation of the status quo. Which isn't a problem, normally, because how many of us really change once we've reached adulthood?

But just occasionally something happens that can't help but upset the status quo, change you for good.

That's when you really know who your friends are.

Chapter 26
Illyngophobia – Fear of Vertigo

I'm in trouble again. First of all, Dennis discovered my squirrel feeding. Then the new edition of *Civil Protection Chronicle* arrived this morning, with a fascinating snippet on the diary page:

> Courtbridge Council Deputy DPPCD Dennis Diffley seems set to attract the wrath of the nation's bakers with his new campaign, if an email sent to the Diary is to be believed. Diffley, 40, is apparently deeply concerned about the hazard represented by cakes and scones, responsible for 493 injuries a year. The email suggests 'it's only a matter of time before Dennis launches "Courtbridge Against Cakes", the nation's first campaign against baked-goods-related accidents'. And though it's possible that it's a joke, the fact that the email's author is none other than Diffley's live-in partner suggests there could be more than an element of truth there. Standby for the backlash campaign. May we suggest 'Save Our Scones' as a slogan?

Bloody Mikey must have forwarded the email to the magazine. Dennis, predictably, fails to see the funny side.

'Oh, well done, Jo. Now I'm a nationwide laughing stock.'

My chest hurts from suppressing my giggles but I know I

daren't let them out. 'But anyone who knows you will know it's a joke. And isn't all publicity good publicity?'

'No, it isn't. And supreme timing, as well, what with –' and then he stops, mid-sentence.

'With what?' I ask, hoping he'll leave soon so I can go into the bathroom to laugh myself silly.

'Oh, nothing,' he snaps. 'I'd better go to work and get the worst over with. I'll be late tonight. Meeting in the Midlands. Safety thing. You know.'

After a truly satisfying fit of the giggles, I pick up the phone to share the joke with Lorraine, but then realise that it'll probably only result in another lecture about Dennis being a paragon. And calling Mikey at work is too risky. Not to mention rather disloyal.

I potter about a bit before deciding I need to do something. Mum's busy sussing out possible studs she's found on the internet for Beatrice, her youngest Maine Coon cat (even though Timmy thinks it smacks of eugenics), and the prospect of a day with only squirrels for company makes me edgy. Actually, I feel edgy all the time at the moment, a kind of restlessness that reminds me of the time before I took my finals, or moved in with Dennis. Except I have nothing to be nervous or excited about. And no idea how to spend my day.

Frisky! I bet he'd appreciate some company, and perhaps I could offer to run an errand or two. The perfect way to make myself useful. Ha! Now who's self-obsessed, eh, Lorrie?

I leave the house before I have time for second thoughts, strolling along Salzburg Avenue, making more of an effort to notice my surroundings. It's the last day of May and the skeletal trees that greeted me when I arrived home from hospital have filled out nicely with plump leaves. In the distance, I see the mega-fit pensioner who lives opposite jogging ahead of me, with her fatter sister. They're both clad in yellow Lycra, like resting actors hired by a supermarket to promote the health benefits of bananas, and they slow down as I approach. Usually I'd ignore them, but the new self-improving Jo greets them with an open smile.

'Hello dear,' the fitter one says. 'Out for a constitutional?'

'Something like that,' I say, nodding manically. 'And you two?'

'I've been persuaded to take up running,' the fatter one says, sweating and out of breath. 'She says my love handles have turned into love mountains.' She giggles between puffs.

'Right,' I say, trying to avoid looking at the rippling flesh under her bodysuit.

'And how are you *feeling*?' asks Fitter, in a voice which instantly tells me that she *knows*, although we've never spoken before.

'Better, thank you.' Now doesn't seem the right time to confide my recent realisation that my entire life is a void and I'm in desperate need of something to fill it.

'We came round the day after you came back from hospital, to ask if there was anything we could do, but your partner said everything was taken care of.'

'Right,' I say. Dennis never mentioned that. But then he has a pathological hatred of prying neighbours, after social services kept turning up on his mum's doorstep in response to anonymous tip-offs of neglect. 'He likes to keep himself to himself.'

'Oh, don't worry. Nothing worse than curtain-twitchers. We know what *that's* like,' Fatter adds, nudging her sister. 'When we first moved in, oh, we couldn't leave the house without some nosy parker coming over to offer cups of sugar, when they clearly only had one thing they really wanted to know.'

Fitter laughs, a meatier sound than Fatter's girly giggle. 'Yes, we wouldn't have minded if they'd asked us outright, "are you a pair of dykes"?'

I look from Fitter to Fatter and back again. Come to think of it, they look nothing like sisters. 'Are you, then?'

'Oh, *bless* her,' Fatter says. 'You hadn't realised, had you?'

'I suppose I didn't expect anything . . . um . . . *unorthodox* on Salzburg Avenue.'

Fitter grins at me. 'So I suppose you didn't know that your next-door neighbour has a sideline as an escort?'

'What? Mrs Cronin with the flowery washing-up gloves?'

'Uh-huh.' She nods. 'With a specialism in rubber. And then you know Mr Davies at number six has been in the local paper with his prize-winning marrows?'

'Not quite as shocking,' I say.

'No, but not all the contents of his greenhouse are what you'd exhibit at the Courtbridge Horticultural Show.'

Fatter giggles again. 'Yes. Though his other *produce* should win prizes. I'm sure he'd be happy to offer you a sample if you need help relaxing.'

'Camomile?'

She shakes her head. 'No. Cannabis.'

I try to imagine what Dennis would say if he came home to find me halfway through a joint. And God only knows what effect the stuff would have on my flashbacks. 'I think I'll stick to coffee, thanks.'

'Fair enough,' Fitter says, 'but do remember, if you ever want some company – and either coffee or something stronger, you know where we are.' She punches Fatter lightly on the arm. 'Now no more gossip for you, madam. You're not going to get a beach body standing at the street corner yacking, are you?'

They trot off, waving as they go. I look back at the cul-de-sac: Salzburg Avenue seems a very different place now. How stupid of me to judge it on appearances. I could have made an effort, talked to Mrs Cronin across the fence, asked Mr Davies for gardening tips, gone jogging with Fitter and Fatter. Instead I battened down the hatches and let my suspicions about the rest of the world grow . . .

Still, maybe it's not too late to learn to look outside instead of in.

By the time I get to Frisky's, my face is the colour of chewed cherry Hubba-Bubba. My hair is damp with sweat. My breath smells like feet because I forgot to brush my teeth before leaving. And I am ravenously hungry.

If it hadn't taken me over an hour to get here, I'd turn around now. I started the journey hoping that perhaps Luke would be at home. With my new-found curiosity about other people, I was determined to discover more about him.

But now I really don't want Luke to see me like this. It's bad enough that I 'fainted' in the back of the car after the Fisherman's Friend incident, without greeting him on his own doorstep looking like a bag lady.

I ring the doorbell. After a few seconds, there's movement behind the frosted glass panel in the door. The figure seems too sprightly to be the lugubrious Luke and, sure enough, it's Frisky who opens the door. He beams when he sees it's me, but then his face changes.

'Good God, Joanna. What the blazes happened to you?' He ushers me inside.

'I . . . ' I'm about to tell him my new plan, but then I stop. It does seem rather patronising, offering to run errands for a man with more va-va-voom in his little toe than I have in my entire body. 'I'm absolutely fine, just thought it would be a nice day for a walk.'

He frowns. 'Really? I mean, it's lovely to see you, but you look a little . . . how should I put this . . . dishabille?'

'A mess, you mean?'

'That's another way of putting it. No matter. Why don't you *freshen up*?' He leads me up the stairs, with bare treads and stripped ornate balustrade. I wonder what state the bathroom's in: two men together won't have made cleaning their top priority.

He pushes open the rough pine door. 'Use whatever you like, Joanna. Fresh towels in the airing cupboard. And shall I toast you some nice teacakes? I always find they're just what the doctor ordered when I . . . ahem . . . am feeling absolutely fine.'

My mouth waters. 'Yes, please, Frisky.'

The bathroom is not what I expected at all. The suite is old, but it's *properly* old, chunky and manly. The toilet has a heavy chain and porcelain pull, the bath taps have spouts as wide as my wrist, and every surface shines. Including the speckled mirror.

Shit. I look worse than I thought. Circles under my eyes so dark you'd think my mascara had run, and sweaty hair drying in uneven clumps. Not so much dragged through a hedge backwards, as dragged upside down, backwards and forwards, from Greenham Common to Savernake Forest. On a more than averagely drizzly day.

Oh, and look at my fuzzy patch. It's now two-tone, red on the top, with pure white growing through, like Santa's fur-lined cloak.

Inside the cupboard, a dozen navy towels are stacked neatly next to a hot water cylinder that's taller than I am. I take one, then inspect the contents of the oak cabinet above the basin.

The top shelf is straight from a 1950s' chemist: royal blue glass jars full of obscure tinctures, a pot of Vaseline, a big bottle of Original Listerine, six creamy squares of Imperial Leather soap, a large natural sponge and a pumice stone.

The bottom shelf tells a different story: expensively packaged vitamins promising better immunity (and possibly eternal life), hair gel, individually packaged eye drops and male moisturiser. At the back there's a black metallic bottle of aftershave so trendy that it doesn't have a name. I take the top off and spray some into the air, then sniff.

A longing so powerful it makes my legs feel wobbly, takes my body hostage. Then, almost as quickly, the scent evaporates.

I think that aftershave might belong to Luke . . .

When I look into the mirror again, my reflection is slightly less scary: colour has appeared in my cheeks to counter-balance the black circles under my eyes. I dig my fingers into the male moisturiser, which seems a lot like female moisturiser but with macho blue colouring, and it sinks into my thirsty skin. The hair gel makes my fringe look quirky rather than greasy, and the eye drops restore a little sparkle. I round it off by gargling with Listerine. I don't look glamorous, but more importantly, I no longer look scary.

The spicy smell of teacakes wafts towards me as I walk downstairs. I find Frisky in the kitchen. He wasn't expecting company, but he's perfectly turned out: starched blue shirt, belt with polished buckle, tweedy trousers that emphasise how slight he is. His presence is so imposing that I always imagine him as a giant, but as he moves, the bottoms of his trousers ride up, revealing old men's ankles, gnarled from sun and walking.

'Now that's a transformation, Joanna,' he says, kissing me on the cheek. 'I don't know how you women do it, but golly, it's nice when you do! Come on through.'

The table in the conservatory is beautifully laid: tablecloth, huge hotel plates and the kind of posh silver cutlery that always feels too big for my hands. There are toasted teacakes, plus thick toast in a wire rack, bright yellow butter in a pottery dish, and jars of Marmite, Tiptree Little Scarlet strawberry jam, Seville marmalade, and clover honey, with the comb submerged like a sticky shipwreck. Plus a pot of coffee and a crystal jug of orange juice.

'Juice from a carton, I'm afraid,' he says. 'If I'd known you were coming . . . '

'It's fine. No, it's five star, Frisky. I can't believe you'd go to this much trouble.' My stomach gurgles in anticipation. 'Unless you're expecting Luke for breakfast too?'

He gives me a curious look. 'Ah, no. The grandson is otherwise occupied. Why? Hoping to see him, were we?'

I shake my head a little too eagerly. 'Oh, no, I'm enjoying spending time with you, keeping my fingers crossed he wouldn't turn up. He can be . . . temperamental,' I add, hoping Frisky will fill in some of the gaps.

'Well, I dare say I'm not the easiest person to live with either,' Frisky admits. 'But he's a good boy, really, considering . . . ' And he leaves the sentence unfinished, so that Luke seems more mysterious than before. Eventually, he pours the coffee. 'So this is all ours, Joanna. Sometimes we all need a little TLC. Toast, love and coffee. Now don't let it go cold.'

I take a first, satisfying bite. Fantastic. Frisky peers contemplatively into his cup of coffee as I demolish the bread and teacakes, munching noisily, with the occasional *mmmm* for good measure. Finally I push the plate away from me, proud to have left one last quarter of toast in the rack.

'Better?' Frisky asks.

'Much.' Though the pleasure fades as I remember I was meant to be looking after Frisky, rather than the other way around.

'You don't have to tell me, Joanna. Whatever it is.' He tops up my coffee for me. 'I'm very happy to keep secrets, of course, but I'm equally happy to accept this as a nice, spontaneous visit from a friend.'

A friend . . . I feel warmer, suddenly. It's all so simple. 'Let's just say I am feeling a bit inconsequential.'

'Oh dear. The old, "What am I doing here? What's the point?" state of mind, eh?'

'Yeah, that's the one. It's not the fact that life's been passing me by. It's the fact that for so long, I didn't notice.'

'You've noticed now. That's the main thing. So, what are we going to do to help you kick the "woe is me" feeling?'

I sigh. 'Thanks, but I think it's down to *me* on my own, isn't it? I've spent enough time navel-gazing and not nearly enough time *doing*. Isn't there something I could do for you for a change, maybe something round the house?'

He takes the final piece of toast and spreads it with the thinnest scraping of butter. 'I'd *never* ask a guest to do chores . . . but let me think. Ah! How's your decorating?'

I shrug. 'Never done it.'

'Perfect. A challenge for you – and a freshly painted room for me. Prepare yourself for a brush with interior design, Joanna. That'll sort you out. Nothing like decorating when you feel a bit so what-ish. Just what you need.'

I smile as graciously as I can. I did ask, after all, but why is it that everyone – from Lorraine to Mum to Dennis to Frisky

– knows what I need? Can't I be allowed to work it out myself? The difference today is that I believe only Frisky has my best interests at heart.

We buy paint at the DIY store near the hospital. I've never been to a DIY store before: always had a dad to buy nails, a landlord to fix blocked U-bends, or Dennis to stock up on lawn food. It's Pensioner Discount Day today, so I'm surrounded by wrinkly couples, and balding builders. The skyscraper aisles make me light-headed but everyone else is unfazed.

When Frisky asks me to choose the paint, the selection is mind-boggling: rows of pure brilliant white fill two aisles, and there's an entire section devoted to 'hints of' blueberry and lime blossom and toffee. Probably beetroot and spring onion and Heinz ketchup too, for all I know.

Silenced by choice, I point at an inoffensive cream.

'Oh, Joanna! Magnolia?' Frisky's voice is teasing. 'All the colours of the rainbow, and this is what you choose?' But he takes out a calculator and does some sums before loading four vats of magnolia into our trolley. In the long queue, I don't recognise most of the things in people's baskets: lengths of plastic *stuff*, tubes of specialist solvent, and boxes of fish, blood and bone, which my mother would probably make into a nutritious milkshake to 'build up my strength'.

Back at the house, he finds me an old pyjama top which would look charming on Gwyneth Paltrow, but makes me look like an inmate of a secure hospital. An elastic band holds my hair out of my eyes, while Frisky looks ready for action in pristine blue overalls. 'Ready to see the Herculean nature of our task?' He leads me into the front room. 'I'll fetch dust-sheets.'

At first, I only see the room's scale – newly plastered walls double my height, and the floor-to-ceiling bay window that looks even bigger from the inside than it does from the street. Then I begin to notice details. The ceiling rose, the coving, the picture rails and ... oh, that fireplace. A masterpiece in grey-veined marble, dominating the space.

Was this a room designed to impress visitors? I imagine a Victorian patriarch pacing the floor (a rather sorry-looking set of bare boards now, but in its heyday, perhaps adorned with exotic rugs shipped from the 'colonies'), waiting for vital news in a new-fangled telegram. Or, later, perhaps a group of chic flappers downing absinthe from sugar-heaped teaspoons and sighing over the futility of love.

Frisky comes in, a pile of old sheets in his arms. 'What do you think?'

'It's a wonderful room. But, Frisky, I might mess it up. The last time I painted anything was a bunch of flowers at primary school. And no one could tell what they were.'

'Luckily, painting a room requires no artistic ability whatsoever. There's an old expression, "if you can piss, you can paint". Excuse the vulgarity.' He lays out the dust-sheets, stained with splats of old paint. 'Anyway I need your help because I am *banned* from stepladders on account of the old vertigo.'

Frisky admitting to weakness – whatever next? It does the trick, though, because I feel useful for the first time in months. He leaves the room again and returns with brushes, rollers and a plastic tray. He shows me how to load the roller – 'better too little than too much, but you'll find that out soon enough' – and explains when to use the brush – 'for the fiddly bits, the skirting-boards and so on'.

I take my roller and sink its woolly coating into the paint tray. When I lift it again, it's twice as heavy. I stalk my patch of wall, raising my roller arm tentatively, but before it makes contact, a cold slick of paint drips down my wrist, past the sleeve of my pyjamas.

'Euch.' I swat at it, feeling the paint soaking into the fabric.

'Ah. I forgot that bit,' Frisky confesses. 'The bit about speed being of the essence if you don't want to end up painting yourself.'

'Now you tell me.' I try again, this time moving the roller

so fast it sends a splatter of cream spots across the bare wall. 'Shit.'

'The beauty of painting is you can cover up your mistakes,' Frisky says.

Finally I make contact, drawing the roller across the smooth beige plaster. I keep walking, pulling the paint along the wall in fascination, like an Andrex puppy dragging a loo roll through the house. By the time the paint's wearing thin, the stripe stretches halfway to the window. 'Ooh. I've done it.'

'Great! But you will need to go over it a few times more. Build up a rhythm!' He disappears back into the hall, reappearing with a stepladder and a radio. A thunderous beat comes from the speakers.

'Not rap again, Frisky.'

'Spoilsport.' He retunes to a rock station, playing a track I don't recognise but I'm sure Luke would love, by Bon Jovi. 'This'll work for painting. Follow the beat . . . one . . . and a-two . . . and a-three . . . '

'Time for a breather.' Frisky is right behind me.

I'd forgotten anyone else was here. I've been up the ladder (trying not to dwell on the fact that fifty Britons die every year from falling off ladders, and another 200,000 accidents are caused by DIY), while Frisky works on everything below the picture rail. I felt faint at first, but then I became so absorbed that after a while I couldn't hear the music: all that mattered was avoiding streaks and lumpy bits, making the paint as even as possible, focusing on the area nearest me.

'Now shut your eyes,' Frisky says, 'I'll keep hold of the steps. There's nothing like an aerial view.'

I do as I'm told. 'It's like one of those TV makeover shows, except they usually wait till everything's finished.'

'Go on then. Open 'em.'

I hesitate, then go for it. 'Oh. OH! It *is* finished. I hadn't realised.'

One coat of magnolia and it's a different room. There's

hardly any sunlight now, yet everything looks brighter, fresher. *My* walls seem flawless, though my first attempts were all over the place.

'Wait there,' Frisky tells me. Standing still, I notice how achy my arms and legs feel, how my shoulder feels sore. But the euphoria is much stronger: today I've actually *achieved* something, made a difference.

'Ta-da . . . ' Frisky comes back with two glasses of amber-coloured wine, and a biscuit barrel. 'Time to celebrate.'

'Bit early for me.'

'It's ten past six, Joanna. Sun's definitely over the yard-arm and besides, we've been working for five hours. You deserve it.'

'Five *hours*?' I reach out for my glass, trying to ignore my conscience. Poor Dennis must be worried.

'Ah, hold your horses, Joanna. A finishing touch is called for.' He reaches into a pocket of his overalls, and pulls out a thin brush and tiny tin of model paint. 'I know it's silly, but I always like to sign a room when I've finished.' He helps me down from the ladder, holding my hand. He flips the lid off the tin, revealing shimmering gold paint. 'On the far side of the chimney breast should be safe, Luke wouldn't approve.'

'He's bound to see it in the end, though, surely?'

'I usually cover it with a second coat. But I know it's there, and I like to think of people in years to come, stripping back the paint and wondering who I was.' He bends down and paints 'Frisky' in curly gold letters. 'Your turn.'

I reach out and write 'Joanna' half an inch above the skirting-board.

'One last thing,' he says, taking the brush back and painting a tiny golden fish below our names. 'This is for luck.'

'Where is Lucky the goldfish by the way?' I ask, as we sit down on a dust-sheet and toast our achievement with wine and chocolate chip cookies.

'Ah, Luke keeps him in the caravan, in case of break-ins.'

'Right. How . . . unusual. Frisky, what do you think Luke

will think? He won't be annoyed we've gone ahead while he's away?'

'He's got bigger things to worry about than the colour of the parlour walls, Joanna.'

I stare at him, not wanting to sound too eager to know what the 'bigger things' might be. 'It's none of my business, of course.'

Frisky seems to be thinking it over. 'He's a terribly private sort, but I think as you're spending time with us, you ought to know the facts. It's his parents. My daughter, and her American husband. They died, you see, five years ago. Very suddenly.'

'Oh. I see.' I feel sick. And ashamed of myself for being nosy. 'You must have been devastated, too. I'm so sorry.'

He gazes into the distance. It's almost as if he's trying to remove himself from here, from pain. 'Thank you, Joanna. It was very shocking, but then being an old man brings a certain familiarity with death. Whereas Luke . . . well, as an only child, I think he's struggling with being alone in the world.'

I wonder where Luke is. How do you get over losing both parents? That must be why he left America, but spending time with his grandfather doesn't seem to be any comfort. They should be united in grief, but all they do is bicker. 'I . . . I suppose it ought to help the two of you, being together,' I say eventually.

'Yes,' he says, 'it ought to.' And there's so much pain in his voice now that it seems to expand to fill the room. 'Golly, I can't believe I'm burdening you with this, Joanna. One has to try to move on. Let's drink to more cheerful times, my dear. To progress.' We clink glasses.

'Progress. And paint!'

He smiles. 'Ah yes. Now, about paint. Lovely job you've done, but before you get going, you *might* like to take a little peep in the bathroom mirror.'

*

'OH MY GOD!'

'It's not *that* bad,' Frisky soothes. 'Although admittedly, it is something of a mystery that we had enough to finish the walls, when you got quite so much on yourself.'

There is paint *everywhere*. Streaked across my fringe like the highlighting efforts of an unsupervised salon junior, splodged across my forehead, cheeks and chin like a drunken clown, across my hands and under my fingernails like a French manicure gone awry. On the plus side, my white fuzzy patch is very effectively camouflaged.

'How do I get it off?'

'Ah . . . well, the thing is that paint seems to stick to skin more effectively than it sticks to walls. Mind you, at least this is only emulsion. Gloss is practically indelible.'

'So?'

'After years of experimentation, I've concluded that the only way to remove paint from hair and skin is with a nailbrush, soap and a heck of a lot of elbow grease.' He reaches into the bathroom cabinet. 'Here are the first two. The last one you'll need to supply yourself.' And he leaves me to it.

I unwrap the soap from its cardboard casing: a brand-new cake from Frisky's stock of Imperial Leather. I run the hot tap, and the ancient boiler supplies steaming water. I start with my hands and wrists, scrubbing with the nailbrush until the skin is pink but the paint itself holding firm.

I decide to change tactics. I fill the basin with water as hot as I can bear, then rub the soap between my hands, until the water turns opaque like Pernod. I duck down, to splash my face with water, in preparation for the Great Scrub. I'd forgotten how well this soap lathers up. My father used it for shaving and Timmy and I would stand in the bathroom, watching him turning himself into Father Christmas with his foamy beard, then slicing through the froth, turning back into Daddy again. One of the few unambiguously happy memories of my childhood.

But if it's so happy, why does that clean smell, tickling up my nose, make me feel lost? Why am I feeling dizzy, even though I'm gripping the basin?

Oh bloody hell. This is the last thing I . . . .

Chapter 27
Xyrophobia – Fear of Razors

'But why doesn't it make your skin bleed?'

I tut at my brother's stupid question, although it's something I've often wondered myself. If a razor-blade is sharp enough to slice through Dad's spiky stubble and reduce it to iron filings in the basin, why doesn't it cut his skin to ribbons?

My father turns round to look at us, his chin striped foam-white and tan, like the lawn when he's halfway through mowing it.

'That, young Master Morgan, is a very good question,' he says, dipping his blade in the soapy water, 'but one, sadly, I cannot answer.' Dad's been speaking like Lady Marjorie from *Upstairs, Downstairs* ever since he brought the house down with his performance as Professor Henry Higgins.

The *Newbury Weekly News*, as he keeps reminding us, pronounced that 'Ted Morgan could give Rex Harrison a run for his money.' He doesn't repeat the next bit though, the part where the reviewer said Charmaine's cockney accent was inconsistent, but her performance was saved by the obvious *chemistry* between the two central characters. When Timmy asked how you could tell if people had chemistry, I thought Dad might snap at him, but no. My brother can officially get away with anything these days.

'But Timmy's wrong, because the razor does cut you sometimes, Dad, doesn't it?' I chip in. 'And you have to use pieces of toilet paper so you don't bleed.'

'Another good observation, Bean. The risk of skin damage is considerably reduced by the application of a generous lather. But quite why that is I have no –'

'Where ARE they? Where the bloody hell ARE they?'

My mother enters the bathroom shrieking, and pushes my father out of the way. She flings open the medicine cabinet, attacking the shelves and sending brown bottles and packets of Elastoplast plopping into Dad's shaving water.

'Lynda. Will you calm down? What are you looking for?'

She moves away from the cabinet and the soapy soup of medicines: it looks like the sea after a shipwreck. 'My pills. I can't find my pills.' Her eyes are glazed, she doesn't seem to recognise us.

'And they're not in the bedside drawer?'

She shakes her head and begins to cry. I'm used to Mum crying, but the tears are falling faster and faster, like she's lost control of her eye muscles. Dad looks at Timmy and me. 'Jo, take your brother to play downstairs will you, while I look for Mum's tablets?'

Dad pleads with his eyes. His face is still half-covered in foam. 'Come on then, Timmy.' My brother is staring at our mother, and resists my attempts to pull him away. If I hold on too tight, within minutes the shape of my hand will appear as a bruise on his skin.

'Go on, mate,' Dad says, snapping out of Henry Higgins mode and doing his best to sound reassuring. 'Nothing to worry about. Mummy's just . . . '

And he stops and I wait for the familiar excuses. 'Mummy's just tired . . . Mummy's just not feeling well . . . Mummy's just a bit dizzy and needs to lie down.'

But he doesn't say anything at all and now his eyes look weirder than Mum's. Eventually he says, 'Do as you're told, please, Timmy.'

Without any more persuasion, my brother leaves the

bathroom and I follow him. Mummy isn't tired or dizzy or poorly. She's crazy. I want to live with Lorraine and her sisters. Never mind the chaos and the mess and Lorraine's mum's varicose veins and gristly casseroles and hand-knitted beige cardigans that make you itch just to look at them. Her house smells the way a home ought to – of garlic and Tweed by Lentheric.

I switch the TV on and promise Timmy a Nesquik if he sits quietly and does a jigsaw. He doesn't protest. The illness means he's sleepy most of the time. At first I preferred him sleepy, but it seems all wrong. I almost miss the old Timmy.

I can hear thumping and crashing and raised voices from upstairs, as they hunt for the tablets. I asked Dad about them once and he said they keep Mum happy but I said I didn't think she seemed all that happy and he smiled the way Arthur Daley does in *Minder* when Terry's caught him up to no good. Then Dad said, 'You don't remember how she was before.'

I mix up the Nesquik – a scoop of banana from one carton, and a scoop of chocolate from the other – and stir in the milk splosh by splosh, like Dad does. I open the serving hatch and Timmy's watching *Tiswas*, which Mum hates because it's so noisy (and Dad loves because of that girl Sally with the dark hair).

I close the hatch. Maybe now could be a good time to add to my stockpile.

The more my parents worry about Timmy, the more I can save. I could have a battalion of Russian spies hiding in my bedroom and no one would notice. On the downside, no one gets time to go to Sainsbury's, so the cupboards are nearly empty and there's not much choice.

So far, the space under my bed contains:

A copy of my 'bible', *Protect and Survive*, which I bought for 50p from the council offices during a school trip. If there is an impending threat of war, the booklet will be given away for free, but then I read somewhere else that it'd take four weeks to print enough copies, and I don't hold out much hope of getting hold of supplies once everyone's in a state of panic. Lucky for Mum, Dad and Timmy (and Misty) that I'm prepared.

Cutlery: a knife, fork and spoon. The booklet says 'cutlery, crockery, tin-opener, bottle-opener' and doesn't specify whether every member of the family needs their own, but I guess we can take it in turns and I daren't take more than one set. I also don't really understand the bottle-opener thing as we are going to be short of space, but maybe the government thinks grown-ups need beer or wine to cheer them up. It *will* get pretty boring sitting in the inner refuge for fourteen days, until the fall-out subsides. Kids are allowed magazines and favourite toys, so maybe wine is the adult equivalent.

A torch (nicked from the garage), candles, matches and a radio with spare set of batteries. My old wind-up Sindy alarm clock and a calendar. I think the idea behind the calendar is that if the radio breaks, you can tick off the days. I look at the calendar. July already. I wonder if we'll make it to the end of 1982 without war starting.

Sometimes it doesn't seem very likely.

I've also hidden tissues, loads of carrier-bags, two stolen toilet rolls, and a notebook and pen 'for messages' (are we meant to get Rover to deliver them to the outside world?). I'm collecting plasters and aspirin from the bathroom cabinet, though Mum's raid this morning is a set-back.

There are lots of things I can't hide under the bed, even if Mum and Dad never go in there, e.g. two bins (one for our *toilet* waste – yuk – and one for rubbish), sleeping bags, thick clothes, wellies so you don't get fall-out on your socks, a spade (as if we're going to do some gardening to take our mind off Armageddon), a lavatory improvised from an old dining chair and a bucket, and containers for the two pints of water we each need to drink every day.

So for now I'm focusing on food. The government says every person aged over five needs six pounds of biscuits or cereals, four and a half pounds of canned meat or fish (e.g. pilchards, I've got some under my bed but I can't imagine eating them if they were the last food on earth so I've been buying Spam with my pocket money), four pounds of canned vegetables, a pound of butter or peanut butter, a pound of jam or honey, six cans of soup, tea and coffee, a pound of sweets, a pound and a half of sugar, and *fourteen* cans of evaporated milk.

This is meant to cost £15 per person, i.e. thirty weeks' worth of pocket money times four, which means either I need to get a paper round, hope that the bombs don't drop before I am fourteen (might have kissed a boy by then, too), or improvise. The canned veg has been a doddle: having tasted cold carrots, cold peas and cold baked beans, it's got to be Heinz every time. Dad's going to fart whatever we eat, after all.

I've been eating everything cold, not that anyone's noticed. The Pot Noodles were a mistake. I tried them on their own, and the noodles were like chewing fingernails, and the powder caught in my throat and made me choke. I added cold water – there won't be any hot in the inner refuge – and it was no better. The water went a rusty colour, but the flavouring sat on the surface, crusting like a spot. I flushed the liquid down the loo, and buried the carton and the still-rigid noodles at the bottom of the kitchen bin.

The Nesquik would be good in the shelter, so I transfer enough of the banana powder into the chocolate carton. *That'll cheer Timmy up*. But then I stop: cheer him up, when we're crammed into a space no bigger than a tent, waiting for the all-clear? Cheer him up when we get ill and we can't tell whether it's the awful food or radiation sickness? Cheer him up if one of us doesn't get home in time when the four-minute warning goes? Or if poor Misty panics and makes a run for it, out into ruined Greenham Lane?

I feel tears stinging in my eyes. I can't think like that. Because what else can I do but try to save our lives? The alternative is to bury my head in the sand like Mum and Dad and every other adult I've ever met except Mr Blake. But even

Mr Blake's moved on from war . . . we're doing the New Ice Age at the moment, with Test Tube Babies to follow.

I take a carrier-bag from under the sink, and fill it with the Nesquik container, a couple of dusty tins of beans from the back of the larder, a small bottle of disinfectant, and a tea towel. Before I sneak it upstairs I take my brother's drink into the living-room.

'Here's your favourite, Timmy . . . *Timmy*?'

The TV's still on – a child dressed in full school uniform is about to get covered in pink gunk by Suggs from Madness – but there's only a Timmy-shaped dent in the sofa cushion where my brother should be. 'Timmy?' I raise my voice, but not enough that they'll hear me upstairs. Misty bounds in, ears pricked and hoping I actually said 'walkies'.

I peer through the French doors into the garden, but there's no sign. He's probably gone upstairs. That's it. Gone to look for Mummy.

But when I go into the hall to follow him upstairs, I see something frightening. The front door is open: not wide, but as if whoever left went quietly, without shutting the door, in case someone heard it slam.

'Dad . . . ' I call out but my voice is small. I run up the stairs, two at a time, and find my parents in their bedroom. There's a pile of pill bottles on the duvet and Mum is still crying, mewing like a kitten. They look up at me, as if they'd forgotten they had a daughter.

'I can't find . . . The front door. I mean, Timmy's gone. Open. Disappeared. TV's on but . . . ' The words come out in all the wrong order.

'Calm down, Jo,' my father says and I hear the careful, reassuring tone he uses on my mother. Except even as he speaks, he's crabbing towards the door.

'I left him to make him a Nesquik. He was watching TV. But he's not now. And someone's left the front door open.'

Dad's coolness is gone. So is he: he thumps down to the hallway and shouts, 'Timmy? TIMMY! Stop playing games.'

Mum gets up and walks into Timmy's bedroom. For a

moment, I'm convinced he must be there, and I wait for the inevitable telling-off for scaring everyone. But over her shoulder, I see what she sees: stillness. When my brother's in his room, it's never still. He throws jigsaws and games across the floor, *literally* throws them and plays with them where they land for a few minutes, before finding something else to throw. When he's asleep, his limbs thrash about as if he's drowning and the toys on his bed are tossed into the air like ship's passengers.

The stillness is eerie. Before I can stop myself I think, this is what it would be like if Timmy doesn't make it. *This* is what my brother would leave behind ...

When my mother turns, her face is warped like a melted candle and I'm convinced she's thinking the same thing. 'Timmy. My Timmy.' I'm invisible as she races down to where my father is crashing about, hunting not a lost packet of pills, but a lost son.

'How long did you leave him for?' Dad asks when I walk into the kitchen.

'I don't know ... a few minutes?'

He faces my mother, grabbing her upper arms. 'Lynda. We need to look for Timmy, you understand that, don't you? We need to look now. He won't have gone far.'

'But where *could* he have gone, Ted? He's eight years old.' She sounds confused.

'Oh, bloody hell. Lynda, if I knew that ... ' Dad pushes past her into the hall, grabs two sets of door keys from the *Country Diary of an Edwardian Lady* rack above the telephone table, and beckons to me. 'I need both my girls to be very sensible now. Timmy will be somewhere nearby, we know that. I need both of you to search together – and you must *stick* together.' He turns to me. 'Jo, you keep hold of the keys. I'll go towards town and you two head towards the common and the base.'

'But what if ... ' I know I shouldn't say this, but I have to. 'What if we don't find him?'

'Then it means I've probably found him already. But

whatever happens, we'll meet back here in an hour. Hang on, let me get some food, he's bound to be hungry by now.' He goes back into the kitchen, and returns with a bag. *My* bag, for the stockpile. 'What's this, Jo?'

'It's . . . ' I hesitate. 'I was packing for a picnic.'

He stares at me, obviously not believing I'd take beans and Nesquik on a picnic. But he shakes his head. 'It doesn't matter. Don't let Mum out of your sight, Jo. And keep your eyes peeled for Timmy. He can't have gone far.'

'You said that already, Dad.'

He smiles, but his eyes don't and it makes me more afraid. 'Yes. I suppose I did.' He kisses me on the forehead. 'If I say it often enough, it has to be true.'

He pulls my mother's shoes out of the understairs cupboard. It smells of leather and damp. Mum lifts her legs as he pushes the shoes on to her feet. He kisses her on the cheek then pats her bottom. 'Off you go. One hour. That'll be all it takes.'

It's hot and sunny outside, and Mum and I blink as we walk up the hill, peering up the drives of dozens of houses like ours. Or not quite like ours: outside each one I mentally calculate the chances of each building surviving a one-megaton blast. As we move towards the common, there's a mix of flimsy new semis which will be blown apart like matchstick models, and sturdier Victorian houses. Though, of course, the closer we get to the common, the closer we are to ground zero. And nothing but a lead box buried a mile below the earth will save you there.

Mum is going through the motions of looking for Timmy, but her eyes are glazed. I'm not sure whether she took too many pills when she found them, or whether this is shock at my brother's disappearance.

'He's probably playing hide-and-seek,' I say. Then, as a test, I try, 'You know how naughty he is.' If she's even half with it, she'll tell me off for that.

She doesn't. Instead she calls out, 'Timmy. Where are you, Timmy?'

The houses are more scattered as we walk towards the air-base perimeter, with privet and gorse hedges shielding the well-heeled occupants from the chaos. A big sign reads 'Women's Peace Camp' in green, white and violet letters, and it's spawned lots of smaller boards picturing doves and that female sign, the one that looks like an O with a + sign attached. We've driven past often enough, but I've never been here before: it seems like a waste of energy to protest against a few more bombs, when there are already enough in the world to kill all of us twenty times over. Better to protect yourself.

I can see their tents in the distance; the different colours and shapes make it look untidy, like a hurricane at a rubbish tip. No wonder Dad's mates at the Rotary hate this place. They're the sort who think women should be seen, not heard, and *always* tidy.

But as we get closer, order emerges from the chaos. As well as tents, there are caravans painted with flowers and fruit, toilet cubicles, and a huge central structure made of canvas and polythene.

Mum and I approach nervously. I couldn't look much less like a peace woman, in my pink stripy pedal-pushers and T-shirt with a glittery gold lion on it. My mother is more of a hippie, in her long, floral skirt (like the one Lady Diana Spencer wore in that photo where you could see her legs) and a creased lemon-yellow blouse. She forgot to put on a bra this morning, so her boobs jiggle as she walks and – yuk – her nipples are sticking out. Her legs are unshaven, covered in little crescents of hair, but she's still too clean to be one of *them*. They're probably going to shout at us for gawping, throw a bucket of dirty water to make us go away.

But what choice do we have? My little brother loves drama, and this is the most dramatic place on our doorstep right now.

'Shall I go?' I ask Mum, and she nods. I walk up to the first tent. It's like a Red Indian wigwam, decorated with ribbons and symbols. The camp is smaller than it looks on TV: next to the high fence, it seems no scarier than the Cub Scout weekend Timmy went on last summer (Dad had to go and get him after one day because he was missing his mummy).

'Hello?' I hover at the entrance to the tent, not knowing what to say. 'Anyone in there?' I wait but I can't hear anyone inside. 'Hello?'

'Looking for someone, my love?' I turn round to see a very pretty woman, a bit older than Mum, behind me. She has a Welsh accent like Ruth Madoc in *Hi-Di-Hi*, bobbed mousy hair with a grey streak in the fringe, and pointy features that make her face look wide awake. No BO or piercings, but she does wear a purple peasant waistcoat with muddy frayed jeans.

'Actually. Yes, we are.' I wave at Mum, who doesn't notice. 'My brother.'

She laughs. 'We don't tend to get too many men round here. Unless they've come to make trouble.'

'No, he's my *little* brother. He's eight and about this tall –' I hold my hand up to my shoulder, '– with light brown hair. Well, he doesn't have much hair at the moment. Just tufts, like a new baby. Blue eyes. *Very* pale.' I feel queasy as I picture him. 'He's not well.'

Waistcoat Lady looks concerned. 'I haven't seen a little boy. But don't worry, if he's here, we'll find him. Maybe he's hiding in one of the benders. Come on.' She calls across to Mum, 'You too, dear. We don't bite, whatever it says in the *Evening Post*.'

Mum approaches reluctantly, and we follow Waistcoat Lady, zig-zagging between tents and washing lines. I wonder how they dry their clothes when it rains. Or dry themselves. Some of the tents look as though they'd float away in the lightest shower. A couple of tents further in, we reach the campfire area, where women sit on deckchairs and orange boxes drinking tea; they stare at us, but they don't seem hostile, simply curious. At their feet, two tiny little girls dressed only in flowery pants are playing marbles.

'Wait here,' Waistcoat Lady says. 'Biscuits and tea are on that table. I think your mum could do with some.'

I approach the trestle and take a few digestives for Mum while I scan the area for mugs and a kettle. I can't help glancing over at the women. They're mostly quite young, teens and twenties, and they could be art students from Newbury College, except they're not wearing lipstick and their hair is either cropped or tangled-looking. The boys on the pull at the Wagon and Horses wouldn't like that.

I know what Dad thinks of them. He's said so often enough. '*Bloody scroungers.* Russia is a big fat bully and will invade us if we can't protect ourselves.'

I've seen how bullies operate so maybe he's right about needing our own bombs. I don't think I'm going to say that out loud, though. Instead, I spot a cauldron of water hanging over a fire. It must be what they use to make tea.

'Timmy!'

Mum cries out and I look up and there is my brother, walking towards us from the far end of the camp, one hand held by Waistcoat Lady, and the other by a younger woman with blue-black hair. He looks like a little prince with his devoted courtiers. My mother races forward, snapped out of her trance, and takes him in her arms.

However much he annoys me, my heart feels like it's growing too big for my ribcage. It must be relief.

Waistcoat Lady beams at Timmy. 'What a charmer your brother is. He's been learning how to play the drums with Mags.'

Mags with the blue hair shrugs. 'I thought he was one of the weekenders' kids. We get people coming on Saturdays, you know. Day-trippers.' She spits out the words in angry cockney.

'Ah, Mags. Don't be such a hard-liner.' Waistcoat Lady ruffles what's left of Timmy's hair; people can't help doing that kind of thing. No stranger ever touches mine, unless you count the nit-nurse.

I see it happening before they do: with Timmy still in her arms, my mother's hairy legs begin to buckle. I race forward and Waistcoat Lady notices too because she catches my brother as Mum crumples, rather elegantly, to the ground.

'Don't grip him too hard!' I scream. 'He's got leukaemia!'

All the women look at me now, and Mags gives me one of those grown-up *meaningful* looks. Waistcoat Lady eases Timmy to the floor and he crawls towards my mother, who is awake but has dreamy eyes, her skirt splayed out and her doll-legs straight ahead of her.

'Leukaemia.' Mags gives me a second serious look. 'Did you hear that, Gillian?'

Waistcoat Lady nods.

Mags touches my hand. 'This is important. You live round here, right?'

'Yes. All my life.'

Mags sighs. 'I knew it. Gillian, we need to –'

My mother moans and I think she's going to faint again. Waistcoat Gillian places her hands on Mum's shoulders and whispers, 'You're all right now, my love. Everything's fine.'

'But, Gillian, we have to let her know what this is –'

'Later, for pity's sake, Mags. Sometimes a protest march isn't the first thing to organise. Sometimes,' she says pointedly, 'a cup of very sweet tea is more of a priority.'

Mags pouts but scuttles off to fetch one. Gillian crouches down next to Mum now. 'So what's your name then?' Mum doesn't seem to hear her.

'She's Lynda. Lynda Morgan. I'm Joanna.'

'And this little ruffian?' She strokes his hair again. I wish she wouldn't do that, it only encourages him.

'Timmy.'

Timmy beams at her, cute as a flipping button, and Gillian beams back. 'And would Timmy like some chocolate?' She frowns. 'If he's allowed, of course. With his *illness*.'

'He doesn't have much of an appetite,' I say, 'but funnily enough he always seems to have room for chocolate.'

'I've got some in my teepee,' she says. 'Come with me if you like.'

I follow her back towards the edge of the camp. 'Have you been here since the start?'

'No. I saw it on the news last summer when the marchers first left Wales and I thought the women were so brave. Never thought I'd have the guts to do it too, but I came for a visit back in January, brought some food and then . . . I can't explain it. It felt like the right thing. The only thing to do.' She pushes through the flap in the teepee. 'And it's so much easier now the weather's drier. The mud! You wouldn't believe what it's like. Right. Chocolate.'

I peer through the flap. There's not much room, but Gillian's made it cosy, with photographs of mountains pinned to the fabric, and a leather pouffe with ethnic embroidery next to the red sleeping roll. Hanging up there's a toilet bag like my granny's. A big black umbrella is propped up against the wall of the tent, and there's a pile of books next to it, with titles like *Woman-Hating* and *Gyn/Ecology: the Metaethics of Radical Feminism*. Right at the bottom, there's a battered copy of *Jane Eyre*.

She rummages through numerous carrier bags. 'Everything gets soaked when it rains, even with all these bags. Right, what about a Mars bar? Helps us work, rest and preserve world peace.'

I giggle. 'You're different from what I thought.'

'What, because I look like I might wash occasionally?'

I blush. 'Yes.'

'You seem a sensible girl, Joanna. So here's a good lesson for you. Don't believe the papers. They have just as much of an agenda as we do. Except ours is about saving lives. You can work out for yourself what theirs might be.'

I nod, though I don't really understand. 'Gillian?'

'Uh-huh,' she says, pulling out a crushed Kit-Kat and giving it to me.

'You know what the other lady, Mags, with the blue hair . . . what she said about Timmy's illness? About something we needed to know?'

'I don't think . . . ' Gillian hesitates. 'No, you're old enough to hear it. We're not scientists, Joanna, so this isn't definite or anything, but we read all the research. You know that Greenham isn't the only military establishment round here? There's also Burghfield and Aldermaston. That's where they invent the weapons and test them.'

'I know about Aldermaston.' It was on the map in the book I borrowed from the library, of sites the Russians would bomb first.

'Good girl. Well, there's anecdotal – that means, unofficial, unverified – evidence that more children living around there might be getting cancer than usual. Cancers like leukaemia.'

'And you think . . . ' I can't say it.

'It's *possible*, no more than that, but possible that your brother's illness could be part of that, what shall we call it, that *trend*. That something the plants are putting out into the atmosphere could be making people ill. Especially children.'

I nod. I don't even feel surprised. As usual, most grown-ups ignore the damage they're doing to the planet. 'But what can we do?'

Gillian touches my arm as she emerges from the teepee. '*Here* is what we do, my love. The camp's not only about bombs. It's about the planet. About you. The next generation. People can laugh as much as they like but I look at your brother and I know we're right. Things have to change.'

'But nothing ever changes, does it? The Russians are bullies. They won't respect us unless we can fight back.'

She raises an eyebrow. 'Is that what *you* think, Joanna? Or what someone else thinks? We ought to talk it through properly. But for now, I think chocolate is the priority, eh? Can't have you fading away.'

Chapter 28

Dromophobia – Fear of Crossing Streets

At last I have a theory about where the flashbacks are leading me.

Right now, they're leading me to London, Dick Whittington style, as I try to follow the trail. I wouldn't normally go out of my way to visit my brother. Even crossing the road would feel like too much effort. But I can't get the latest flashback of the camp out of my head and I know that Timmy must be part of the answer.

When I rang his mobile, he tried to use his '*horrible* diary' as an obstacle to meeting much before the 2012 Olympics ('you could come as my guest, bound to be hundreds of champagne receptions and I'm brilliant at blagging'). But I played the head-banger card, told him my own diary was horribly empty, and offered to be on standby 24/7 for a free slot. He then fired below the belt.

'But you hate London. It scares you silly.'

'I must face my fears,' I said solemnly. He relented with a sigh.

He's right about London, of course, and I consume a whole bottle of Rescue Remedy before I board the train. At Paddington, I'm unsteady on my feet, but wobble through the crowds to the taxi rank. The cab to Timmy's offices costs me twelve pounds though it can only be a mile away and most of the journey we're in stationary traffic.

The ad agency is based in an old varnish factory, now known as the Shiny Happy Place. It's a tall, narrow building in city-browned brick, and probably once had a quiet dignity. Not any more.

Through the high lead-framed windows, I can see malnourished blonde receptionists perching on bar stools, alongside an espresso machine the size of a family saloon. After fiddling for several minutes with the entryphone (this area of town is what Timmy calls 'high energy' and what the cabbie called 'well-fucking dodgy'), I finally catch the eye of one of the girls. She manoeuvres herself slowly off her bar stool, so her skinny jeans don't split, and opens the door two inches.

'Are you lost? The Tube's back up that way,' she says, peering through the gap.

'No, I think I'm in the right place. I've come to see Timmy. My brother.'

She stares at me. 'Timmy?'

'Timothy Morgan. Your boss?'

Her eyes flicker in recognition. 'Oh, the Morg. And you're his ... sister? You know, I'd *never* have guessed that.' She opens the door fully. 'He's in the penthouse.'

The smell hits me first: varnish. But I bet it's fake, created especially for the factory by a Parisian 'nose' to hint at the place's history without giving everyone solvent headaches. Then I look up: this handsome industrial building seems to be midway through conversion to a children's play centre, all primary colours and climbing frames. The receptionist points to a tiny glass bubble lift, but I feel dizzy looking at it, so take the spiral staircase instead. On my way up, I pass more tight-jeaned young women, and several forty-something men trying to compensate for receding hairlines with ponytails and George Michael beards. I can't quite believe my little brother is their boss.

The stairs go on and on and I'm nauseous by the time I

reach the 'penthouse' – more like a balcony placed strategically and, knowing Timmy's inflated ego, symbolically above everyone else. There's a huge bed, a suspended plasma screen the size of a pool table, an actual pool table, plus a metal desk hanging from the ceiling on thick dungeon chains. Behind it sits a woman who ...

Bloody hell! A woman who is the spitting image of my mother. Well, my mother twenty years ago, if she'd had the benefit of £300 highlights and a wafty-fabric wardrobe from Ghost.

'Aha! Jo, isn't it? You do look a bit like the Morg ... I mean, Tim.' She gets up from her ergonomic chair and shakes my hand. Then she leans into a microphone on her desk. 'Will the Morg return to base immediately?' Her voice echoes round the building.

She makes me a camomile tea and I wait. *Come on, Jo.* You can stand up to your brother. You've seen him naked. You know his secrets.

Out of the blue, I think of Luke. What was it Frisky called him, an only child who's struggling with being alone in the world? I remind myself that I should be grateful to have a brother.

After several minutes, the lift slides up to our level and Timmy steps out, with all the humility of a rock god. He wears tweed breeches with a neon green thread, and a matching T-shirt. 'Yo, sis!' he says, air-kissing me from three feet away. He turns to our Mum-a-like, 'So, who got the good looks in the Morgan family, Karine?'

She tuts at him, then reaches forward and *ruffles his hair*. And he makes a noise I can only describe as a purr. I have to look away.

'Join me on the bed, sis,' he says and beckons me over. I balance on the edge of the silk Playboy duvet cover, and sip my tea. 'So, what on earth's so important that you've ventured into our dangerous capital?'

'Well ... ' I'm not prepared for such a direct question, so

soon. 'I wanted to see you. The last time I was only semi-conscious, after all.'

'The only way to survive Courtbridge, if you want my opinion,' he says. Then he lights a cigarette. 'Is that what you want? My opinion?'

'What do you mean?'

'Let me guess what's going on, sis. Some kind of road to Damascus, seen the light, the future's bright, the future's Orange, near-death experience moment that's made you want to bond with me. Lovely. But can I be brutally honest?'

'Can I stop you being?'

'What have we got in common? Apart from *les parents*. And if we've nothing in common, well . . . is there a point?' He lies back on the bed, eyes closed.

In a few blunt words, my perfectly honed speech about letting bygones be bygones, my questions about happiness and childhood memories, has been rendered redundant and naïve. 'Just a minute, Timothy EDWARD HORATIO Morgan.' I always hated the fact he had three names when I was plain Joanna. 'You got away with it when you were eight, but you're not going to bully me now. And when did you become a bloody mind-reader?'

He opens one eyelid – God how I hated it when he used to do that – and smiles lazily. 'Now don't get those knickers in a twist, sis. You might dribble on the duvet. Silk stains terribly.'

I stand up: it's difficult to be assertive on the bed. 'Stop it! Yes, I would like us to be closer, but I'm fully aware that having the world's most arrogant *twat* as a brother makes that impossible.'

Timmy waves his hand in the air. 'Hold on a sec. Karine, would you mind taking an early lunch? And telling Liam at Saatchi's that I can't make it for the one fifteen appointment? Looks like this might take a while . . . '

I look at the time, projected on to the warehouse wall in pink letters. Three minutes past one. 'So you had generously allocated *fifteen minutes* to this? Well, lucky old me.'

Karine backs away, muttering about working from a hot

desk downstairs. As she leaves, Timmy presses a switch, and a metal blind descends from the ceiling to the floor, so no one below can see us.

'All right, Jo. What is this *really* about? Do you need some money? I'm more than happy to write you a cheque if I can take a raincheck from the family therapy.'

'Money? God, you've got no idea, have you? No. I want to make sense of the past.'

'I *knew* it!' He punches the air like a footballer. 'I knew it had to do with the Meaning of Life.'

'Can't you ditch the sarcasm and actually listen to what I've got to say for once, Timmy?'

He shrugs, but his face is softer. 'I suppose I could try.'

I take a big breath. 'I'm not mistaking you for the Dalai Lama. I don't want your views on the afterlife, or my progression up the career ladder, or my image.'

'Ah, now that's probably the only thing I'd be any use at. Those pastel colours, Jo, they're so draining. I've got a mobile number for the best personal shopper in London.' He withers under my glare. 'No? Sorry. Carry on.'

'I don't envy your stupid job or your gaudy clothes. But I'd like to claim back my share of confidence that somehow got allocated to you. And that certainty you've always had about what you want out of life.'

For the first time, he looks interested. 'They're not *that* gaudy, are they? My clothes? Gaultier is the only designer that always works for me. As for the confidence thing, well, I've never really thought about it.'

'Could you try now? Just for me?'

He stubs out his cigarette between the breasts of a nymph-shaped onyx ashtray, and picks up a Rubik's Cube. 'Helps me think,' he says and begins to click and twist the rows. 'Um . . . knowing what I want. Let's see. Nearly dying as a kid probably helped.' He peers up from the cube, to see whether this is enough.

'No, I don't buy it Timmy. I've nearly died and it's made me *more* confused. And anyway you were rocky from birth.'

'Fair point. Maybe it's down to Mum.'

'So you'll admit you were her favourite?' I snap.

His eyes open wide. 'What, and you weren't *Dad's* favourite?'

'No way. You were the apple of *everyone*'s eye.'

'Bollocks, sis. Always the same in families. Mummy's boys and Daddy's girls. Way of the world. But that's not my point. My point is we both had a parent on our side.'

I'm too intrigued to argue the toss. 'Go on.'

'So in theory we should *both* have grown up with high self-esteem.' He's frantically twisting the cube now, thinking aloud.' But maybe . . . OK. How about this? Mum was the underdog in our family, wasn't she? Had to support Dad, all she got a say on was what was for dinner, or what brand of washing powder to use.'

'I suppose so.' I decide not to tell him about what I learned at the barbecue: that Mum had made that choice consciously, aware of what it might cost her.

'And all the time, he was knocking off endless girls at the bank or the operatic society.'

I flinch. No one's ever said it out loud before, and the bluntness makes me realise that however pragmatic my mother was, she couldn't have predicted quite how bad it would be. 'But you didn't know that till you were older.'

'Well, no, but I did sense that she was unhappy and put upon. What if she spoiled me precisely because she wanted me to live the life she couldn't? Make me believe anything's possible? Wouldn't be the first mother to live vicariously through her kids.' He stops fiddling with the cube and holds it up, each side the same fluorescent colour.

It does make a strange sort of sense. Except . . . 'How come I didn't grow up feeling the same? Like I could have anything I wanted?'

He folds his hands behind his head and lies back against the pillow. 'Well, it was only a theory. Maybe I was born with the selfish gene. Like you said, I always was a brat. But

Mum's lessons worked. I do have everything I want.' He waves at his surroundings.

'Really? No deep longings? No horrible inadequacies below the surface?'

'No. Sorry, sis. Just a bad boy who never intends to grow up.' He grins and for once, I allow myself to fall for the charm.

'Great if you can get away with it,' I say. And why shouldn't he? I've focused on Timmy for so long, blaming him for my insecurities, and all he's done is pursued what he wanted.

'The thing you need to remember, Jo, is that sometimes selfish is *good for everyone*. Sometimes selfish is the *right thing*. Look at this place,' he stands up, peering down at his domain through the blind, 'being selfish has got me here, sure, but it's also given jobs to twenty people. And created some of the best ad campaigns the British public could hope for.'

'So I should look after *numero uno*, for the sake of everyone else?'

'Yup. You know, people *like* being manipulated, if it's done with panache.'

'Ri-ight.' And I wonder whether that's what he's doing to me.

'And don't forget, some would say shyness is only another form of selfishness. The passive-aggressive sort. The trick is not to think *too* much. Go with your gut.' He presses a button and the privacy blind begins to retract. 'Speaking of guts, now we've cracked the code, why don't you join me for sushi? Might as well use the booking Karine made. Think of it as an open apology for making your entire childhood a misery.'

By the time we've got a cab to the sushi bar, Timmy's all smiles. He greets the waitresses like he lunches there every day – for all I know, he does – with treble air-kisses and an enquiry about the availability of *anago*.

'What's that?' I ask, as we take our seat in front of a conveyor belt.

'Conger eel,' he says. 'Only in season for a while but when it is . . . ' He smacks his lips. 'So. Just pick off the dishes you like and stack up the plates, that's how they work out the bill. Beats the conveyor belt in *The Generation Game*, eh?'

I hesitate. If I really want to turn my back on my fearful days, I should be diving in, stuffing myself with raw fish and eels so fresh they probably twitch on your tongue, but the thought makes me want to retch. And then I think of Timmy every Christmas, demanding circumcised sausage rolls: if I'm really turning into a woman who knows her own mind, then surely I can eat exactly what I like. Go with my gut. Even if my brother mocks me for it, as he undoubtedly will.

Timmy looks at me. 'You know, if you don't fancy raw fish, the omelette *nigiri* is *really* good, here.' And he picks up a saucer with three blocks of rice with bright yellow toppings.

It's probably the most considerate thing my brother's ever done for me. 'Thanks,' I say. To stop them, I pick up the *nigiri* with my fingers and chew carefully. I wouldn't say it's the best thing I've ever tasted, but it doesn't make me puke.

I follow it with some more veggie stuff – a salad, some of the same chewy rice topped with avocado and peppers. Timmy tries hard, making enquiries about Dennis and Lorraine, and it's only because I recognise that too rapt expression from years ago, that I know he's not really listening. But I can't expect miracles.

My brother pushes a single wodge of tuna around his plate before eating half of it.

'That all you're having?'

He pats his chest. 'This six-pack takes a lot of sacrifices, sis.'

No, I definitely wouldn't want to make those kind of sacrifices.

On the train back to Courtbridge, I feel slightly resentful that Timmy didn't have an instant solution, but then again maybe he's right. Maybe shyness *is* plain old egocentricity and everyone would be happier if I swapped my self-obsession for good old-fashioned selfishness.

I decide to start by ordering myself a double vodka and orange from the buffet bar. The fact that Dennis would disapprove makes it taste ever sweeter.

Chapter 29

Taphephobia – Fear of Being Buried Alive

Selfishness is harder than it looks. I've been busy telling Mum I don't like quinoa casserole (and having to admit that all the other casseroles she's supplied since the accident have ended up in the bin). Telling Dennis that I *like* squirrels and will go on feeding them, whatever he says. And telling Lorraine that I'm going to keep seeing Frisky whatever happens.

Maybe when you've done what you want for as long as Timmy, you get used to the way people look at you. Like you've kicked their puppy or criticised their children.

Frisky, meanwhile, feels so responsible for the two 'funny turns' I've had while he's been around, that he's on best behaviour.

'I've taken very special care with your latest . . . what shall I call it? . . . date with danger. This one took some string-pulling, my dear, but it's worth it. You'll love it. Oh, and make sure you wear sensible shoes.'

So now I'm back in the Red Peril, wondering how I got myself into a situation where I'm at the mercy of a madman's whims, while Frisky hints at his other plans for summer outings.

'We're definitely going to have to find a way to get you airborne, Joanna. In a strictly non-acrobatic sense, so as not to aggravate the good doctor. But there's nothing like seeing the English countryside from above for making the pulse race a little faster.'

'I did fly once, when I was nine. To Spain.' I don't add that I was too busy screaming to appreciate the countryside, and that the stewardess threatened to lock me in a lavatory ('She'll provoke hysteria in the other passengers!'). After that, all our holidays were in draughty four-star Norfolk hotels full of clothes moths and old people.

'Oh, I'm not talking about a *charter* flight,' Frisky says ominously. 'Then there's water. Messing about on rivers, like *Wind in the Willows*. I'll be Toad, you can be Mole. And I'm afraid Luke is *definitely* ratty.'

Luke catches my eye in the driver's mirror and looks heavenwards. I caught a trace of *that* aftershave when I climbed into the car, and it made me blush all over again. I try to work out his mood, how his loss is affecting him, but his face gives nothing away. I was granted a flash of his all-American teeth when he smiled earlier, made more dazzling by his tan. He looks out of place in boring old Courtbridge, like a stretch limo at a car-boot sale.

'So that's air and water. We've done speed and thrills . . . '

'Don't forget public humiliation by making me sing karaoke. Oh, and advanced DIY. I can honestly say you've changed my life, Frisky.' It comes out flippant, so I try again. 'I know it might not seem that obvious yet, but you have. Both of you,' I add, including Luke in my thank you. 'You're my favourite men.'

Frisky chuckles. 'I wonder what your *partner* would have to say about that,' he says, and guilt nibbles at my contentment, until my brother's voice kicks in. *Sometimes selfish is good for everyone.*

The drive goes on and on, with Luke consulting a series of maps, enclosed in protective plastic covers, as though we're on an army expedition. Once we get off the main roads and into proper countryside, his face relaxes and he manoeuvres the Peril with confidence *and* delicacy, so that the car seems to transcend its mechanical limitations and float along the hedgerows. It's a glorious June day, and the view is straight from the pages of a 'Visit England' brochure.

Finally he pulls up and turns round: his cheeks are pink and his eyes wide. 'I think we're here.'

Here is the corner of a meadow, somewhere an hour to the west of Courtbridge. Unless those sleepy-looking cows turn into raging bulls on demand, I can't see anything that's going to test my courage.

Perhaps it's a nice, straightforward picnic. How lovely. Then it occurs to me: it could be a test of self-sufficiency, where we'll be expected to catch *and* kill our lunch.

Frisky's out of the car, peering all around. To our right there's a small woodland glade, and a wall with a derelict, pebble-dashed bungalow behind it. He whistles, but it's not a casual whistle. In fact, I'm sure it's the tune the aliens used in *Close Encounters*.

'You haven't brought me to meet little green men, have you?' It's not that ridiculous. Wiltshire has so many crop circles in summer that they barely get a mention on the local news any more. Space invaders clearly have a soft spot for this area as a holiday destination.

'Ha ha, not quite,' he says, as an unmistakable whistled reply drifts towards us from the area by the bungalow. 'This is *such* fun. I always wanted to be in the S.O.E.'

He repeats the whistle again as he moves towards the densest patch of trees. Out of the corner of my eye, I glimpse a camouflaged shape. The shape emerges from behind the branches: it's not an alien, but a bald middle-aged man in combat jacket, waterproof trousers and a khaki baseball cap pulled down so far you can only see his lips and chin.

'Wing Commander Freeman Van Belle?' he hisses.

'That's me,' says Frisky, holding out his hand. I wonder if Frisky really was that high up, or whether it's a little white lie. Combat Man's wearing fingerless gloves, although the temperature's in the mid-twenties. 'And you must be Lionel?'

The man nods. He's slightly overweight and his teeth are veined with nicotine stains. 'No one followed you?'

Frisky seems to be fighting the urge to giggle. 'Nope. There are only three of us. This is Joanna, a friend of mine, who shares our fascination. And then this is my grandson, Luke.'

Lionel acknowledges Luke but ignores me. Whatever his fascination is (Paint-balling? Radical far right survivalism? Taxidermy?), I very much doubt we share it. But I *am* intrigued . . .

'It's not covered by Official Secrets no more, but we still like to keep it *need to know*, yeah?'

'Mum's the word, old chap,' Frisky assures him.

Lionel finally looks at me, but only from the knees down. 'You told her to wear sensible shoes. Good girl. Birds usually turn up in heels. You wouldn't believe it.'

'Oh, Joanna always dresses appropriately,' Frisky says, then winks at me. 'Shall we make a start then?'

We follow our prickly guide towards the derelict bungalow. He pulls out a huge bunch of keys to unlock the heavily padlocked gate, then leads us up the path and opens the front door. Maybe he has some kind of uniform in there for us? But as we step inside, there's no paramilitary kit room or secret stash of Kalashnikovs. Instead, we're in a white-washed tunnel that stretches way beyond the length of the bungalow. It's completely disorientating, until I smell the distinctive smell of municipal grade disinfectant, and suddenly know where we are.

I turn to Frisky. 'It's a bunker, isn't it? A regional command centre?'

He claps his hands together. 'Well spotted, my dear. Our friend Lionel here is a local enthusiast – took me a while to convince him, but he's agreed to give us a little tour. Isn't it fun?'

I stare down the tunnel. *Fun?* No, but oddly thrilling. I dreamed of places like this when I was twelve, of being one of the Chosen Few. Now I'm here, twenty years too late. 'Thank you, Lionel. I'm sure it'll be very interesting.'

He nods solemnly. 'Best untouched example in the south of England, this one. You wouldn't believe what some bastards have done with shelters. Mushroom farms. Conference centres. Party venues. I mean. Parties? No bloody decorum.'

Lionel doesn't look like much of a party animal. We walk in silence along the corridor, which slopes downwards. A set of stretcher-like beds projects from the wall, shelves for people. I wonder who'd have slept here, outside the shelter; the lower ranks, perhaps, dispensable enough to be endangered by a light scattering of fall-out. Or maybe these were for sentries, tasked with shooting desperate civilians whose only hope of survival lay underground.

Lionel stops and I look up at the enormous metal doors that shield those inside from blast and intruders. They must be twice my height at least. He takes yet more keys from his gaoler's bundle, before winding back the metal wheels that control the door levers. Finally the doors begin to slide open.

'This would have been what they called a Regional Government HQ – which evolved from the more basic War Rooms built after the Second World War. These were the Rolls-Royces. The next level up, the top of the range Aston Martin, was unique. Codenamed "Turnstile", meant to be top secret, but everyone knows it's twenty miles up the road, in a quarry near Corsham. A complete underground city, with roads and a pub.'

'Ah, that's the spirit,' says Frisky, 'raising a pint glass to the end of the world.'

Lionel looks at him. 'Well, you can bet the Russians would have stockpiled the vodka too. Anyway, that's where you'd stand the best chance of making it, but this would have been the next best thing.'

The door slams shut behind us. Slam is too small a word, somehow. When this door closes, it feels like the metal separates us from all that's good about the world: no more trees or flowers or animals or art ... the smell of damp overpowers the smell of disinfectant, and the only colour is accidental, rust-red watermarks bleeding through grey concrete floors and cream-painted walls.

The corridor continues more steeply downhill now, towards another barrier: an even bigger pair of doors, like the opening to a bank vault. 'The second blast doors,' Lionel explains as he manoeuvres one of them open, 'always open into a dog-leg corridor, to absorb the shockwave. These buggers literally weigh a tonne. But engineered so you can still open them if you're the one human left alive.'

He flicks a switch and illuminates a dead-end. 'We're on mains, but there are diesel generators outside, on the left-hand side of the bungalow. National Grid would be a goner if 200 atom bombs landed on the UK. And the air purification system here uses the same filters as your average Dyson.' He looks at me, because as a woman, presumably vacuum cleaners are all I understand. If only he knew.

We turn sharply down another corridor. The first door is marked 'Decontamination'. I peer inside. There's a shower without a curtain, and a large bin marked 'Contaminated Clothing'. 'It's like that film with Meryl Streep, where they almost scrubbed her eyes out.'

'Fat lot of good that'd do. They didn't keep spare clothes here, so if you did make it back in the bunker after a recce outside, you were presumably supposed to wander about starkers. Or maybe just go back to your dorm to die,' Lionel says and ushers us back into the corridor. Luke frowns, surveying the space from floor to ceiling, as if he's planning to build his own bunker.

'How long would they be underground?' Frisky asks.

'Councils were meant to have rations for thirty days, for 200 staff. Trouble is, most councils didn't plan to buy stores till the preparation phase, which meant they'd be joining the queues of terrified civilians at Tesco's. Only grub here is a few tins of salmon from panic buying during the Cuban Missile Crisis.'

He leads us to another door. 'This was the telephone exchange, linked to every other bunker in the country. No bugger wanted to admit you might never hear a dicky bird from the outside world. No way of knowing if you were on your own down here.'

The exchange seems to date back to the 1950s, with row upon row of wires and sockets. I imagine women down here, waiting for the call. Were they chosen for telephony skills, or their potential as the brood mares of the post-nuclear generation? 'How did they pick the staff?'

Lionel smiles: now he's in his stride, he seems to have forgotten that I'm a pathetic *girl*. 'The controllers – basically, the new prime ministers for each area – knew they had a place, and so did senior staff. Then they could pick who they liked. No one with faddy diets or claustrophobia. First you'd know would be a letter when the authorities thought war was coming, telling you to report to HQ with clothes, a toothbrush and maybe a few magazines to read.'

'And their families?'

Lionel shrugs. 'No room at the inn. But the authorities did promise to pay your salary into the missus's bank account though.'

'As if there'd be any banks left standing.' It's the first thing Luke's said since we got in the bunker.

'Bang on,' says Lionel. 'Then this is the sick bay.' It's a tiny room with a couple of bunks and a small first-aid cabinet. 'Not exactly geared up for major operations. The canteen had better kit, which tells you all you need to know about the plans for anyone who got sick.' He draws a heavily bitten finger across his throat in a slicing motion.

The canteen is the most normal place we've seen. It could be a school or hospital dining-room, with an adjoining kitchen that Gordon Ramsay wouldn't turn his nose up at. Huge ovens, freezers and a hostess trolley arrangement. I wonder what they'd make from the tinned supplies: apple crumbles and custard, to remind the occupants of homes that no longer existed?

'Time to go deeper.' Lionel leads us down some steps. 'Where the real action is.'

This is more like what I expected. There's a control room, with Perspex curved windows at waist level on two walls, a cross between a submarine and the Starship Enterprise. Plastic covers protect maps of our bit of England, each one divided into smaller zones. I spot Swindon and Newbury and Courtbridge too.

'Ah, bit more sophisticated than the old RAF control rooms,' Frisky says.

'Same principle, though. They'd write casualty estimates on the plastic sheets with chinagraph pencil, so they could change them easily. And then here's the boss's office.'

It's like the set of a '70s cop show, with wrinkled tobacco-brown carpet, padded swivel chairs, and a melamine bookcase that, above ground, would display darts trophies and photographs of ballet-dancing daughters.

'This is where the controller would make the life or death decisions. Shooting looters on sight, abandoning the walking dead, who'd already taken a fatal hit of radiation. Civil servants would become gods.' He pushes open the door to an ante-room. 'And this is where the Voice of God was broadcast from. Every bunker had a radio studio, though the chances of hearing the news depended on finding a radio under the rubble that was once your house.'

I think of hiding in the science prep room, of my painstaking plans for the 'inner refuge' at Greenham Lane: the stockpile of food, the improvised toilet, the radio that I later found out would probably have been knocked out by the shockwaves within seconds of the blast. It seems at once very sad and hilariously funny. Was I the only person in Britain daft enough to take that advice seriously?

'Do you mind if I take another look?' I gesture back towards the control room.

'Take your time,' Lionel says.

I walk up to the largest map, with Oxford at the top edge, and the Isle of Wight at the bottom. USAF Greenham Common is marked and I find Aldermaston and Burghfield, picturesque Berkshire villages that should be famous for pub cricket teams or local ale, but instead became notorious worldwide for marches and bases. Strange, strange times.

'So when your children ask you what you did in the Cold War, what will you say?' Luke is standing behind me.

'You wouldn't believe me if I told you.'

He smiles. 'In America, we were told to duck and cover.'

I smile back. 'We were meant to protect and survive. I was so frightened. And so jealous of Americans – I used to watch all your TV shows and in every one there was a yellow sign in the background, pointing to the fall-out shelter in the basement.'

He shakes his head. 'You know, I was more worried about the San Andreas fault. Russia seemed one hell of a long way away.'

'Were you ever in an earthquake?'

'Nothing big. As kids, we got used to waking up to tremors. But we all knew about 1906. Hundreds, maybe thousands, died in the Bay Area. I was kinda fascinated as well as scared. Like being a soldier, maybe. You don't want bad stuff to happen – but if it never does, what was the point of all the drills?' He laughs at himself. 'Final twist was, when the last one hit in 1989, I was on a study tour to Japan.'

'Was it the fear that made you choose your career?'

He nods. 'Kinda fear, kinda fascination. But also, I love my city. Wanted to help beat nature. Save us all, you know, like a seismic Superman. But sometimes danger comes when you least expect it.' He stares at the floor. 'But I guess you know that already, from what happened to you.'

Luke looks so unhappy that I want to reach out and hug him, but I don't think he'd appreciate it. I wonder whether Frisky's told him that I know about his parents. Eventually I say, 'I only chose my job with the council to try to get a place in a bunker like this. So my whole career was based on fear.' I shake my head. 'I didn't want to save the world. I wanted to save myself. Now I've seen this, I think I'd have preferred to go up in smoke like everyone else.'

'Funny, most kids think they're gonna live for ever,' he

says. 'Not us, huh?' He smiles at me and there's such warmth, such understanding in his face that for the first time, I feel good about being different.

Frisky emerges from the controller's office. 'Joanna, my dear, have you seen all you want to see? Only Lionel doesn't like to spend too long here, in case he gets into trouble. And he's already done us a huge favour, hasn't he?'

Lionel shuffles on the spot. 'I'm only supposed to have the keys to show round prospective purchasers.'

'What? They'd turn this place into a nightclub, like the others?'

'Or a mushroom farm, yes. Ruddy unbelievable.'

'Thank you for showing us round, Lionel,' I say. 'I appreciate it.'

'It's good to be with people who *get* it, you know. Most people think I'm nuts.'

That makes two of us, Lionel. 'Can I ask you one last question?'

'Fire away.'

'It's just . . . I mean. I never realised, till now, quite how futile it was. All that effort.'

'This ain't the half of it. They even built a shelter at Eton. And there was a masterplan for moving paintings from the National Gallery. But none for moving the population of London.'

'Exactly. Doesn't it make you angry?'

'I know it sounds weird,' he says, 'but it makes me feel better. They wanted to save paintings . . . well, it makes me think they believed – against the odds – that the human race would survive.' He shrugs, embarrassed now.

Maybe it's the stale air making me all emotional, but now I feel like hugging Lionel as well as Luke. I settle for saying, 'That's *such* a positive way of looking at it.'

Lionel narrows his eyes, unsure whether I'm being sarcastic. 'Better show you out, before you get too comfortable.'

When we surface, it feels like we've been underground for days, not minutes. After those government-issue beiges and browns, the million shades of green in the fields make me light-headed. And the sounds . . . I'd got so used to the hum of the ventilators that the birdsong and even the distant traffic makes me want to sing 'All Things Bright and Beautiful' at the top of my voice.

We say goodbye to Lionel, and board the Red Peril. 'So?' Frisky asks me.

'It was brilliant. Really. But what was my lesson meant to be?'

'Whatever you choose, my dear. Although . . . ' Frisky grants me a mischievous smile, 'there was an element of proving that life's about more than preparing for the worst. Oh,' and he reaches into his trousers, 'I nearly forgot. Your latest fishy souvenir.'

He hands me a slightly rusty tin of sardines, complete with tiny metal key. 'Um. Thanks.'

'Vintage. *Borrowed* it from the bunker canteen. You never know when you might need a long-life snack. And while I remember, date for your diary. Three weeks on Sunday. This one you'll never forget.'

Three weeks on . . . shit. 'Um, well, Frisky. That's tricky. Family celebration.' It's only a little white lie. Actually it's the Emergency Readiness and Resilience Exercise – the first one Dennis has ever commanded. It's all he's talked about for weeks.

I shiver slightly as I imagine what my boyfriend would have been like during the Cold War. Would he have left me to die above ground while he saved the world from below?

Frisky looks put out. 'Well, I'm sure you can make an excuse. This one is *important*, Joanna. Find an excuse to skip the celebration. You won't regret it.'

I catch sight of Luke in the mirror. He raises his eyebrows as if to remind me, *there is never any point arguing with Frisky.*

Chapter 30

Arachibutyrophobia – Fear of Peanut Butter Sticking to the Roof of the Mouth

'This is probably the least ethical thing I have ever done', says Dr Williams.

I am lying on Dr Nathan Williams' examination couch, my eyes shut, my nostrils flared and my arm attached to a meter that's monitoring my pulse, as he prepares for what I hope will be the last phase of my treatment.

'I could sign a consent form, if it helps.'

'What, that you consent to have the smelliest things I could find in the supermarket waved under your nose, like a reality TV contestant? I'd be laughed out of the hospital.'

'If this is reality TV, does that make you Big Brother?' I open my eyes as he rummages in the carrier-bags. 'Seriously, Nathan, I appreciate this.'

The idea came during the last appointment we had, when I told him I felt frustrated because I knew the flashbacks were trying to tell me something. 'But they're not coming fast enough.'

After lots of prevarication, he finally suggested attempting to trigger a flashback by exposing me to a range of smells, under medical supervision. It does seem a bit barmy, but no more so than the last few months of my life.

'Have you had any more since the one where your brother went missing?' he asks, his back to me as he spoons out the stuff he's bought into Petri dishes. Maybe it's his way of reassuring himself that this is medicine and not domestic science.

'No. Haven't had one for three weeks.'

'But the ones you've had are still in chronological sequence?'

'Yep.'

'That's the strangest thing. I'd expect the flashbacks to bounce around time, like the ball in a pinball machine. This is more linear, which suggests there may be an end point.' He turns around, a solemn expression on that kind, lined face. He's wearing a lab coat today, the first time I've seen him in 'uniform' since I was an in-patient, and his long fingers are encased in rubber gloves.

'Unless the flashbacks are going to continue until the present day.' The thought makes me queasy. 'All my worst moments since the age of twelve. If only my memory would throw up a *nice* flashback: the day I learned to swim, say, or passed my A-levels.'

'Do you know what's going to happen, when you're having a flashback?'

I think it over. 'No, not really. But when I come to, God! It's so frustrating because I want to put right all our mistakes. Especially mine.'

'Like what?'

'Well . . . you know what I said about being a scaredy-cat? The thing I've understood is that I got so much worse after my brother got ill. I mean I was always worried about nuclear war and the bogeyman and the dark before that, but it didn't stop me having fun.'

'And afterwards?'

'Afterwards, I was full-on weird. The hoarding of baked beans began the same weekend that Timmy was diagnosed.'

Nathan shakes his head. 'Yes, but they were scary times. Midge Ure dancing with tears in his eyes. That German girl with the hairy armpits singing about ninety-nine red balloons. And it's all part of puberty. The obsessions, that is, not the armpits.'

'I know. But most people grow out of it.' I pause, trying to decide whether to confess how pathetic I really am. I take a deep breath: if I can't confide in my doctor, who else can I talk to? 'I didn't grow out of it, you see, Nathan. I've spent my entire life blaming other people. *Oh poor little me, no wonder I am frightened of heights or whatever, it's because my brother was spoiled, because my mum was out of her tree, because Dad had affairs and let me down.*'

'So now you're blaming yourself for everything, including world poverty and the price of potatoes. There is a happy medium, Jo. And don't forget that having a brother with cancer is a big thing for a twelve-year-old to deal with. It sounds to me as though your hoarding was a coping mechanism for a situation that was out of anyone's control.'

I stare at him. 'Go on.'

Nathan thinks it over. 'Well, your family was facing a disaster that you couldn't understand. So instead of looking into that abyss, you focused on trying to prevent another disaster and I suppose, living where you did, it was the obvious thing to capture your imagination. Protecting *to* survive?'

His words startle me. Didn't I reject that theory as bonkers a few weeks ago? But the way he explains it, I don't feel like such a freak any more, just a child trying to deal with scary grown-up things. 'You're right. You're bloody right, doctor.' He looks hurt. 'Sorry, it's the white coat. You're a star, Nathan.'

'Yeah, well,' he says. 'So long as you let me write it all up in the *Lancet*.'

I nod vaguely. All those years fearing the worst, but missing the obvious point: Timmy survived. *I* survived. And the flashbacks are like a big fat alarm clock going off in my head, saying, *wake up, Jo, there's still time to get things right.* An image of Luke, pruning the hedge in Frisky's garden, pops into my head. I chase it away. 'Mind you, Nathan, it's one thing knowing my problem. Quite another doing something about it.' Though maybe I'm already changing, whether I want to or not.

'All in good time, Jo. Remember what you've been through since the accident. You're doing brilliantly so far. Your physical recovery is astounding,' he breaks off, looking at me so intensely that I feel almost like squirming, 'so cut yourself some slack, eh?' He seems impatient now, pulling at the end of his rubber glove. 'Right, are you ready for the first smell? We can stop at any time, remember that. Now close your eyes . . . '

I let my lids droop, and take a deep breath. When I first came round from my coma, I used to lie in bed with my eyes closed, and my other senses became more responsive to compensate. That's what it's like now: my skin tingles, my tongue moistens, as if to taste the air. The tiny hairs in my ears strain to interrogate my surroundings, although Nathan has closed the curtains to block out noise and light.

But it's my sense of smell that's on highest alert.

'Ready, Jo? Number one, coming up.'

I hear the surprisingly light foot steps I heard when I was first emerging from my coma. There's a draught across my face before the smell hits me.

'That's easy,' I said. 'It's coffee. Fresh ground.'

He sighs. 'This isn't a guessing game, Jo. Your flashbacks are about the chemistry in the smell reacting with your brain. So work harder to *really* smell it. Don't tell me what the thing *is*. Tell me what it's *like*.'

'Umm. OK. Well, it's bitter. Burned. With . . . a tobacco-like smell behind it. Not cigarettes, but the dried leaves old men buy in boxes.'

'Very good. And are you feeling anything yet? Any pull back to 1982?'

'No. Sorry. We weren't the kind of household to brew fresh coffee.'

'Never mind. Plenty more smells to play with.'

I hear a knife slicing through something crunchy and before Nathan gets near me I know what it is. 'Apple.'

'Go on, describe it,' he says, holding it so close to my nose that I'm sure I can feel the juice, spitting like bubbles from a glass of freshly poured champagne.

'Right, it smells of ... I know it's apple, but when I concentrate it smells more like a lemon. Acidic. Or maybe I can taste that.'

'Does it have any associations?'

I squeeze my eyes together even more tightly. I want to produce a real, live flashback for Nathan, after all he's done for me. But all I can summon up are images straight from a women's magazine: happy families round a dinner table eating apple pie, children in playgrounds munching core, pips and all.

'Nothing yet.'

He takes the fruit away. The next smell is earth and malt vinegar. 'Beetroot. Yuck! Take it away.'

'Might trigger something, if you hate it that much.'

'It might trigger a wave of vomit, if you keep it there any longer.'

He replaces it with a smell that's simultaneously sweet and savoury, cloying and nutty. I get a weird sensation in the roof of my mouth, dry and uncomfortable. 'It's peanut butter, isn't it? Evil stuff.'

And so it goes on, a production line of aromas: fresh orange juice ('citrus and sulphur ... no, really. It smells of fart!'), Marmite ('it's tickling my nose ... molasses and toffee and beer'), and honey ('that smells of summer, but not specifically the summer of 1982, sorry').

By now, Nathan's voice is flat with disappointment. I try to figure out why it's not working. 'I think perhaps it's because the things you bought, well, they're all a bit *wholesome*. We didn't eat anything without E numbers in it when we were kids.'

'Ah. Well, the next one doesn't have E numbers, but it is a bit more *fast food*.'

He wafts the dish under my nose. 'I'm getting vinegar

again. But fruit, as well, mature fruit. Garlic. Something spicy. I know! It's HP sauce, isn't it?'

'Yes. Dead right. But remember, it's not "name that sniff". Concentrate, Jo.'

I'm getting bored, and feeling a complete failure, but I try again to show willing, inhaling furiously.

Finally ... an image that's all mine. A plate of steaming chip-shop chips, covered in stripes of brown sauce, on the kitchen table. Sitting opposite me, my father, scowling, not at me but at life. No, he's scowling about my mother, who isn't here. 'She'll make me a laughing stock, hanging round those women. Tell her to stop, Jo, she takes no bloody notice of me because I'm part of the male conspiracy.'

'You're having one, aren't you? Your pulse has shot up.'

Nathan's voice cuts across my father's, and the image evaporates faster than the steam from the fish supper.

I open my eyes. 'I *was* having one.'

'Ah. Shouldn't have said anything, should I?'

I feel very tired and very hot. The atmosphere is overwhelmingly intense, because all my senses are so heightened. 'I'm not sure I can face having another go, Nathan.'

'Oh, please. For me. I've only got one smell left. I promise I won't talk.' He looks strange in the semi-darkness. Concentration makes the lines on his face more defined.

'All right then. The last one.' I close my eyes again and wait. 'Syrup ... sugar syrup. It smells artificial, like perfume ... it's a strawberry, isn't it?'

He doesn't say anything, which seems odd until I remember he's promised not to. 'Strawberries. I love strawberries.' I feel the coolness of the fruit as he holds it closer to my nose and it brushes against my lips, tiny hairs catching on my skin. An impulse makes me open my mouth and bite into the strawberry.

It's perfect. Intensely sweet and yet tart enough to save it from being sickly. A drop of strawberry juice leaks out where my teeth have sliced the berry, and slides down my chin. I lean forward slightly to taste the other half and ...

My lips meet someone else's lips. Images flood my brain, not of childhood but of *now*, of a man's face, close to mine, of black pupils enclosed in pale lilac-grey irises, not Dennis's eyes but . . .

My own eyes snap open just as Nathan springs back. For moments, no, it must be several seconds, we stare at each other: Nathan's eyes seem to be begging me to speak first, but I can't. Finally, resignedly, he says, 'Jo, I am *so* sorry. I can't . . . I have *never* done anything like that before. With a patient, I mean. It's utterly the last thing I would ever do.'

I shake my head slightly, not quite trusting my eyes and my ears and my lips. 'Um. It's fine. Really. I mean. Extraordinary situation, quite clearly. Not typical in any way.' I sit up a little too quickly and tiny sparks of light appear at the edge of my vision. 'Forget about it.'

Nathan pulls back the curtains and lets light back into the office. 'Are you sure?'

'I know it wasn't serious. It really doesn't matter.'

He nods, but looks terribly glum. 'I don't know what came over me. It must be the situation. Serves me right for meddling in things I don't understand.'

I sigh. 'But that pretty much rules out the entire brain, doesn't it?'

He seems bashful now. 'No. Just women.'

There's another pause as I try to decode what he's said. Does he mean this wasn't an accident after all? That the resemblance between this experiment and *9½ Weeks* was part of some grand plan? That he thinks I was leading him on? 'Right.'

'I think it might be better, Jo, if I transfer your case to one of my colleagues.'

'OK.' I'm still confused. I have never, ever, inspired recklessness in a man before, still less provoked them to an act that could lose them their job. After all, I am Joanna Morgan, the less attractive half of the Lorrie-Joey double act, the wallflower to Lorraine's *femme fatale*. Unless . . . maybe I got that wrong too. Maybe Dennis isn't the only man who fancies me. The thought makes me even more light-headed.

He seems relieved. 'But one thing, Jo. I think that whatever happens, you're nearly there. Your brain will tell you when everything's sorted.' And he taps his forehead.

'I'll take your word for it,' I say, wondering if he's right. And whether my good old brain also holds the key to another mystery.

Because the eyes I wanted to see, the lips I wanted to be the ones touching mine didn't belong to Dennis. Or even Nathan.

They belonged to Luke.

In an ideal world, after an excruciating moment with a strawberry and a consultant, it's best to go your separate ways with the minimum of delay. Especially when your head's so full of new ideas and possibilities: that you might not have been a crazy child, that you might just be attractive, that your future is potentially more exciting than you'd ever imagined.

However, there's a hitch. When you've spent days planning a blind date between the aforementioned consultant and your best friend, and when that date happens to be scheduled for precisely forty-five minutes after the embarrassing moment . . . well, it's tricky, to say the least.

We drive to the centre of town in Nathan's car, a sporty black VW. He keeps his eyes straight ahead and his hands welded to the leather steering wheel. When he absolutely has to change gear, he does it *very* quickly, his arm shooting out on to the lever and back to the wheel in a blur. Because the gear stick is only inches from my knee.

Lorraine is waiting for us in Matches, sitting at the long purple glass bar, chatting to – or rather, chatting *up* – one of the owners. Nathan trails behind me and when I step aside, so she can see him properly, I know instantly it's not going to work. She appraises him as if he were a dog at Crufts, and from the curling of her lip, I know she won't be declaring him 'Best in Show'.

'Nathan, this is Lorraine, my oldest school friend. Lorraine, this is my specialist.' They swap fleeting, going-through-the-motions smiles, and it's all I can do not to groan. Can't we all admit there's no point being here, and go home now? Then I can start planning my new life.

'I need a drink,' I say, with feeling.

'Seconded,' Nathan says. 'Lorraine, you look like a girl who knows her way round a cocktail menu. What would you recommend?' Oh God, he's actually *trying*. Hasn't he worked out that she'd eat him alive? If she could be bothered ...

Lorraine reaches over for the menu and flicks it open, with a hint of a sneer I hope Nathan doesn't see. 'Whatever floats your boat, doc. I know what Jo will want though.' She winks at the barman. 'Give us one of those,' she says, pointing at the menu.

He does his bit behind the bar, throwing bottles about and showing off, before placing a glass of dark purple liquid in front of me. 'Go on,' Lorraine says, 'it's Charlotte Church's favourite tipple apparently.'

I raise the glass to my lips. It smells familiar, but then after my afternoon's sniff-a-thon, I'm probably imagining things. I take a tiny sip. 'It tastes of fruit. Blackcurrant maybe, a bit like ... '

Lorraine is impatient. 'It's a Cheeky Vimto, a grown-up version of your favourite drink when we were kids.'

But I work it out for myself, as the glass begins to go out of focus. And as I realise that Nathan is going to witness one of my funny turns after all ...

Chapter 31
Enochlophobia – Fear of Crowds

I suck hard on my straw to savour the last drops of pop and there's a loud gurgle as the liquid travels towards my mouth.

'Ugh.'

Warm Vimto tastes like jam, hot and sticky on my tongue. I finish the can, even though it could be a while before Mum remembers to get me another drink. After all, today she is Saving the World.

I should be grateful, because she's saving it not for herself, but for the Next Generation, meaning Timmy and me. Six weeks ago she barely had the energy to get out of bed. Oh yes, there's been a change in my mother.

Her pills have been replaced by a small brown bottle of flower essence, and her flowery dresses exchanged for baggy tops and bottoms in greying unbleached cotton. But the real change is in how she behaves, and it's not an improvement. Instead of whining, she snaps. Not just at me and Dad but, unbelievably, at Timmy too.

And he can pout all he likes but the fact is, this is all his fault.

If he hadn't run away that day, we'd never have ended up at Greenham. We'd never have met Gillian and Mags and the other women. And Mum would never have been *activated*.

'How are you getting on?' Gillian peers into my carrier-bag.

'It's getting harder,' I admit. 'I can't find any of the big ones any more.'

'I know. I don't think any of us quite grasped how tricky it would be to get our hands on 100,000 stones.'

'If we were allowed to count gravel, then we'd have it done in no time. Couldn't we say the tiny ones represent the little children in Hiroshima?'

'Hmmm.' She looks dubious. 'Nice idea, Jo, but I don't think that's quite the dignified effect we were hoping for.'

I was suspicious when Mum announced we were off to the camp for a 'treasure hunt'. It sounded a bit conventional, and anyway what would the treasure have been? Carob brownies? Instead, I was told to look for stones. The idea is to collect one beautiful stone for each person who died thirty-seven years ago today, when the Bomb dropped on Hiroshima.

One of the women had read that 100,000 people were wiped out in seconds on 6 August 1945. The images from Mr Blake's film still appear whenever I close my eyes. There were bodies on the newsreel, but hundreds, not hundreds of thousands. People must have been turned into fall-out, then returned to earth as radioactive rain.

I want to make a good job of the collection, but the area nearest to the camp has been stripped of stones, so Gillian, Mum and I have followed the perimeter fence for a mile or so, towards the Forgotten Gate, where the ground hasn't yet been harvested. Timmy has been excused, of course, he's in one of the teepees, being presented with bagfuls of sweets to tempt his temperamental appetite. He's on a break between treatments, but you can still tell he's ill. Last summer his skin turned light gold in the sunshine, but this year he's stayed the colour of typing paper.

I crouch down, rub away at the hot earth with my hands. My nails are black and my fingertips sore, but I keep telling myself *this is nothing* compared to what the people suffered in Hiroshima.

My excavations reveal two smooth stones, one as big as a crab-apple, the other slightly smaller and flatter. I hold the smaller one in my hand and wonder who this might represent: the woman with her skin burned in the pattern of her kimono? No, she survived at least long enough to be filmed. Perhaps it's her sister or her husband or her son.

'This is really important to you, isn't it?' Gillian says. 'After that film you saw?'

Gillian's easy to talk to. Dad thinks that the women at Greenham spend their time plotting to overthrow the government, 'and at the bloody taxpayer's expense', but actually, they talk about everything. Cruise missiles, yes, and Aldermaston, and die-ins. But also Northern Ireland and favourite foods and Nicaragua and *ET* and Russia and the big fire on *Crossroads* and how to be happy. They plan mischief and non-violent protests, paint banners and answer letters from all over the world. They open bottles of wine and drink it from plastic picnic mugs, and someone will get out a guitar or a clarinet, and I wonder whether the baby-faced American soldiers ever hear the music through their dormitory windows.

It was the talking that made Mum flush her pills down the toilet, and take up the flower remedies instead. Mags told her that her drugs were 'a chemical cosh, prescribed by male doctors as part of the plot to keep women enslaved'. Gillian said that was all very well, but any drug was difficult to withdraw from ('and you should know, Mags, I'd like to see you lay off pot') and so Mum should tail off gently, but Mum ignored her and apparently that's why she's been having nightmares and headaches, and a million other symptoms. But 'that proves what the Valium's been doing to your system' (no prizes for guessing that's Mags again).

'I want to do it right,' I tell Gillian. 'For the people who woke up in Hiroshima that morning pleased it was a sunny day.'

'I think it's time to go back.' Mum appears, shielding her eyes from the bright sun with her hand. I lean on her as we walk back the way we came. The unfamiliar sensation of her hand gripping mine makes me feel fizzier than the Vimto.

It's only since we've been coming to the camp that I've realised how beautiful she is. Camp dress code doesn't suit most women but with no make-up and those horrible loose clothes, she *shines*. I can almost see why Dad fell in love with her.

And I wonder when he fell *out* of love with her.

Even though she's more beautiful than ever, he's furious with Mum, for 'messing around with things she doesn't understand'. Actually, I think he's more worried that some bloke from the Rotary could come down to the camp after a night at the pub to hurl abuse and might spot Mum. Dad's convinced this would be the end of his career.

The camp is ahead of us now, busier than usual because of the final preparations for the demo. I can see a TV crew: a cameraman, a guy with headphones, and a young male reporter sweating in his navy suit. As we approach, one of the women points at Mum, and I spot that Timmy is being filmed.

'Are you Mrs Morgan?' The reporter has a posh accent, and looks like Sebastian from *Brideshead Revisited*. 'I'm James Donaldson, from *Thames Valley Today*. And I've been chatting to young Timothy here. What a *brave* little chap he is.'

Mum frowns at the journalist. 'What have you been talking to him about, exactly?' Her voice is steely, no longer softened by pills.

'Give us a minute.' Mags takes Mum to one side. 'I told him about Timmy's illness and –'

'What the hell did you do that for? Mags, I can't believe you'd do that.'

'Look, I know he's a scumbag reporter and we can't trust him any further than we can throw him, but he's here and he's keen and there *is* more at stake here than just Timmy. You know that, don't you? And telling the world about Timmy is our only chance when the newspapers are full of stories about whether Ling-Ling the bloody panda is pregnant.'

'But I don't want my family's business broadcast on the news.' Mum sounds less angry now, and I can already tell who's going to win this argument: Mags is as determined as her namesake at Number Ten.

'Family is political, too, Lynda. You know that, don't you? Timmy's illness is *evidence*. He bears witness to what the authorities are doing to all our kids.'

I don't think now is the time to remind Mags she hasn't got any kids, and regards motherhood as a further form of enslavement. Oh, and has even said if she ever did become pregnant and gave birth to a boy child, she'd have it adopted.

Mum sighs so deeply that for a moment it reminds me of pre-peace camp days, then she trudges back to the reporter. 'So what do you want to know?'

The reporter gives the thumbs-up to his crew. He ushers Mum towards Main Gate, and positions her so the camp is behind her while the cameraman sets up his tripod.

Gillian stands next to me, watching. We're too far away from Mum to hear what she's saying. 'Your dad's not going to like this much, is he?'

I shake my head. 'Maybe we have to do this, like the children in the Hiroshima film. Maybe it's the only way people will take notice. But do you believe it, Gillian? About the bombs and the experiments causing Timmy's leukaemia?' She's the only adult – apart from Mr Blake – I trust to be honest with me.

'Jo, I don't know. I wish I did. I do believe we're doing pretty terrible damage to the world, and that humans are suffering as a result. But whether that's directly to blame for what's the matter with your brother? I can't see how any of us could ever know for sure.'

The reporter beckons Timmy to stand next to Mum, and the cameraman crouches down to film his face close up.

A fleet of cars pulls up alongside the camp: old bangers, Volvo estates, a shiny metallic green Cavalier. 'That'll be the cavalry then,' Gillian says, then slaps her own wrist, laughing. '*Naughty* Gillian. This is strictly a military-language-free zone.'

Women spill out of the cars, embracing the camp dwellers. Boots are opened, and bags of stones stacked inside, the suspensions dipping slightly with every new load.

Gillian and I walk towards the cars and a woman who's driven from Bath specially for the occasion offers to give us a lift into Newbury. A dozen women have gone ahead, with still more stones. I sit in the front of the car, and as we approach the outskirts of town, I see kids doing normal school holiday things. Boys Timmy's age eating blue Slush Puppies and Cornettos outside a newsagent's; girls my age queuing outside the Corn Exchange to try to get in to see *An Officer and a Gentleman* despite the 15 certificate. For a moment I long to be normal, not to feel the weight of the world on my shoulders.

But if I didn't feel that, I wouldn't be me.

The woman keeps getting lost in the one-way system, taking the ring road off in completely the wrong direction, and then getting stuck in traffic. I begin to panic: what if we're late? What if Mum hates me for letting us down?

Finally, Gillian manages to navigate us to where we need to be. We stop a couple of streets away from the war memorial, and take a bag of stones each; mine is only a small carrier, but it still digs into my palm. I open my mouth to complain but then remember why we're doing it, and close it again.

There's a crowd around the memorial now, and as we approach, I realise not everyone's there to congratulate us. In fact, there's a lot of shouting going on.

I look around for Timmy and my mother, but I can't spot them among the angry faces. A woman of Mum's age is jabbing her finger in the face of one of the camp women, screaming, 'My father died in the war under the Japanese, how dare you do this? How bloody dare you.'

Other people in the crowd murmur in agreement, and I feel torn. Are we being disrespectful? I think it's right to take a stand, but I still don't know whether Mutually Assured Destruction will save us or destroy us. That's why you have to act personally as well as politically: my stockpile is the Morgan safety net. Not that I'm making much progress with it. Mum's more or less stopped shopping because she spends all her time at Greenham – and when she ever is at home, she'll be sneaking in some of the women for a soak in a Badedas bath (sometimes they run out and have to use Timmy's Matey), or making cabbagey stews to take back to the camp.

Where *are* Mum and Timmy?

A man in his late teens breaks ranks and takes one of the larger stones from a bag that's been left open on the ground. For a few seconds, I think he's going to throw it at the protesting women, but instead he moves forward. I peer through a gap in the crowd: the concrete steps of the memorial are piled high with stacks of stones, like the Cornish dry-stone walls we studied in geography.

Finally I see Timmy and my mum, at the front of the group of protestors, next to Mags. I bet Mags pushed them forward, knowing it would make a good photo. She hates the media but doesn't seem to mind playing them at their own game.

The man takes his stone and places it carefully on top of others, on the lowest step. 'You're doing the right thing,' he tells the woman who was being hectored. 'If we fought for nothing else, it was the freedom to speak our minds.'

I look around me, to see what the reaction is, and on the other side of the street, I recognise a figure in a navy suit who's stopped to watch.

'Dad,' I whisper, hoping he hasn't seen me, but knowing from his expression that he has. He looks smart, his hair is perfectly styled. Of course. Savannah's salon is round the corner. While Mum has been saving the world, Dad's sneaked away from the bank for a cut and blow dry.

'You bloody idiot!'

It's the woman with the jabbing finger, turning on the young man who placed the stone. There's a horrible pause, and then she turns round and thumps the man in the arm, a proper *thwack* that reverberates around the crowd and I swear I can physically *feel* the change in mood, as people turn on each other, shouting and jostling and pushing.

'Come on, Jo,' Gillian says, trying to guide me out of the way, but the crowd is closing in on itself. I can see Mum and Timmy being shoved, right at the centre of the protest, and both their mouths contort into 'O's of panic.

'My little brother,' I shout, pummelling at a man's blue T-shirted back with my fists. My nails are lined with earth, from digging away at the soil, and our bagfuls of stone-souls are trampled as people push and push . . .

'TIMMY! LYNDA!'

It's my father's voice. 'Get out of the bloody way! That's my son in there, he's very poorly, he'll be hurt, let me through.'

Sweat drips down my forehead. I try to call my father's name, so he knows where to find me, but my body's squashed and my lungs don't seem to be working and neither is my voice. *But he saw me just now*, I tell myself, *he'll be coming for me too.*

My sleeve is damp and I turn my head as much as I can to see that Gillian is crying. 'Jo,' her breath is short. 'This isn't . . . how it was meant to be. Not at all . . . the way it was meant to be. But we'll be out soon. I promise.'

The man with the blue T-shirt moves, and through the space below his armpit, I see – thank goodness – that Dad has reached my brother and Mum and is elbowing the protestors and the angry women out of the way. 'Shift, go on, bloody MOVE IT, my son has leukaemia.'

Finally that section of the crowd seems to hear my father and the people disperse like ripples in a pond, leaving my family huddled together, like the silhouettes in the circle on the cover of the *Protect and Survive* booklet. Except there's one person missing.

Now my father will come for me.

But as blue T-shirt man moves again, I get a last glimpse of my father ushering Mum and Timmy away, even as I feel the crowd crushing me.

He's abandoned me.

Someone shouts that the police are on their way, but that only inflames the people around me, and Gillian is praying now, mumbling under her breath, and although she's right next to me, I have never ever in my life felt more alone than I do now …

'Jo! JOOOOOO … '

Chapter 32

Optophobia – Fear of Opening One's Eyes

'At zero eight zero four hours this morning, reports were received of a large explosion in the Courtbridge industrial zone. At zero eight twelve hours, the first local residents began calling to report breathing difficulties and eye irritation.'

Dennis looks up from his notes, fixing his audience with a steely stare. 'Let us synchronise watches. It is now zero eight thirty-seven hours and the District Emergency Plan is officially in action. Good luck.'

My soul mate pauses at his podium, as if he's expecting a round of applause. Luckily his colleagues realise that, even though this is only a readiness and resilience exercise, applause would be unseemly. That can come later, in the pub.

The different teams scatter to corners of the school hall, which is the nerve centre of today's activities. Each area has a sign, crafted by yours truly last night, using Clip Art and a colour printer. At the back, by the netball hoops, there's Command Control, which I typed in a bright red Courier font, set off nicely by an image of two manly hands shaking. Shaking each other, that is, rather than shaking in fear at the prospect of having to command or control anything.

Command Control is staffed by Dennis, plus the Police

Sub-divisional Superintendent, the Regional Chief Ambulance Officer, the Divisional Head of the Fire and Rescue Service, and, of course, good old Mrs Fothergill. I wonder which of the three she's currently screwing; perhaps there'll be a performance-related bonus to the one who makes the best impression today. She's steered clear of her usual outlandish colours and is wearing black, presumably as a mark of respect to the 'un-dead' – our volunteer victims who will be arriving over the next few hours. Though whether the plunging neckline and soaring split in her skirt can actually be regarded as respectful is open to debate.

By the gym monkey bars is Communications, which I put in a nice clear navy Arial Narrow, accompanied by a picture of a microphone. Our public relations officers, used to issuing press releases about Trading Standards unsafe toy campaigns and Christmas tree recycling services, are looking positively ravenous about disaster management.

The Casualty Bureau (a user-friendly buttercup yellow Nimbus Script with a picture of a syringe) could be mistaken for the telethon team after a gruelling night of *Children in Need*, while the Scientific Advisory Panel (green Verdana, microscope) are colonising their tables with maps and books, and a very nifty laptop which models weather fronts and cloud formations. Though I think the fact that Dennis pre-warned them they 'might be advised to have wind patterns and the industrial chemicals database fully updated' is borderline cheating.

He is *determined* nothing should go wrong.

Triage don't have a table or a sign (shame, really, I have a lovely purple Times New Roman left over) as they are going straight outside as soon as the first casualties get here. The playground currently resembles a camping and outdoor pursuits trade show, with an impressive line-up of decontamination tents, toilet tents, treatment tents and rest tents. Unlike in a proper disaster, the tents were requisitioned from central stores seven days ago and they've all been put up overnight, but Dennis will be insisting the medical staff delay using the facilities until what he calls 'average erection times' have elapsed, to keep the exercise realistic.

I've been happy enough to do little jobs for him this last week. He sees it as a form of rehabilitation, I think: beginning with an unsupervised supermarket shop for teabags and instant coffee (I passed this test, though Dennis felt my choice of luxury chocolate biscuits rather than own-brand was reckless). Then I collated and stapled eighty-five briefing documents (a tick in the box for basic admin skills) before I was let loose on the signs.

But I'm not trying to prove anything. The reason I've been volunteering for mind-numbing tasks is that since my last flashback I've been fighting to keep myself together. I keep replaying my father's betrayal, over and over. I've avoided his phone calls, told Mum I'm busy and decided my scaredy-ness was, in fact, the right approach after all. So much for misjudging Dad all these years, and for Timmy's theory about me being a daddy's girl. One thing my flashback proves is that you can only rely on yourself in this life.

Admittedly, Dennis comes a pretty close second in the reliability stakes, but even he's been sneaking round like a spy, planning today's drama.

'Hey, Joanna,' Mikey calls across the room. 'Great to see you back in action. You're looking gorgeous.'

I let Mikey kiss me on both cheeks. 'Yeah, right.' Before I can stop myself, my hand darts up to my head, to cover my fuzzy patch.

Mikey and I are without portfolio. Presumably as our non-emergency jobs involve accident prevention, we've already failed in our duties. We're going to work as runners, relaying messages, fetching refreshments and, unofficially, snitching to Dennis on any team that isn't taking the exercise seriously enough.

'Surprised he let you come back for this,' Mikey says. 'Won't all the excitement endanger your health?'

'Nah. I'm as normal as I'm going to be now. And I wouldn't have missed his day of glory.'

'Wanted you to see him being all *masterful*, I bet. There'll be some action in the sack later, no doubt, girl.'

'Don't be coarse!' I giggle and hit him on the arm. 'It's good to see you, though, Mikey. Listen, I've got a bit of a favour to ask.'

'Let me guess ... you want to borrow my fluorescent tabard for a kinky quickie with our emergency planning superhero.'

I shudder, and I can tell Mikey's noticed. There's been no sex since Coventry. 'I wouldn't want to tear him away, even for a minute.'

'Yeah, but it wouldn't take him that long, would it? What, thirty seconds, tops?'

This time I don't giggle. 'Not everything in life is about sex, Mikey,' I say primly.

He nods over towards Councillor Fothergill, who is leaning unnecessarily low over a map of the area, revealing so much over-cooked cleavage that I catch a glimpse of both nipples. 'Mrs F appreciates the importance of a good dollop of sensuality to keep up morale.'

'Hmm. They'll be pulling the fire chief and ambulance boss apart within the hour, I think. Hasn't she bonked both—' I stop mid-sentence, remembering that Mikey's not meant to know that. 'Anyway, that favour. Basically, I have somewhere else I need to be later on and I wondered if you'd cover for me.'

Mikey looks like Christmas has come early. 'Ooh. Subterfuge. I love it. But only if you tell me why.'

'I have to go and meet someone ... about my accident.' *There*. How innocent does that sound?

'I didn't realise the NHS did routine appointments on a Sunday. And why would you need to keep that secret from the lovely Dennis?'

'It's more of a ... psychological thing. More *ad hoc*.'

'You can't be mysterious with your mate Mikey, you know, Jo. *Especially* when you need me.'

'OK, OK. I know it might sound weird, but there's this guy called Frisky.'

'Ooo-er. And is he?' He actually skips on the spot.

'Frisky is eighty-five years old, Mikey. He's a nice old chap I met at the hospital and he's, well, taken me under his wing. We go on trips together. He wants to show me life beyond public protection.' I decide not to mention Luke, but just thinking about him makes me feel wobbly. I haven't seen him for three weeks, but I've decided today will be the last time. I need to stop kidding myself. Dennis is my destiny. He might not be perfect, but neither am I and he will never let me down. All Frisky does is make me believe things could be different, but they can't.

Mikey whistles. 'Eighty-five? Now that's what I call an older man. Not that it means he doesn't still fancy his chances, Jo. The male capacity for self-delusion is one of the last faculties to go, you know.'

'He's a kind person who wants to help me.' Even though I'm about to let him down. 'So you'll do it?'

Mikey winks at me. 'Course I will. So where's he taking you?'

'Now that is something I'd like to know myself. Frisky has a terrible fondness for surprises.'

Three hours on and Courtbridge is in the grip of a major disaster, but Dennis hasn't broken a sweat. Two chemical tankers have exploded (admittedly, in a factory that doesn't actually exist: all our industry is small-scale, making catnip toys or organic chutney) and, though initial indications suggested a terror attack, it's now clear that the blasts probably resulted from a factory supervisor falling asleep on the job.

The playground is full of 'casualties', volunteers with cards in their pockets to remind them what symptoms they should be exhibiting. A few have emptied out capsules of fake blood from their own personal am dram collections, though in fact no patient at the Casualty Reception Centre is meant to have been caught in the explosion itself. They're workers at other factories or local residents, all struck down by breathing problems, eye irritation and a rather worrying yellowy-green discharge from the lungs.

I've been allocated the job of relaying patient information to the woman who updates the 'facts and figures' electronic display. It's a cross between a cricket scoreboard and the Eurovision totaliser. So far, I have passed on the sad news that three people are known to have died at the factory itself, two have expired here after their lungs filled with gunk, and we have six stretcher cases and twenty-three walking wounded. The latter are being forced to endure decontamination showers, although it's chilly for early July. Funny how their method acting ceases abruptly when they're ordered to strip to their undies. 'Do I have to? It's only an exercise . . . '

As part of my escape strategy, I've been trying to get in Dennis's line of sight as often as possible, so that he will remember me being here. That *was* the plan, anyhow, but today he doesn't seem to see me at all. Because I am neither important nor feigning injury, I don't count. I'm invisible.

I try one last time, as he strides towards the boffins. 'Dennis,' I whisper.

He stops, looks around him. Eventually he spots me. 'Jo. What's the matter? Another death?' His eyes shine with excitement, though he must know how many casualties there'll be, as he was the one who planned the entire bloody thing.

'No, no. Nothing like that. I just wanted to say how well it seems to be going. You're in your element.'

He frowns as he processes the information. 'So no update then?'

'Well, no, I thought you might like some . . . ' I try to find an important-sounding phrase. 'Performance feedback.'

Dennis tuts. 'When I need feedback, do you think I'd want it from you?' He must register the shock in my face, because he adds, 'I mean, no disrespect or anything, Jo, but you're not really an expert in this area, are you?'

'No,' I mumble.

'Not that you aren't doing a fantastic job, I'm sure.' He looks around him, at the dozens of people darting to and fro, and nods in satisfaction. 'But it would really be best if you refrain from talking to me until the exercise is over, unless you have urgent data. We need to stay in our respective roles, and there is no chain of communication established between the head of operations and a . . . a . . . runner.'

'Right.'

'No offence. We'll celebrate later though, eh? Just the two of us.' And he gives me such a leer that I realise faked death and destruction has done what I couldn't, and given Dennis his mojo back.

He resumes his journey towards the scientists, and I stand in the corner of the room, wanting to scream or sob or both.

But I don't. Instead I watch him as he interrupts two of the scientific advisers, snatching their papers and ticking them off for something, because he can.

My *soul mate*. The most reliable man I know. The one constant in my life.

I don't think I love him any more.

Oh God. I wait to feel something, a sharp pain or a blow to the head. But instead I feel a leaden certainty, like an indigestible meal sitting in my stomach.

He's moved over to Communications now, pushing that misbehaving kiss-curl off his forehead so he looks more weighty in interviews. But it isn't just Dennis, it's all of this, the pretence that you can prepare for the unthinkable, seems so *futile*. I can't think of a worse place for a scaredy-cat to work, dwelling on the worst that can happen, to the exclusion of the best. Don't let this happen, Jo. Focus on his good qualities, that confidence and certainty . . .

This feeling will pass, it must. I am not a wicked person. Loyal is my middle name. Dennis has nursed me and cared for me and stood by me. I *won't* let him down.

I'm tying myself in mental knots, so to stop myself, I go to look for Mikey. I find him sitting on a wall behind the school, rolling a joint.

'Talk about risky, with all these police around.'

He shrugs. 'They're a little preoccupied, don't you think? I needed to chill, mate. Whole things makes me feel sick.'

'Yeah.' I look back over my shoulder at the tents and ambulances and people and it reminds me of that awful bunker: I have to escape. Now. 'Listen, I need to get going. Are you OK to take over?'

He abandons his rolling, and tucks the unlit joint back into his tobacco box. 'Such sacrifices I make for you, Jo. Off you go to your octogenarian. Whatever he's got lined up, it's gotta be more fun than this.'

Chapter 33

Pyrophobia – Fear of Fire

I power-walk to Frisky's villa, forcing myself to go faster and faster, to block out the confused thoughts that might derail me totally. I must stick to Plan A: stay loyal to Dennis. Count my blessings. Turn my back on Frisky and Luke before they get bored and reject me.

I can't meet Luke's eye when he answers the door, but fortunately he's equally cool with me. I've convinced myself that he can *tell* I imagined being kissed by him in Nathan's office.

Frisky's in the front of the Red Peril, giving Luke directions, and they're bickering like a pair of old women. But at least neither of them is checking their solemn, yet reassuring facial expression in the wing mirror of an ambulance, as I spotted Dennis doing earlier.

'Stop the car!'

We're in nowhere land, a big slice of 1960s' suburbia. The kind of place where wife-swapping and ouija-boarding flourishes, a place like Salzburg Avenue, where everything happens below the surface.

Luke's already opening the door, but Frisky puts his mottled hand out to stop him. 'We're not there yet, but I wanted to say something important.'

He turns around and those sharp brown eyes scrutinise me. Don't tell me he's guessed, too? About the snogging fantasy?

But he smiles and says, 'I've asked a lot of you up till now, Joanna, and though it hasn't always been entirely painless, I like to think it's made a difference.' He waits for me to say yes.

'Um. Yes. It has. I mean, I know I haven't become Wiltshire go-karting champion. Or set up my own decorating company. But you always make me think.'

'Indeed. Well, today, I am going to ask you to do more than think. It means you must trust me like never before. But believe me when I say I have researched this thoroughly and it is *not* dangerous. And I did gain the permission of Dr Williams.'

I blink. 'Ri-ight.' As if Nathan would dare to object to *anything* after what happened in his office. And the fact that Frisky's never bothered with this preamble before is worrying: the emergency planning exercise is suddenly looking a much safer place to be.

'As usual, of course, I will participate fully myself. Go first, in fact.'

'Frisky, you know I trust you. But I can't absolutely promise I'll do whatever you want. I do need some discretion.'

'A get-out clause, you mean?' Frisky frowns at me. 'I would have hoped that by now you'd understand I have your best interests at heart.'

He looks so vulnerable. So what if it's jumping out of a plane or diving into a reservoir in an aqualung? Surely I can do it, for him. Especially as it'll be the last time. 'Sorry. I was being silly. If you're happy it's safe, then I'll try whatever you want.'

He nods, unsmiling. 'Now Luke, to be blunt, I know you regard spending time with me less desirable than facing a firing squad, but you've shown an admirable level of self-sacrifice for Joanna's sake. From which I conclude that you do want to help her?'

Luke shrugs. 'You know I do.' He does look adorable when he sulks. *Stop it, Jo.*

'And so when I tell you that today's challenge *may* cause a little initial alarm, and that what Joanna will need is a promise that both of us are willing to be at her side . . . you assent to this?'

'Jeez, can you not speak modern English? Yeah, I promise whatever it is. It's not like I have a choice.'

'Good,' Frisky says and taps the dashboard. 'On we go then. Straight ahead. Don't spare the horses!'

I shiver in the back of the car, wondering what Luke and I have agreed to. I've always assumed that Frisky's accident is such ancient history that it no longer affects him, but what if all that Battle of Britain *bonhomie* has cunningly disguised the fact that he is flipped-lid, crazy-horse, full-on bonkers? That we're part of some plot to take over the world?

'Right, then immediate left, then pull up on the left.'

The building doesn't look like World Domination HQ. It's a modern community hall, in bright yellow brick, far too cheery for this overcast day. There's a handwritten sign taped to the glass door: 'Inner Strength Workshop, straight ahead in Citadel of Mental Powers (also known as the English Country Garden Seminar Room)'.

'Inner strength?' I say, feeling reassured. 'As in, bit of chanting, a few self-affirmations, and maybe some yogic breathing?'

'Something like that.' Frisky coughs. 'Though there may be some more *physical* activity required.'

'Great,' Luke says. 'I've always wanted to know how to tear up a telephone directory.'

'Shhh,' Frisky says as we push open the door to the Citadel. Every surface has been Cath Kidstoned. Tea roses on the walls, the curtains, the tie-on chair cushions, and an air freshener in every corner, pumping out synthesised flower fragrance.

The man at the front glares at us. He's rather short for a guru, though he does have the prerequisite grey ponytail, held back by a thin piece of leather. 'You've missed visualisation,' he says, then checks himself. 'But greetings, friends, and welcome to the journey.'

We take seats behind everyone else, our bums sliding on the flowery cushions. There are about twenty delegates: New Agers, seeking the secrets of the universe; Trendy Old Dears looking for the secret of eternal youth; and balding Mid-Life Men, looking for meaning after redundancy or divorce.

No wonder the guru looked confused, we don't fit into any of his categories.

'So, once you've found your harnessing image, you can call on it any time you are feeling under pressure, or wish to reconnect with your life mission statement.' Our guru wears loose linen clothes, and sandals. He has *horrible* feet, like a gorilla's, all gnarled, with rust-coloured nails that have begun to curl back into the tips of his toes. Can I really take advice from a man who neglects his soles?

'Time for refreshments,' he says. 'Though you three may like to join me for a catch-up before the walk.'

The *walk*? Is this what Frisky's been making all the fuss about, an inspirational stroll round mystical Courtbridge?

The guru lets us queue for a herbal tea and take a millet flapjack, then we follow him into a corner. He begins to drone on about mind-power and sixth senses and inner cores.

' ... and I always find that the real proof of the visualisation is when people tell me they still feel their feet are being bathed in cool spring water, even in the midst of the fire-walk.'

'Fire-walk?' The colour has drained from Luke's bronzed face.

'That's why we do it, really. I mean, the walking on hot coals thing is a bit of a cliché, can seem a bit city wanker, but it has *such* a positive effect on self-image and inner resources, that I had to reinstate it.'

Now Frisky's warnings make sense. I feel terrified, but oddly curious. Could I do this? After all, I promised I'd try ...

'You bastard,' Luke says to Frisky, and marches out of the room.

The guru scowls. 'I sense some tension here, guys. Can we talk out the issues?'

But Frisky's already followed Luke, and I am right behind him. I nearly collide with a woman walking her chihuahua before I spot the two of them next to the Red Peril.

' . . . and all that bullshit about helping Jo, when this was about some weird, screwed-up mission to fuck with my head. You're unbelievable.' Luke is rather magnificent in full flow.

Frisky seems calm. 'You know, Luke, I wouldn't mind being on the receiving end of your anger, if I thought it was actually helping. But it's not helping, is it?'

'Cut the psychobabble. You know what this is about.' Luke is fumbling with the car keys, trying to unlock the door, but his hands are shaking too much.

'So running away again is how you're going to deal with it, is it, Luke? Because it worked so well in the past, didn't it? Leaving America was *such* a bright new beginning.' Sarcasm makes Frisky's voice sour.

'I didn't leave America because of that. I left it because of you.'

'After four score years, I think I can look after myself.'

Luke shakes his head. 'Oh yeah. I remember. They wouldn't let you out of hospital on your own after the stroke, or have you conveniently forgotton that bit?'

Stroke? Frisky told me he'd had a 'cerebral accident'. I stare at him and his jaw goes slack, a picture of defeat and shame, as if getting sick is the ultimate humiliation.

'They . . . they would have done. Fuss about nothing. And don't change the subject.'

'You'd be in a care home if I hadn't come over,' Luke says, then stops. 'Not that I didn't want to help, Gramps, you know that I did. But I won't have you rewriting history.' His voice is softer now.

Frisky notices me at last, and looks more embarrassed. 'In

case you've forgotten, Luke, you promised me you'd do this, for Joanna.'

'It doesn't matter,' I say, and Luke seems surprised to see me.

'I don't . . . ' he begins. 'Jo, I don't want you to get the wrong idea. I would do it, but . . . '

'Luke, it's fine.' I don't know what's going on, but I know this isn't only about fire-walking.

'Yes, that's right, Luke,' Frisky says. 'Stay holed up in that caravan for the rest of your days. Never let anyone get close or see you're frightened. It's your life to throw away.'

Finally, Luke manages to unlock the door to the Red Peril and, without meeting my eye, climbs inside and drives off. Frisky looks sheepish. 'It's a long story.'

Maybe if I was planning to stick around after today, I'd feel I had the right to hear it, but instead I nod. 'Right.'

'Oh, Joanna. I just wish I knew how to help him . . . ' He sounds desperate, and I realise that our friendship isn't only about helping me, it's about rescuing all three of us.

'Sometimes people have to help themselves,' I say. I try not to let myself dwell on how he's going to feel when I let him down.

'Yes. Yes, I have always had trouble realising that.' He nods towards the community centre. 'I'll understand if you don't want to . . . '

It's such a tempting no-fault get-out that I nearly accept, but I can't do this to him. I want him to see me as someone who can, just once, show some mettle.

Whatever that is.

'Let's go back inside. These feet were made for fire-walking, I reckon. So long as my nerve holds.'

We endure sessions on incantations and the deity within, before our guru gets to the all-important science bit. Apparently we won't burn the soles of our feet because: number one, the skin there is much thicker than anywhere else on the body; number two, we barely make contact with the burning coals so, like putting your finger through a candle flame, there'll be no damage; and number three, when properly aligned, our chakras will protect us.

Somehow I find three reasons less convincing than one. He's protesting too much.

I keep drifting off, staring out of the window and wondering where Luke has gone, and why this particular activity had the effect it did. Intimacy is what most little boys are afraid of, isn't it? Only little girls are allowed to be afraid of pain and suffering. Luke stood up to the thugs at the fairground, and fell in love with earthquakes despite their dangers. Yet he wimps out now. It makes no sense.

The guru tells us how to approach the coals. It'll help if we're sweating, as most of us will be, because water is another barrier between us and the heat. 'Ladies, think how you always wet your finger before testing the temperature of an iron. And finally, remember, this is essentially a spiritual experience, but even so it's as well not to dawdle.'

Finally, we troop out to the back of the centre, past the children's playground and sandpit to an area that's already glowing like the barbecues Dennis opposes so fiercely on health and safety grounds.

I giggle at the thought of Dennis's reaction to the idea of walking over hot coals. 'But *why*?' I imagine him saying. 'What on earth would be the point?'

The doubts I have about the wisdom of the fire-walk drift away like smoke. Anything that Dennis would dismiss as madness seems instantly appealing.

The guru has a young male helper who has already prepared the trench: judging from the precise lines and concrete step up, the fire-walks are a regular event. Which must mean that it's safe. The trench itself is only ten feet long, but the heat the fire is generating is intense, primeval against the grey overcast sky. I think, suddenly, of the people at Hiroshima, of the choice between burning to death as the fires spread, or jumping into the boiling river.

'How do you feel?' Frisky asks, his face reflecting the red of the coals.

'Apprehensive. I heard what the guru said and I can believe it in my head. But when we stand here, I can't quite believe in my heart that we'll get across it unscathed.'

He nods, back in the relentlessly positive mood I no longer quite believe. 'Yes, but experience has shown me that whenever I'm afraid of something, it's almost always something worth doing.'

The guru ushers us into line on the far side of the fire pit. 'There'll be elderflower cordial and more flapjacks after the walk,' he says.

So all that stands between me and an organic treat is ten feet of red-hot coals. I jostle with the others to get to the back of the queue. Not like Frisky, who steps confidently towards the front. We take off our shoes and socks, lining them up like children doing Tumbletots.

Frisky turns around, gives me an emphatic thumbs-up. 'Here we go, then,' he says, spitting on his hands as if he's about to wrestle the fire, rather than walk through it.

We all take a breath and hold it as Frisky's gnarled yet very patrician left foot lifts up to take the first step. 'I'm tempted to misquote Neil Armstrong,' he announces, 'one small step for an old bugger and so on, but I do so hate to be predictable. Bottoms up!'

And he launches himself on to the coals, moving so fast that we barely have time to 'ooh' and 'aah' before he reaches the other side, grinning and laughing. 'I couldn't feel a thing! Might have to do it again!'

The guru smiles a tight smile. 'You'll have to go to the back of the queue. Right, who's next?'

I watch as the New Agers and the paunchy men and the right-on grans take their turn. Some whoop with joy afterwards, others are in tears – but not, our guru points out, due to injury. It's because they're ecstatic.

I *can* do this, can't I? I look ahead to the building only twenty feet away. My eye is drawn to the doorway where a tall figure, rendered wobbly by the heat haze, is standing quite still.

'Luke.'

He walks slowly towards the fire and past it to me. 'I shouldn't have run away,' he says. 'I don't break promises.'

'I'm sure you had your reasons. But it's good you came back.' As I speak, I realise it's more than *good*. 'So are you going to watch me? Frisky's already done it.'

He leans into me so close that I feel the warmth of his breath on my neck and it feels hotter than the fire pit. 'Actually, I want to try it myself.'

'But ... is that a good idea? I mean, it's none of my business what happened but I know you must have your reasons.'

'I want to tell you, Jo. Afterwards.' And he turns to take a good look at the fire pit. 'Sheesh. It looked a lot smaller from over there.' His eyes glow in the firelight.

'You don't have anything to prove, Luke.'

He shakes his head. 'Really, I do. Maybe not to you or to my grandfather, but to myself.'

Only an elderly woman is ahead of us now and she steps on to the coals, walking steadily across them as if she's on a sponsored hike. She turns when she gets to the other side, and waves across the heat haze, beckoning for me to follow.

'Do you want to go first?' I ask Luke. His hands are trembling as he takes off those dirty trainers, and fluffy sports socks.

'No. You'll give me something to cross the coals for.'

I frown at him, trying to understand whether it's a joke, but before I can work it out, the guru calls across the smoke. 'Right. Wish me luck, Luke.'

'Good luck.'

I approach the bed of coals and all I can smell is fuel. Surely it's not right to pour petrol on a fire we're about to walk on. I hold my foot above the pit and feel the heat, like a pulse, on my sole.

The guru wags his finger. 'Heart over head, friend. You can't think about this too much.'

Ah, thinking too much. My life would be so much simpler if I could break that habit.

Now's my chance.

I see Frisky at the other end of the pit. Ten feet. Five steps. Go, go, *go* . . .

I feel the heat on my legs, but not on my feet, as I take the first step on to the coals. They shift beneath my toes and all I can hear is crackling. Strangely, there's no sensation on my feet, and before I know it I'm on the other side, and the grass suddenly feels spikier than ever before and then Frisky takes me in his arms and gives me a huge, slobbery kiss. 'Yes! Joanna! I knew you could do it.'

I expected to feel euphoric or faint, but actually my main sensation now is of being grounded, balanced, capable of anything. No one else did that for me. I managed it on my own. I turn and there on the other side of the pit is Luke, still shaking. 'It's easy,' I shout across. 'If I can do it, anyone can.'

He bites his lip, and despite his height, he looks like a boy. Then, just like a boy, he plunges himself into the midst of the fire, taking great heavy steps that leave gaps between the coals.

He makes it to the other side, large drops of sweat running down his face.

'There! We all did it,' I say, and even Frisky dares to get close.

'Well done, Luke. Never thought you'd manage it.'

But then I look more closely at Luke's face and realise he isn't sweating. He's *crying*.

'It's the emotion,' the guru says. 'The harder they are, the harder they fall.'

I feel a terrible sense of disappointment in Luke, and then a rush of guilt. I shouldn't judge a man because he's in touch with his sensitive side. That's what us girls want these days, isn't it? But I can't help it, I expected more of him.

He seems to be fighting for breath and I compose my face

into an expression of sympathy, though I actually want to tell him to pull himself together.

Finally he manages to mumble. 'It's not . . . it's not the emotion. It's my feet.'

I peer down at his soles. They are blistering before my eyes, angry shapes like balloons inflating.

'Fuck,' says the guru. 'This has never happened . . . I mean, it's perfectly safe. It must have been the way you did it, yin and yang out of kilter. This is not my fault –'

Frisky pushes him out of the way. 'Save it for the compensation claim. Now make yourself useful and help me lift him into the car. This boy doesn't need elderflower cordial. He needs a doctor.'

Chapter 34

Oneirophobia – Fear of Dreams

Somehow I manage to drive the rickety Red Peril to the hospital, abandoning it on the double yellows outside casualty. It didn't exactly make an ideal ambulance. The guru travelled with us, mumbling about public liability insurance, and now he holds Luke's head, while Frisky clutches his calves and I, rather embarrassingly, an allocated his . . . um, well, his bottom. Not that it's a bad bottom to have to support. On the contrary. It provides an extremely firm surface to grasp hold of.

He's been very stoical so far, the tears dried up within two minutes of leaving the centre and the only peep out of him has been an apology for weeping. He tried to insist on walking into the hospital but when Frisky touched his feet, ever so gently, with the tip of his finger, Luke began to retch, so instead we decided that we had to carry him.

It's not until the casualty nurse races forward with a wheelchair that we work out that might have been an easier way to bring him in. Perhaps fire-walking has singed our brain cells.

'Next of kin?' the nurse says, while Luke clenches his fists so he doesn't moan. They've propped his feet up on a plastic chair.

'Me,' says Frisky.

Luke grunts. Then he says, 'But if it's OK, I'd like *her* to stay with me.'

The nurse stands up. 'No skin off my nose. But you and your girlfriend could be in for a bit of a wait.'

I blush again. The guru sees his chance to escape, mumbling about needing to realign the chakras of the other students, and Frisky looks from Luke, to me, and back again. 'I can walk home,' he says, 'as you don't need me here.'

'Don't go,' I say, but Luke won't look at his grandfather.

'I think I should, Joanna. Now, next time, I'll pick something easy. Ballroom dancing or . . . ' But his voice tails off as he understands that there can't possibly be a next time. In the worst way, this has taken the decision out of my hands. 'Luke, I'm sorry. I know this is my fault. Playing God has become rather a habit of mine, hasn't it? Time to stop meddling now.'

Before we can answer, he walks towards the sliding doors. I try to go after him, but Luke reaches out. 'Leave him, Jo. I need you here.'

'Do you?' I feel flattered and flustered. 'Would you like a drink? Tea, coffee, water. Or I could go and see –'

'I said, I need you *here*, Jo. I'm feeling woozy. And my feet hurt like crazy.'

I take a peep: the blisters are oozing yellow liquid that's crusting at the edges. And the ends of his toes are bright red. 'Well, at least they haven't dropped off.'

He manages a weak smile and then closes his eyes. I look around the department: it's full of fit young men, nursing sporting injuries, laughing and trying to outdo each other with Sunday afternoon war wounds.

'Everything OK, kid?' Luke asks.

'Yeah. Fine. I've just realised that this must have been where they brought me after my head injury.'

'You don't remember?'

'No. My memory's a big black hole about some things, and totally hyperactive about others.'

'What do you mean?'

I *wish* I hadn't said that. 'Oh, it's nothing.'

'Go on. Distract me from my agony.'

'OK. But you have to promise me you won't think I'm mad.' He nods. 'Well, ever since the bang on my head, I get these weird flashbacks to things that happened to me years ago.'

He stares at me and I realise he *does* think I'm mad. One of the football players switches on a portable radio, and 'Bohemian Rhapsody' fills the waiting room. I'm trying to think of some witty comment about the karaoke evening to change the subject, perhaps a joke about my singing voice, when he says, 'Thing is, I get flashbacks too, Jo.'

'Right.' Now it's my turn to look gob-smacked.

'What are yours of?' he asks.

'Um ... school. Home. All kinds of different stuff that seemed really important when I was twelve. And yours?'

'The same thing, every single time.' He winces.

I wait for him to explain. Freddie Mercury's voice fills the space as Luke takes his time.

'I've always been a heavy sleeper,' he begins. 'It was a joke at home. But in the flashbacks, the faintest crackling noises wake me up. And intense heat, like sunbathing at midday, but it's dark. The heat's coming from the corridor. I touch the hotel room door and it stings my hand and then I smell burning wood.' His eyes are closed.

'You don't have to do this ... '

He holds up his hand. 'It kinda makes me choke so I go to the window and pull open the doors to the balcony and then when I step out the air feels so good but I see fire-tenders. Rows of 'em. And people on the sidewalk, in gowns and PJs.'

'Go on.'

'I lean against the front rail of the balcony and I crane my neck so I can see more of the building above me. The suite seven floors above me where my parents are, the room with one of the best views of Manhattan. We paid extra for it, for me to share with my grandfather because he'd flown all that way, a treat for his birthday. The big family reunion, like in the movies. But he insisted they take the suite. "Suites are for couples," he said. The suite that's leaking orange flames through broken windows.'

'When was this, Luke?'

'Five years ago,' he says, then opens his eyes. 'Then nightly, seven days a week. With matinées on the weekend.'

'They didn't make it, did they? My words sound too blunt. 'Sorry. But Frisky told me your parents had died. He wouldn't give me the details.'

He nods. 'The fire started on the floor below them. My mom bust her ankle skiing at Whistler so we think that when they heard the alarm, they decided to stay where they were. Wait for help. Gramps woke same time as me, and we both tried to get to them. Ran down our corridor, up to the stairs, but the doors wouldn't budge. We pushed and pulled and we didn't notice the bars were red hot till much later.' And he holds out his right hand, where the scar that matches Frisky's suddenly makes sense. 'We gave up when the smoke got too much, Frisky dragged me downstairs. I wanted to stay. Keep trying.' His eyes are dull now, and his voice resigned. 'They said they were probably dead before we even left our room, from smoke.'

I want to reach out and hug him. 'Luke, I am so, so sorry. You tried. That was all you could do, wasn't it?'

'I guess I know that in here,' he says, touching his head, 'but I will never believe it in here.' He holds his fist to his chest.

The song on the radio's changed to 'Walking on Sunshine', until a nurse walks over and switchs it off.

'And Frisky?'

Luke looks down. 'Mom always said we were so alike but as we'd always lived in the States, and my grandmother died when Mom was twenty, I'd never spent time with my British family. And that time was running out, you know. That's why he came over. Now what we have in common is watching that building burn.'

'No wonder you two seem so spiky all the time.'

'Yeah. We'd had two days to get to know each other, then the fire. He stayed a while, helped with all the funeral arrangements, then had a stroke six months after flying home. Maybe Mom dying brought it on, though the doctors won't say so for sure.'

I wish I could hold him, tell him it'll be OK, but it seems too trite. Instead I say, 'It was good of you to come to Britain, look after him. Give it all up.'

He shrugs. 'Had to get away from the States for a while anyhow, and I thought being in the house where Mom grew up might make me feel closer to her.'

Three young lads come into casualty, the one in the middle supported by his friends. They're singing 'Yesterday' with all the mournful enthusiasm of a pack of spaniels.

'It hasn't helped, though, has it?'

'Maybe a little.'

I hesitate before saying more, wondering how far I ought to pry. Getting this right seems so important. 'I suppose you've heard all the stuff about time healing?'

'Sure. One day maybe I might even be ready to quit the caravan.'

A thought occurs to me. 'That's why you live in the caravan. Because of the fire?'

'Yeah. I tried to sleep indoors but the nightmares . . . worse than the flashbacks. Always trapped somewhere.' He blinks hard, as if he's trying to banish the images. 'Why, what did you think it was about?'

'Frisky told me you loved animals. That you were sleeping outside because local cats were being stolen.'

'I'm allergic to cats.' He begins to laugh, and I can't help joining in. The other patients give us wary glances. 'I got to hand it to Frisky,' Luke says, when he finally stops, 'he's got one hell of an imagination. I guess he didn't want you to think I was a psycho.'

I nod. 'No, just a vigilante. But he did tell me about how you need to get away, sometimes. Where do you go?'

'Go?'

I feel embarrassed at my directness now. 'Well, you know when Frisky and I decorated the parlour. He said you'd gone away.'

'Yeah, sure. To Tokyo. I was giving a paper to a conference on how to earthquake-proof cities.'

'Oh,' I manage, after a while. 'I didn't realise you were still working. I thought . . . '

'That I was a drop-out? No. Great thing about my job is I can work anywhere in the world. Laptop, modem, brain, that's all I need. Apart from anything, work helps me stop thinking. Jeez, he's really painted a great picture of me. Must be the world's worst matchmaker.'

'Matchmaker?'

Luke looks down. 'Well, yeah. That's what he's been trying to do, isn't it? Fix us up. Like any girl would go for a guy who has to sleep outdoors like a dog.'

'Or any guy would go for a girl who is scared of her own shadow.' We smile shyly at each other, united in self-deprecation. 'He does care, though, Frisky does. Even this,' I point at his poor feet, 'was about wanting to help you, wasn't it?'

'Yeah. I worked that one out, in the car. I came back because I made my promise, but also because I don't *want* to be this way. No one would want to be this way. But this is part of me, now. I don't know if I can ever go home. Memories, you know.'

We sit in silence and I can tell Luke's in a lot of pain. I keep talking to distract him. 'Well, my flashbacks aren't quite like yours, but they're still scary. You know you said you were afraid of earthquakes, until you understood them? And I was scared of the A-bomb. Seems stupid now, doesn't it?'

'No, not stupid at all. Different times.'

'But it's not just fear. In my flashbacks, I get so angry with the adults because they did nothing. I stop. 'Sorry, I'm rambling. Shall I get you a drink? A chocolate bar?'

'No, keep talking. You're interesting.'

'Me?' I blush. 'Right, well, when you're a kid, you don't

see why things have to stay the same. You fight. That's why I tried to protect us from the Bomb, though any idiot could see it was naïve. But then you grow up, you give in. That's what I did. Gave in to being afraid, so that the stuff I was scared of grew and grew, until it outnumbered the things I loved.'

'And then came the accident, right?'

'Yes. Then came the accident and I understood that my self-imposed bunker had done me no good at all, made me make wrong decisions about my job and my . . . ' I tail off. It's disloyal to mention Dennis. That fire-walk tricked me into feeling I'm invincible, when I should know better. 'Anyhow, I'm not saying that's what you're doing, Luke, but if you leave it too long, well . . . I'm a warning, that's all.'

'A warning, huh? Well, you're the nicest warning I've ever had, Jo.'

'Oh.' I don't know what to say. 'Right. Thank you.'

'And does your story have a happy ending?' he asks.

I sigh. 'Um . . . ' I think about my life ahead with Dennis, and my resolve falters. But I must be able to work things out. I'll invite the lesbians over for dinner, cultivate a friendship with the dope-grower. Encourage Dennis to be more outgoing, get over his resentment of nosy neighbours, forget the way his mother let him down, make him realise that, like John Lennon said, life is what happens when you're making other plans.

As if he'll ever accept that. My confidence in the future drains away faster than bathwater. Luke is staring at me. 'So does it? Have a happy ending?'

'Well,' I manage, 'it's not an *unhappy* ending.'

He blinks. 'Right. Sure. Not unhappy. I guess I'd settle for that these days.'

Well, that really was *terrific*, Jo, wasn't it? You're such a bloody inspiration.

Luke leans forward to touch his feet.

'Are they hurting again?' I ask and he nods, not looking at my face. I suddenly remember how I'd pictured his feet when I was in bed with Dennis in Coventry. Even with singed edges, they're every bit as tanned and perfect as I'd imagined. I stand up, anxious to get away. 'Let me see where you are in the queue for being seen.'

I walk towards the reception area, and wait for the nurse to get off the phone. Against my better judgement, I look round at Luke. He seems so lonely, in the midst of the joking footballers. I can't turn my back on him now.

But I must. I pinch myself hard on the inside of my arm as I repeat in my head what Timmy told me, 'sometimes selfish is good for everyone'.

The middle-aged doctor, when we finally get to see him, is thorough but crotchety. As he examines Luke's feet, he mumbles under his breath, 'bloody self-inflicted injuries'.

'I beg your pardon?' I say. Luke is beyond speech.

'Every Sunday afternoon it's the same. Football injuries, rugby injuries, drinking in the pub injuries. At least your boyfriend's original.'

'He's not my . . . '

'Though quite what makes anybody walk on coals is beyond me. Doesn't exactly help this afternoon that half my nurses are at some ludicrous emergency exercise. Great timing.'

Shit. I look at the wall clock. Six thirty. The exercise must be nearly over by now, and Dennis will be wondering where I am. Or maybe not: he's probably cracked open the beers with the other bigwigs, backslapping away.

But I owe him my support. I need to work at loving him again, because he's the only person in the world who'll put up with me. 'So how bad are the burns?'

'They look worse than they are. They haven't gone too deep, so we'll dress them and then your young man will have to keep his feet up for a week or so. Ever fancied yourself as a nurse?'

'I'm not his . . . ' And then I stop. I'm making it worse.

While they dress Luke's feet, I order a taxi. Once he's been wheeled to the car, I chat inanely to the driver about the weather and the football results. Anything to stop Luke asking me for help that I can't give.

At the villa, the taxi parks near the front door, as I tell Frisky what the doctor said.

'We'll either kill each other or end up best buddies by the end of the week,' he says, and I hover round the taxi, so he can't ask me to come and visit. I know I'm being horribly selfish, but I have to cut the ties.

By the time Frisky, the driver and I have manhandled Luke on to the chintzy chaise longue in the conservatory, we're all panting.

'Is it all right if I take the taxi on?' I say. 'Only I have another appointment. I'm late as it is.'

Luke and Frisky look at me, then each other, and their faces fall. 'Can't you stay for a tea?' Frisky says.

'She's done enough already,' Luke says. 'Thank you, Jo. You kept me going.'

Before I can stop myself, I kneel down and grab his hand. I whisper, 'What I said. I didn't put it very well, but it matters, Luke. It really matters. Maybe it's a chance for you and Frisky to start over. Talk through the bad stuff. Get to know each other. *Please.*'

He grips my hand back, hard. 'Yeah. I know. Not easy, though. It'll be easier if you're around to remind me.'

I take my hand back. 'I . . . I don't know if . . . '

'I don't mean like a *girlfriend*. I just mean as a friend. I don't exactly have a whole posse of buddies about to show up with dirty movies and a crate of Miller Lite.'

I stand up. 'I'll try,' I say, the guilt burning like the heat I can still feel from his hand in mine. 'I need to go.'

I turn to go but Frisky catches me for a hug. His body feels lighter than I expected, as though I could crush him in my arms.

'Thanks, Frisky. It was fun. Well, until . . . ' and I wave towards Luke.

'Fun. Yes. Such a shame you can't stay. I had a special fishy treat arranged too, smoked salmon. Perhaps not the most tasteful, under the circumstances.'

I wish I could tell him why I need to do this, but know I can't. I return to the taxi.

'Where to, love?'

'St Matthew's School? On the ring road? It's not far.'

I stare through the back window as he accelerates away. The villa looks dark and reproachful, and I imagine the days of bickering ahead. Maybe it was better to leave them to it, force them to settle their differences.

I turn to face forward again. This was only an interlude, a few strange months I'll forget as soon as I begin focusing on my old life again. And a *not unhappy ending* is still one hell of a lot better than most of us manage, after all. Look at my parents.

The playground is deserted, though judging from the soapy water still draining away from the decontamination shower tents, the exercise has only just finished.

I creep back into the hall, where Dennis has evidently finished his speech, and people are helping themselves to drinks from the free bar that's been set up on the scientific adviser's table. Rescuers dressed in chemical protection gear, and casualties with dog tags in paper smocks, sip from cans of Foster's and nibble on crisps. Having satisfied themselves they are invincible (though the scoreboard shows a total of eight fatalities, 200 hospitalised), Courtbridge can sleep easy.

Mikey emerges from the throng, carrying a beer. 'Hey, Jo. You cut it fine.' He offers me a drink and I take it, suddenly realising how thirsty I am.

'I was . . . delayed. Do you think he noticed?'

We both look over at command control, where Dennis and Mrs Fothergill are sharing a joke. 'Nope. He's only had eyes for disaster.'

'I suppose that's a good thing,' I say.

'What's that smell? Like a bonfire?' Mikey says. 'And you

look a bit weird, Jo. Your face is all smudged, like a miner's. What exactly have you been up to?'

Before I have time to think up a convincing lie, Dennis finally spots me and works his way through the crowd, head held high, every inch the conquering hero. 'Jo. *Jo*. It's gone *so* well, couldn't have been better.' And he puts his arm around me. 'Of course, it's not wholly down to me. It's also down to our little *foot soldiers*.'

Mikey scowls. 'Gee, thanks, mate. You're so generous with your praise.' And he walks off in search of more alcohol.

'Yes, that's the secret of my success, motivating my staff,' Dennis says. 'And what about you, Jo? I've hardly seen you. Getting your hands dirty, eh? And your face by the look of it. My lovely Jo.'

I get a sudden urge to tell him what I've really been doing but before I can speak, Dennis moves towards me for a triumphant beery kiss; when his mouth meets mine, the hoppy, yeasty bitterness is overpowering. I brace myself. I'm not going to spoil his day.

As I feel the tell-tale heaviness in my arms and legs, I wonder if I've ever been so glad of a flashback . . .

Chapter 35

Athazagoraphobia – Fear of Being Forgotten

Beer-scented breath and sandalwood aftershave. My father's face, up close, inches from mine. His hand around my wrist.

'Come on, Jo. We need to get out of here. Now! Let me through . . . my daughter is finding it hard to breathe.'

'Daddy.' I don't think anyone hears me. I can't even tell if I said it out loud, because my lungs are empty.

He's pulling me through the crowd now. Dad releases my limbs from the jammed-together bodies, and I see Gillian, still wedged between angry people who can't seem to stop shouting. At least, I think they're shouting. Their mouths are opening and shutting, and the ones with free hands are pointing and prodding, but I can't hear anything. Once the crowd is no longer holding me up, it feels like my muscles have stopped working too, so he has to carry me, all the way across the road, and round the corner and into Savannah's salon.

Dad lifts me gently into one of the padded leather chairs at the back of the salon. In the mirror my face is blotchy, as if I've been crying, though I know I haven't.

I look up, and see Mum, with Timmy asleep on her lap, at the next chair along. 'I'm sorry,' she mouths. Gradually, my ears let in sounds again: the whirr of the hairdryers, the shoosh of the water in the basins, the low hum of speculation about the bedraggled arrivals. A huge poster of a woman with a Lady Diana flicked hairdo stares down at me.

'You came back for me.' My voice is croaky, like an old woman's.

Dad looks hurt. 'Of course I did.'

'But I saw you with Mum and Timmy and I thought you'd forgotten.'

'As if I would. I only got them first because they were nearer the front, where the angriest people were.'

'Gillian! What about Gillian? Is she going to be OK?'

My parents exchange a look, then Mum stares at the ground. Finally my father says, 'Gillian's a grown woman. She can take care of herself.'

'Car's here,' Savannah says, and Dad helps me up. Mum sits in the front and Dad lifts my brother back on to her lap without waking him. Then he joins me in the back. I smell the beer again and I wonder why he's been drinking at lunchtime, when he should be approving people's bank loans. But all that matters is that he didn't forget me.

The taxi's engine drowns out its radio, and I close my eyes. Then I hear my father's whispered voice. 'Bean, listen to me. This is between you and me. I *know*, OK? About your *collection*.'

I open my eyes again, hoping he's talking about the gonk collection I bought from a girl at school, before I spent all my money on supplies.

'The tins and the packets,' he says. He checks in the mirror to see whether Mum's listening, but she seems dazed, her mouth hanging open and her eyelids fluttering as if she's dreaming.

'And that leaflet, about bomb shelters. Under your bed. I knew something strange was going on when I found that bag after Timmy went missing, with the beans and the Dettol inside. At first I thought you had one of those eating disorders, like on TV. Or maybe you were shoplifting.'

'I . . . ' I imagine my father rifling through my painstakingly acquired stockpile. Tins of baked beans that I'd stacked carefully to take up less space, rolling all over the carpet. My lists inspected and laughed at. My sparse first-aid kit emptied on to my Holly Hobby rug. 'Dad, I haven't stolen anything. It's for us. All of us. For when the Bomb comes.'

He nods. 'I know that now. It was almost a relief when I found that booklet.'

I seize my chance. 'The thing is, we really should move house, Dad. But if we can't do that straight away, we need a plan. Most people won't be prepared for nuclear attack, but if we are, then we'll have a hope of survival.' He listens, and it's so rare that I keep talking, let it all out. 'The booklet said the build-up to war might only last a fortnight. The shops will be emptied. We can't rely on the government, we need to look after ourselves.' I don't add *and this is your job, as head of the family, but as you haven't done it, I've had to.*

Finally, I run out of reasons. He puts his hand on mine. 'Bean, it's going to be all right, you know.'

'But they've got hundreds of bombs aimed at us. The Russians. SS20s. Hundreds of them.'

'And we've got hundreds aimed at them. That's why it'll be all right. Trust me.'

We're passing the common now, though none of us dares to look at the camp. I wonder if Gillian will be all right. I wish we'd made sure.

I want to tell Dad it's not up to him, he's not Brezhnev or Reagan, he's a bank manager, and what can he do? Instead I say, 'Couldn't we move away, Daddy?'

'Oh, Bean. This isn't about nuclear war.' He checks that Mum's still asleep. 'Your mum and me have been bloody awful at noticing what's happening under our noses. I promise we'll try harder. Timmy's had the lion's share of attention lately, but that's going to change. We'll have fun. As a family. How does that sound?' He sounds as if he's trying to convince himself as much as me.

'Good, Daddy, but . . . ' And then I understand that

nothing I say will make him move, or persuade him to build a fall-out shelter in the back garden. He believes what he believes and that's that: adults can't change. They're set, like concrete. 'It sounds good.'

He smiles. 'Fantastic. Just two things then. First, we don't tell your mother. She's got enough to worry about and finding out about your stockpile ... well, I don't think it would help her to know.'

'OK,' I say, knowing from experience that Dad always names the easiest thing first. 'And the second thing?'

'You need to get rid of it, Bean. All of it. The tins. The first-aid kit. That bloody scary booklet with the pictures of bodies in bin-liners.'

'But ... '

'But nothing. It's all a reminder of ... a bad time for the Morgans. Time for a new beginning, now.'

I try a different tactic. 'It's a terrible waste.'

He nods, weighing up my point. 'Fair enough. We give it away then. To an old folks' home or something. Though not the leaflet, obviously. Up to you to get shot of it ... I'll give you seven days, Jo, no more than that, then I'll check up.'

'All right.'

'The sheltered housing near school, they'd be glad of the tinned stuff,' he says.

But I've already decided where my precious stockpile is going.

To the peace camp. Lucky they're keen on tins.

The taxi pulls up in our road, and Dad gives the driver double the usual fare. He lifts Timmy from my mother's arms, and my brother wakes up now, rubbing his eyes and insisting on walking, rather than being carried. We could be any other nuclear family, on our way home from an August day trip. Tired but happy.

Except that as my father snakes his arm around my mother's sunken shoulders to lead her up the path, I hear him whisper, 'It stops here, Lynda, the fun and games at Greenham. If you *ever* endanger my children's lives again, I will divorce you and take them with me. The courts won't grant custody to an unfit mother. Do you understand?'

Her lips twitch and her eyes open. And she nods, like a sleepy child.

'Good girl,' he says in the voice he uses when Misty lies on her back, playing dead for the Queen. 'Good girl.'

Chapter 36
Tropophobia – Fear of Making Changes

By rights Dennis should be hanging a banner on the outside of our bungalow: 'WELCOME HOME, JO MORGAN'.

Yes, my fearless alter ego has done the decent thing, and quit town, with her: the tendency to feed squirrels, talk to cold-callers and send inappropriate emails. She's also packed off those peculiar ideas about taking risks or putting herself first.

I feel bad about the squirrels. They eyeball me through the patio doors, their flat-eared faces tight with annoyance. They try ever more impressive tricks to change my mind, and I wouldn't be surprised to look out one morning and see them juggling nuts, or playing a form of squirrel cricket with a magnolia leaf as the bat and berries as balls.

It's such a trivial thing, and I keep wondering what harm it would do to sneak out a few plates of sunflower seeds, where Dennis won't find them. But I'm not going to give in: there's more at stake here than a few hungry rodents. Turning myself back into the old Jo is going to be the hardest thing I've ever done. Like a method actor, I must adopt the mannerisms and behaviour of my former self, in the hope that eventually my performance will be so convincing that I'll fool myself.

But there's no banner yet, or streamers or party poppers.

Dennis barely seems to have noticed the change. He ignored the bonfire I made of the brochures and junk mail. I watched alone as my possibilities of winning a Caribbean cruise or building up my own property empire went up in smoke.

The trouble is, the old Jo Morgan had a million things to think about, on behalf of the citizens of Courtbridge. AIDS, Bombs, Crashes, Disasters, Ebola, Flesh-eating Bugs, GM Crops, Hoodies, Ice Storms, Joyriders, Killer Clothing, Livestock Stampedes, Mobile Phone Masts, Nuclear War, Organised Crime, Plane Crashes, Quack Therapists, Rats, Spontaneity, Terrorism, UV Radiation, Volcanic Eruptions, Wasps, X-rays, Youth Crime and Zoonoses. Not necessarily in alphabetical order.

I've decided I can't face going back to my stupid job, but I'd give anything to be busy. Mum and Dad have downgraded their surveillance operation and Dennis is too distracted to pay me any attention. At first I thought it was because of this stupid stunt arranged by *Civil Protection Chronicle*, who convinced him to pose for a photograph eating a Victoria sandwich with a bunch of bakers, to prevent a diplomatic incident after my cake danger memo. I've seen the picture and he looks like that Tory minister who ate a hamburger at the height of the BSE crisis. But even since the photoshoot, he seems miles away.

So I have all the freedom I was longing for when I first came home from hospital, yet now I crave nature trails and duck-feeding expeditions. Anything to stop me thinking about Frisky and Luke. Every day I think it'll get easier, that this guilt will begin to be replaced by a fond nostalgia. That I won't wake up wondering how Luke's burns are healing, or whether he's exchanged two words with his grandfather, and whether those two words might be 'stupid cow', or 'scheming bitch'.

I've started going for long walks, playing Russian roulette with my feet, which might misbehave and carry me to the villa, although I know it's the last place I should be. So far I've walked to St Matthew's School, where screaming infants have taken the place of fake casualties, and to the field next to the leisure centre, where the gondola ride is long gone and preparations are under way for the July carnival queen ceremony.

When the doorbell goes as I sit eating my organic lunch, I allow myself a moment of imagining it might be Frisky. But I'm not really surprised when it turns out to be my father.

'Bean! You sounded a bit fed up on the phone so I thought you might fancy a movie!' He pushes past me to the living-room and begins to set up the DVD recorder.

I sigh, and go to make some tea. When I bring it in, I recognise the movie's opening sequence immediately: a red sports car snaking round terrifying hairpin bends before exploding in a tunnel.

'Hey, is this meant to be a treat for me or for you, Dad?'

'Ah, I defy anyone to feel miserable after watching the finest British movie ever made.'

We watch *The Italian Job* in reverential silence, except for gasps when the Minis do their stuff, giggles when the boys outsmart the Mafia, and the obligatory bit where we join in with Michael Caine when he says, 'You were only supposed to blow the bloody doors off.'

But I spend as much time watching Dad as the screen: with the cynicism gone from his face, he looks twenty years younger. Still just handsome enough to make heads turn.

As the credits roll, leaving Charlie Croker and his crew on the precipice, Dad sings along with the 'Get a Bloomin' Move On' song, before remembering his tea, and drinking it down, cold, in one long gulp.

'Now, what are we going to do with you, Bean?'

'This wasn't a social call, then.'

'I've been wanting to talk to you properly ever since you came out of hospital, but I knew I'd get in trouble with your mother if I said anything out of turn.'

I open my mouth to protest that he's always been the one censoring her, but then I stop. Actually, he's the only person who hasn't been giving me unwanted advice since my accident. Even when he took me to the pub for those long nutritious lunches, he didn't seem his usual garrulous self. 'So what did you want to tell me?'

'I just want my daughter to be happy. And I'm not convinced all this is doing the job.' He waves vaguely around the room to indicate 'all this'.

I'd like to ask him what makes him the world expert on happiness. Instead I say, 'What makes you think that, Dad?'

He must pick up on the sarcasm in my voice because he smiles. 'I know what you're thinking, Bean. I've known you long enough to recognise *that* look, the one that says, "Dad's 100 per cent wrong, but I can't be bothered to argue."'

Now I'm smiling. 'I'll give you the benefit of the doubt, just this once.'

'Thing is, when you were in your coma, I felt so powerless, Bean. For the second time. I was useless when Timmy was ill and then he got better so it was all right, and then there I was again, nothing I could do to keep you alive, one of those times you wish you could convince yourself there's a God. I said to myself then, if she makes it, I'm going to tell her what I really think. Even if she hates me for it.'

'Why would I hate you, Dad?' As I say it, I realise with a jolt that I *did* hate him, until that last flashback proved that he didn't abandon me, after all.

'Because I think Dennis is the wrong man for you.' He flinches, anticipating a hostile reaction. When I say nothing, he continues warily. 'Because he's ... boring. That's not a crime in itself, Bean. I do realise that you're not exactly a wild-child yourself, and thank goodness not everyone is like me. But the point of a partner is that they should make you *better* than the person you were alone. Not worse.'

'Like you and Mum?' I say, sharper than I intended.

'Ah ... Ah, well, I know you might not see it that way, but actually, yes. I'm a flawed person in so many ways, but if it wasn't for your mother ... I've hurt her too often, Jo, but both of us had a lot to learn about how to treat someone you love. And I know this sounds arrogant, but I think she's better for having me around. She's always needed stability.'

I think back to what Mum said at the barbecue, the way it sounded so clinical, more like an arranged marriage than the discovery of a soul mate, but maybe being unromantic isn't a crime. It's just a shame.

'Jo?'

'Thing is, Dad, if stability's a good thing, then aren't I lucky to have Dennis?'

He sighs. 'Stability was what your mum needed, Jo. I think what you need is someone who will destabilise you, challenge all those neuroses. I was thrilled when you got home and started shouting at people, being a bit bonkers. At last you were standing up for yourself.'

'I thought everyone hated the new me.'

'Ah, but I've always been contrary, Bean. And maybe it's madly controlling of me, but I'd love to see you with a man who likes the new you too. Or at the very least, a man in possession of a sense of humour.'

He's gone too far, now, sitting on Dennis's sofa, accusing him of being a humourless bore. *I'm* allowed to think it, but only because I appreciate his other qualities. 'Dennis looks after me, Dad. That's what I need. Not a stand-up comedian who subjects me to endless practical jokes. I'm feeling tired, now. I think you should go.'

He nods. 'Yes, you're probably right. Pushed my luck, maybe. But I thought it was worth the risk. Take care, Bean. You know where we are if you need us.'

After he's gone, taking the precious DVD with him, I go to the understairs cupboard to look for photos of when Dennis and I first met, to remind myself of those qualities I'm trying so hard to appreciate.

But the first bag I pull out doesn't contain photo albums: it contains a rusty tin of tuna, a carved wooden fish, and an opened pack of Fisherman's Friends. I stick my nose in the carrier and breathe deeply, wondering if the strange cocktail of smells will take me back in time.

All that happens is my eyes begin to sting with tears. So I take the bag and push it to the back of the cupboard, behind the wellies and toolboxes. I ought to chuck it out, but I can't bring myself to do it, even though Frisky and Luke are my past. And Dennis is my future.

Chapter 37
Euphobia – Fear of Hearing Good News

When Dennis announced he was taking today off work (a Monday, too, the day Dennis says 'sets the tone for the working week!') for a 'special trip', I thought it was touching and romantic. He'd finally noticed my efforts to change and was responding in kind. Once he hit the M40, with lots of meaningful looks in my direction, I managed not to groan at the prospect of another 'inspiring' visit to Coventry.

But I wasn't expecting this.

'Would you mind repeating what you just said, Dennis? I think I must have misheard.' *At least I hope I misheard.*

Dennis's smile falters for a fraction of a second and his hand gets halfway towards the lock of fringe he always pulls when he's nervous, before he brings himself back under control.

Oh please God, let me have misheard.

We're not back at the Warwickshire wife-swapping Plaza Hotel. Instead we're on a brand-new estate, with fake heraldic developers' flags at the entrance, and banners that promise 'Your stamp duty paid!' and 'Fab free furniture package! Ethically sourced!' Every road is named after a tree – Ash Rise, Oak Lane, and where we are now, Maple Drive. Though no one's bothered to plant so much as a sapling.

The brand-spanking-newness of everything is scary, as is

the quiet: it makes Salzburg Avenue look like Soho on a Saturday night. But scariest of all is that Dennis appears to know his way round.

'It's ours,' he says, very softly, with a fey, nervous wave at the large detached redbrick house behind him. It looks like it's built from Lego.

'Ours?' That's what I thought he said. 'When? Why? How?' I sound like a Ladybird book.

'So many questions!' says Dennis, interpreting them as enthusiasm. 'Which one shall I answer first?'

'Why?' I say, dully. There's a distinct whiff of *fait accompli* about this, though I can't possibly see how he . . .

'I've been offered a director's job.'

A blow to the belly, as not so much the penny as an entire money-bag full of loose change drops. 'Here? In Coventry?'

'In Coventry, yes,' he says, looking slightly shamefaced. 'You know I didn't want to be somebody's deputy for the rest of my life. And this is a big step up, a full *city* to look after. Population of a third of a million people to keep safe.'

'Oh.' I don't know how to react. '*Congratulations*.' The word comes out acid-dipped.

He doesn't hear the sarcasm. 'It *is* a dream come true for me, Jo. But I wanted it to be special for you too, and I did my research, and this development is apparently the most popular –'

I interrupt him. 'How long?'

'I only accepted a fortnight ago,' he says. 'I was itching to tell you, but with all that's happened . . . I didn't want to get you stressed so I waited till I'd made all the arrangements.' He touches my arm lightly.

'You misunderstand me, Dennis,' I say, brushing him off. 'I meant, how long ago did you apply for the job?' As I speak, I realise he must done it before we went to Coventry for our 'romantic' break. So much for accidentally booking into the wrong hotel.

His face flushes. 'Well, um, I first saw the advert maybe . . . three months ago. And I couldn't discuss it with you then, could I? I mean you were just out of hospital, hardly in the right state of mind ... '

'The right state of mind to discuss my entire future?'

He nods. 'Yes, exactly. Exactly, Jo. I knew you'd understand. Your behaviour was so unpredictable, I wasn't sure there was a future to discuss.'

I think through the implications of this: after my accident, Dennis either thought I didn't have a future *or* that we didn't have a future together.

I'm still digesting this, when a well-groomed middle-aged woman approaches us, brandishing keys.

'Mr Diffley, Mrs Diffley?'

'Miss Morgan,' I say.

'Sorry. So, what do you think of it so far?' she says, her unfamiliar accent the only sign that we're in Coventry, rather than a thousand other identikit estates across the country. 'I'm sure you'd like a look inside ... '

I follow, dumbly, because I don't know what else to do. She regales us with a patter so rehearsed it could be playing from a tape in her handbag. 'The Platinum is at the top of our range of executive homes, a uniquely generous, stylish and architect-designed space for the twenty-first-century family.'

I'm tempted to ask her who usually designs new homes if it's not an architect, but there are more important things to devote my damaged neurons to right now.

'The mosaic-tiled hallway is the first gorgeous hint at the high specification and attention to detail of this luxury five-bedroomed property,' she drones on, 'from the Shaker kitchen, the two reception rooms, the rainforest-friendly west-facing sundeck and the double garage. All with full NHBC guarantee, of course.'

Of course. It *is* a nice house, if you like somewhere with no history and no identity. Virgin appliances, unused baths, empty borders ready for your choice of tropical or traditional planting by Chelsea medal-winning horticulturalists.

We trail behind her, Dennis throwing me nervous glances

which I refuse to return. Upstairs she keeps up the commentary as she shows us four perfect rectangular bedrooms – no awkward fireplaces or uneven walls – before we ascend to the master suite.

She opens the door to the en suite with a delighted flourish, like a parent unveiling a child's first bike on Christmas morning. 'This is the same spa bath two former American presidents have chosen for their homes. *Ten* ozonic power jets. Perfect for relaxing after a stressful day.'

I think she's finished now, but when I open my mouth, she adds, 'You were so lucky to get this one. The last Platinum on the development. All the others went months ago.'

'I'd like some time alone with my . . . partner, if that's OK?' I say, finally.

She nods. 'Of course. I'll be waiting downstairs.'

I listen to her heels on the Brazilian hardwood steps. 'So you've bought the house, then, Dennis?'

'Yup,' he says, sitting on the edge of the president-approved spa bath. 'I knew it was the right one for us. What do you think?'

I ignore the question. 'How, though? I mean, what about number 64?' I never thought I'd feel loyal towards Salzburg Avenue, but then I can't believe he'd toss the bungalow aside like a lover who's seen better days.

'I . . . ' now he seems flustered, 'I didn't want to put you through having people traipse round our home. So instead of putting it on the market the usual way, I had an open day.'

'When?'

'When you went to that health place with Lorraine . . . worked a treat, actually. The market's so buoyant that I had three asking-price offers. It went to sealed bids.'

There's a little trick Lorraine taught me years ago, when she first began her midwife training. Shallow breathing, used by women in labour, also comes in handy during moments of extreme stress. 'You sold our home? Without asking me?'

He sighs now, as if I am deliberately spoiling his big

surprise. 'Well, it is in *my* name, Jo, and it's not like I can commute from Courtbridge, is it?'

'Dennis, have you considered at any point that I might not want to relocate?'

He adopts a serious face. 'Of course I have. That's why I chose a place with five bedrooms, so your mum and dad can come to stay. And you and Lorraine can have girly weekends.'

'You're missing something. I don't have a job in Coventry.'

'Well, we won't need two incomes when we move.'

'It's not just about income,' I say, the pitch of my voice rising with every word, 'it's about the rest of my life. Unless you're expecting me to sit at home for ever like Elizabeth Barrett Browning.'

'I could get you a dog, for company,' he says.

'So long as it's one that doesn't need much exercise, with an invalid for an owner?' I suggest.

'Not a terrier, then,' he says, apparently giving it serious thought. 'But a Pekinese perhaps? Though you'd have to be willing to groom it every day.'

'Well, according to you, I won't need to worry my pretty but dented little head about anything else, will I?'

He stands up, picks away at the tiny pieces of plastic still clinging to the new taps. 'Oh. You were joking about the dog, then?'

'Yes, I was *joking about the dog*. But you're not joking about the *job*, are you?' I find myself raging in a whisper and he has to lean in to listen. 'About dragging me off to a place I never wanted to visit, never mind live there. About seeing my job as so trivial and unimportant that I can happily abandon it to play housewife, without being consulted! Go on. I dare you. Tell me this is some elaborate, side-splitting, practical joke.'

He shakes his head. 'I was trying to look after you, Jo.' He has collected a small ball of plastic, but with no bin to put it in, he rolls it between his hands. 'After everything that's happened, I didn't want to make life any more stressful that it had to be.'

'So you thought it'd be less stressful for me if you ran my life on my behalf?'

'The thing is, I . . . ' he begins. 'I mean, I didn't think you'd . . . ' Now he shrugs apologetically at his complete failure to explain. 'To tell you the truth, I didn't think it would make any difference to you one way or another. I mean, you always told me you had no ambition, except to be happy. You've never expressed any real preference about where you live or what you do.'

I open my mouth to berate him for his arrogance, his cheek, his sheer chauvinist piggery, when I suddenly remember he's right. Until the accident, I didn't take decisions, or express an opinion, if there was any way of avoiding it. My life was about self-preservation, the avoidance of risk, the careful balancing of one improbable danger over another equally unlikely hazard, paralysed by the unknown. I was all too willing to let other people take responsibility.

And Dennis was the perfect man for me, taking control of everything, from the most ethical electricity supplier, to the safest car. No wonder he thought it didn't matter to me where I ended up.

'Jo? I only wanted to take care of everything. A new life, for both of us. A blank slate.'

I look around *our* bathroom suite. 'It's that, all right.' I go to the window and peer down at the identical decks at the back of each house. There are paddling pools and climbing frames all over the place. 'This is a family house, Dennis.'

And his cherubic face lights up, momentarily, and I understand this is part of the plan.

'A new start, Jo.' For a moment, I feel terribly guilty; I know what it must mean to him to be able to contemplate children. It's taken him forty years to get over his mother's neglect, to be able to trust women. And here I am, about to destroy that trust for good.

I screw up my eyes, try to imagine myself here. Our own

paddling pool, full of Maple Drive munchkins, the neighbours coming over for organic dinners, bringing bottles of the same wine that's on special offer at the same superstore where we all shop.

One hundred miles away from Frisky. One hundred miles away from Luke.

'Dennis . . . I don't think I can do this.'

He frowns. 'It's the shock, but I know that when you've had time to let it sink in, you'll see what an opportunity this is for me . . . I mean, for us.'

I shake my head, knowing he won't believe me. I barely believe it myself. 'Dennis. It's not about the house or the job. I can see what an opportunity it is for you and the house is . . . ' I cast around for the right word, 'incredible. Six months ago, it would have been perfect.'

'Before the accident? As I've said before, Jo, you need to give yourself time to get back to normal.'

I speak slowly, now, considering every word. 'Dennis, you wouldn't believe how hard I've tried to get back to normal. With you, and Mum and Dad, and Lorraine, all on the sidelines, cheering me on. It's only very recently that I've admitted I will *never* be the same again.'

'Oh God, Jo. Depression is very common among people who've suffered a life-threatening illness. I'm sure your doctor would prescribe one of the newer anti-depressants, just for a few months, to help you adjust. You *can* be your old self again.'

'You don't understand, Dennis. I don't *want* to be my old self.'

He's pulling frantically at his kiss-curl now, frustrated at my obstinacy. 'That's not you talking, Jo. It's your illness.'

'No. It is me. The illness has changed me for good, like . . . ' I grasp for an analogy he might understand. 'Imagine the bomb's dropped. And the chosen ones have been in the bunker, and after two weeks, they come out again. They're still the same people, really, a bit pasty-faced, maybe, but everything's changed. Their job is to restore normality, but it can't *ever* be the same as it was.'

'I don't see . . . '

'I've been in the bunker my whole life, Dennis. A bunker I built myself. The accident forced me out, and I don't want to go back in.'

He nods, and his eyes look so hurt. 'And that's what your life is like with me, is it? As if you're buried fifty feet underground?'

I shake my head, and reach for his hand. He won't touch me. 'No. Dennis, you were the kindest, most caring man I've ever met.'

'Were?'

I didn't even hear myself use the past tense. But he's right. 'It really is me, not you. I am not the right person for you any more, Dennis. I will stop you leading the life you want.'

'But this house. I've signed the contract, Jo.'

'You mustn't change anything for me. You must take the job. It's what you're meant to do.'

'And what are you *meant to do*?' He can't keep the coldness out of his voice, and I don't blame him.

'I haven't got a clue, Dennis. I think that's what I need to find out.'

He stares at me, as if he's looking at a stranger. 'Well, don't expect me to be waiting when you realise your mistake.'

My once-upon-a-time soul mate turns and walks, with considered paces, out of the bathroom and back down the stairs. I know I'm doing the right thing, but the thought of how much I've hurt him makes me feel so wretched that I race for the unused toilet behind me, to throw up.

There's nothing there but bile, and as I stand up to flush it away – does vomit merit a full-power flush or a low-water eco-friendly one, it's the planet at stake, after all – the smell overwhelms me and I just have enough time to think, *oh no, not here . . .*

Chapter 38

Doxophobia – Fear of Expressing Opinions

'Now, you're sure you're feeling better, Timmy?'

My brother nods as Mum wipes the last yellowy smear of sick from his chin. She sighs at the wet stain that the vomit's made on his new pink tie. Dad protested that pink 'makes him look like a little poof', but Timmy got his way, of course. As my mother said, 'It is being held in his honour, so I think he should be allowed to wear what he likes.'

We leave the loos and return to the foyer, where photographers and a cameraman pace the marble floor. Don't they realise that a child with a serious illness can't be relied upon to smile sweetly and be obediently tragic *all* the time? That they might occasionally sulk or scream or puke up in front of the cameras like a junior Johnny Rotten?

My mother now poses with her arms stretched across Timmy's chest, to cover the stain. Dad's nipped out from backstage in his MC outfit, black tie and shiny shoes. Mum and I are wearing dresses in the same shade of sky blue. Hers is made of silk and swirls when she walks, it makes her look younger. Unfortunately so does mine: it has an irritating lace collar that I'll never live down if the girls from school see me. Though perhaps having a dying brother will get me off the hook.

Actually, I don't believe Timmy is going to die any more.

He looks a little less like a ghost every day, and that must mean his blood is getting stronger, strong enough to put colour in his cheeks.

'So, Timmy, what are you looking forward to tonight?' the TV reporter asks.

'I'm looking forward to the ice cream in the interval,' Timmy says.

'Nothing wrong with his appetite, then,' the reporter says, and I recognise the posh bloke from the stones protest on Hiroshima Day. Dad never saw the report, but the whole thing escalated so much that Timmy ended up in the *Daily Mail*, with questions asked in Parliament and a charity appeal in the *Newbury Weekly News*. Dad stole back the thunder by setting up the fundraising concert to collect money for leukaemia research.

'If you're finished, guys,' my father says, slipping into *Alfie* mode to charm the photographers, 'we've gotta get our show on the road.'

They pack up, and the doors are opened to let in the audience; smartly dressed people crowd around my brother, hungry for their share of our tragedy, cheap at the price of a £4 ticket for this one-off concert. They seem to need to touch him, as if he'll protect them and their families from all the bad things that might happen in the late twentieth century.

As they move away to order their port and lemons for the interval, I hear fragments of conversation. 'Bless him, what a cutie.' 'He had a twinkle in his eye, didn't he?' 'But what about the mother? Do you think she was drunk?' 'Ah, no, probably just a bit overwhelmed.' 'You know she was at the peace camp, I saw her on the telly.' 'No way! She doesn't look the type at all. Her hair's combed for a start.'

The Timothy Morgan Birthday Benefit concert is like a present from my father to my mother, but you only need to look at her to know nothing in life is free. When Mum agreed to turn her back on Greenham, Dad began to pay her more attention. He brings home flowers and organises a babysitter so they can go to the Chinese for crispy duck and pancakes.

He even went to the hospital when Timmy was having chemo, though he threw up more violently than my brother and the nurses suggested it might be better if he didn't go again.

In return, my mother has turned into the perfect wife. I know she's back on tablets, but the new ones seem different. She doesn't get so sleepy and she doesn't cry at all, but then again she doesn't do much apart from wander round with a vague smile on her face, cuddling Timmy at random.

She doesn't have to do much, anyway: Dad's hired a cleaner who comes in twice a week, leaving no carpet unturned. I'd never have got away with the stockpile under the new clean regime.

I took the tins to Greenham, late at night, and left them outside Gillian's tent. No note. I've started again, though it's slow going, because Dad keeps a list in each cupboard of how many tins, packets and sachets should be inside. So I buy a new can with my pocket money each week, and hide it in the garage. Sometimes I feel like giving up, because it's hopeless, but you can't, can you?

Someone rings a bell to let people know it's time to go into the auditorium, but we hold back. It's part of Dad's grand plan to have Timmy march in to a round of applause, 'to remind everyone who this night is all about'.

He means Timmy, not himself. You could have fooled me.

Through the glass I see three late arrivals. 'Mum?'

'Oh God,' she says. 'Oh no.'

She rushes to the door and the few stragglers who haven't yet taken their seats look round curiously.

'Hello, Lynda,' Gillian says, holding out her arms to embrace my mother. Mum hesitates for several agonising seconds, then darts forward quickly to peck Gillian on the cheek. The women have made a special effort – even Mags has softened the spikes in her hair – but Mum's dress would show the tiniest speck of Greenham Common dirt.

'Gillian, Mags. Um ... ' She struggles with the last woman's name and so I whisper, 'Claudette'. 'Claudette.

What are you doing here?' Her voice is light, as if we've run into old friends on holiday.

Mags raises her eyebrows. 'Well, what do you *think* we're doing here?'

'Ignore her, Lynda,' Gillian says. 'We're here for Timmy. For the concert. You supported us when it mattered and we wanted to do the same.'

'Ri-ight,' Mum says. I'm sure I can see her brain working as her eyes flicker from side to side. 'It's very good of you to come.' Timmy runs up to Gillian and jumps into her arms.

'Oof!' She clutches him as he wraps his legs around her waist. 'He's putting weight on, Lynda. That must be a good thing.'

Mum nods. 'We think so. The doctors keep saying we have to be careful not to read too much into anything but it's so hard not to.'

'Timmy, I'll have to let you get down now, or I'll fall over,' Gillian pants. 'We were worried, Lynda, after the demo. And then we saw the concert posters and we thought we'd come along.'

Mum closes her eyes and I think she's going to faint, but as I step forward to take her weight, she opens them again. 'I'm sorry,' she says. 'I'm so sorry to disappear like that, but . . . '

Mags interrupts. 'We're used to it. Better to find out early on who can't cope, than invest our trust in people who aren't up to the job. It's going to get harder, too. There are rumours that bailiffs might be here next week. With bulldozers. No place for *cowards*.'

My mother begins to cry, softly, like an abandoned animal. Gillian glares at Mags, then says to my mother, 'We didn't come here to accuse you of letting the side down. God knows, it must be hard enough to cope, without people wanting you to feel guilty.'

'I wanted to come back, to say goodbye and *explain*, but I wasn't brave enough,' my mother says.

The bell sounds again. 'Time to find our seats,' Mags says, pushing through the door.

'No!' Mum's voice is loud and panicky. 'I mean, wait.'

'Why?' Mags asks. 'Oh, no, don't tell me. You're ashamed of us, aren't you?'

Mum peers down at her new blue shoes. 'It isn't that. I admire you all. You're so much braver than I could ever be.'

'I can hear a but coming,' Mags says bitterly.

'If this was only about me, I'd sit in the front row with you,' my mother says, each word slow and painful, 'but I have to think of my family.'

'Your husband, you mean.'

Gillian looks as if she's about to slap Mags. 'Let her speak, for pity's sake.'

Mum hesitates. 'At the camp, things seem so black and white. Peace or war. Love or hate. Life or death. But I'm not strong enough to forget the other choices I made, before I'd heard of a Cruise missile. I wish I was, but I'm not.'

'Is that *hubby* talking or you, Lynda?'

'I know Ted isn't perfect. But then neither am I, and we've made a joint decision, to try to make things work. For the sake of Timmy and Jo.' She takes my hand and I feel hers trembling.

'Look after your own and sod everyone else's kids, then? Very *Protect and Survive*,' Mags sneers.

Mum stands up a little straighter, though she's crying again. 'I won't stop you coming into the theatre. In another life, I'd want you here. But I don't have another life. I have this one.'

Mags is frowning, Claudette is already turning round, but it's Gillian's face that makes me feel sad. Her eyes are narrowed with hurt and she's biting her lip. Finally, she nods to herself. 'I understand, Lynda. Just remember, we are your friends, whatever happens. And you know where to find us. I have a feeling we won't be moving on for a while yet.'

Gillian stoops down to kiss my brother's forehead and he pulls a face. Then she touches my arm. 'Keep questioning things, Jo. Never feel you have to accept the status quo, because there's no such thing.'

She leans forwards to kiss my mother on the cheek, but

Mum moves back before she can help herself and Gillian smiles. 'Take care of you and yours, Lynda. Stay happy.' And she walks back through the door to join the other two. They don't look back.

The bell rings, as insistent as a siren, and I'm sure it's my dad's hand on the button. There's only the three of us in the foyer now, so I take Mum's hand and she takes Timmy's and we walk towards the stalls.

Mum stops. 'I can't go on stage. I can't.' She's crying properly now, tears running down her face in twin streams. 'You take Timmy.'

I leave her by the door and as the conductor sees Timmy and I walking up the red carpet between the aisle, the music begins.

The opening notes of Art Garfunkel's 'Bright Eyes' fill the auditorium. My father designed the programme for tonight and he likes to lay it on thick. As I climb on to the stage with my brother, the footlights are dazzling, but I'm sure I can still see my mother at the back of the auditorium, one hand wiping away tears.

Dad winks at me from the wings. He couldn't be more pleased with himself. The concert, thousands already in the bag for leukaemia research, leading roles as Master of Ceremonies *and* head of the family, a platform for a little political posturing. Oh, and then there's the present he's bought for Mum, waiting at my grandparents' for the big handover.

'A kitten, Jo,' he told me earlier. 'Pedigree, the fluffiest one in the litter. They're a special breed, from Maine in America, and there's only one breeder in the whole of the UK. She'll love it, won't she?'

And all I keep thinking, as Dad fizzes on to the stage like a shaken-up can of Vimto, is that now I have to add Whiskas to my stockpile . . .

Chapter 39
Philophobia – Fear of Falling in Love

The view from the train is almost enough to make me forget the disaster zone my life has turned into.

Rows of cottages seem to sprout from Cotswold stone like square-topped mushrooms. Un-mad cows graze on what must be the greenest grass in the world. A blue Morris Minor with wooden window frames meanders along a narrow lane.

One of the Armageddon documentaries I watched as a teenager began with scenes like this. Dad must have been out at rehearsals, because I was normally banned from anything that might feed my obsession, yet I kept searching for bad news, like picking a scab. Predictably, within five minutes, the village in the programme was devastated by a blast wave that brought the church spire down on the boys' brigade.

No wonder I never worked out what I wanted from life: Mutually Assured Destruction focused my mind on basic survival, rather than the interesting stuff – careers, boyfriends, a home of my own.

Wrong call, Jo. The bomb never dropped, and while everyone else was filling in job applications and mortgage forms and wedding lists, I notice that the world had changed. Dennis and the job and Salzburg Avenue were my shelter from having to make a single decision of my own.

And now I've lost all three, and I can't think of a time I've felt more terrified – or more alive.

Lorraine will think I'm crazy. My parents will want to pack me off to hospital again. There's only one person I can think of who'll agree with me that my insanity is something to celebrate.

At Courtbridge, I step on to the platform and need to steady myself on another passenger.

'Sorry.'

I'm laying the blame on nerves. My image of Frisky welcoming me into the conservatory, glass of wine and bowl of Greek olives at the ready, congratulating me for following my heart, sustained me on the journey, but now it seems ridiculous.

I walked out on him and Luke when they needed me most. I didn't even say goodbye. I wouldn't talk to me under the circumstances.

But I have to ignore my doubts – what else can I do with no home to go to? I begin the walk towards the villa. It's hotter here than in Coventry, and I tie my cardigan around my waist, like a schoolgirl. I feel light-headed, as I did the morning of the accident, and I remember that I haven't eaten since the motorway service station breakfast Dennis treated me to on the M40.

I turn the corner into Frisky's road. The pavement is sticky with lime sap, and gravity-defying bees bumble around lush front gardens. I look for the Red Peril, but it's nowhere to be seen. Perhaps Luke is out. I'd prefer it if he was out.

Wouldn't I?

But he can't be out. His feet will only just have healed.

Come on, Jo. What's the worst that can happen?

I decide not to follow that particular train of thought and instead focus on putting one foot in front of the other, towards the villa. The stone façade looks perfect, the mellow sunshine bleaching out its many imperfections. I climb the steps and hesitate for a second before I ring the bell.

I hear it sound inside the house, and wait for footsteps. A woman with a pushchair passes the gate, singing 'Ring a Ring o' Roses'. I peer through the thick purple glass in the door. No sign of movement. I push my fingers through the letterbox but there's still nothing, and when I look down I see a pile of post on the doormat.

I feel sick. Why would both of them be out? I try ringing the bell again, pressing hard so it reverberates again and again.

What if Frisky's ill? He's eighty-five, and eighty-five-year-olds can go from fighting fit to terribly sick in days. And then there's the stroke. What if I broke his heart, triggered a terrible decline or a second stroke?

There's no other explanation. Even if Frisky's found himself another lost soul to rehabilitate in my place, then Luke would be confined to barracks because of his feet – and there's been enough time now for him to hobble to the door.

I imagine Frisky lying semi-conscious, mumbling my name.

I run down the steps and turn right, towards the hospital. I'm so out of condition that within a few yards I'm forced to take great gasping breaths, but I won't stop. I can't afford a wasted minute, because Frisky may not have that luxury.

My heart is hammering by the time I get to the hospital. I sprint over to the enquiry desk.

'You have to help me. I'm looking for my . . . ' I hesitate, they may only be letting relatives in, 'my godfather, I think he's here.'

The woman nods. 'Take a moment to get your breath back and tell me his name.'

'He . . . his name is . . . ' Oh shit. What is Frisky's real name? I try to remember that first meeting, outside that ugly clinic, the smoke clearing, the gnarled hand meeting mine, 'Um. Roger. Roger Freeman Van Belle.'

She frowns. 'That's a mouthful.' She types some letters into her keyboard, presses return. Waits. Then she tries again. And for a third time. 'No. Nothing there. I've tried under Freeman, Van and Belle. No one as an in-patient or out-patient.'

I start to cry. On one level, I know this has got to be *good* news, but I feel like I've failed. And without Frisky to tell, how will I know if I've done the right thing?

The woman hands me a tissue. 'There, there, love. Have you tried one of the other hospitals?'

I shake my head. 'No, Frisky only lives round the corner.'

Her face changes. 'Frisky? As in, wrinkly old goat who can't stop talking?'

'Yes, that's him. Oh God, he is here.' *Can't stop talking*. That has to be a good sign, surely?

'I didn't realise he was *really* posh, I thought he was putting on the airs and graces.'

'So he is here?'

She nods. 'I should think so. Frisky never misses the Monday Club.'

I stare at her, as it sinks in. It's Monday. It's two o'clock. Of *course* he's here. 'Thanks.'

I run out of reception, past the car park, a fat man on crutches, the maternity unit, two nurses sneaking a cigarette, the wheelchair repair workshop, a teenager pushing a tea-urn on a trolley, and finally there is rehabilitation.

I am so puffed now that I feel faint. Have I been rehabilitated? Am I a fully functioning human being? Was I ever one in the first place?

There's laughter coming from the open window, and the loudest belongs to Frisky. Not only is he not at death's door, he's sounding very chirpy. I'm not sure that's allowed, shouldn't he be missing me?

No more dawdling, Miss Morgan. Time to face the music. I open the door, and smell the instant coffee. I spot Frisky straight away: he has his back to me and his ice-cream curls bob as he laughs and laughs.

Familiar faces – Nathan, Monster, Falsie, the young chap who couldn't stop crying – peer back at me and the noise in the room fades away.

'Cat got our tongues or something?' Frisky says as he turns. He sees me and frowns. 'Ah. Ah, right.' He moves to one side and there, sitting on the squidgy sofa with his feet up, is Luke. Frisky clasps his hands together. 'There, you see. I told you she'd come back!'

Nathan suggests the others accompany him on a tea and buns trip to the WRVS stall, which is good of him, as I'm sure he'd rather eavesdrop.

'I actually went to your place this morning, to try to talk you into coming to the club,' Frisky says. 'In a taxi, since my grandson here couldn't drive me. And some nice women over the road told me your house had been sold.'

Trust the neighbours to know more than me. 'Yes,' I say. 'Sorry. Bit of a shock to me too, actually.'

Frisky takes out a cigar and lights it. 'I was rather miffed. I always think of myself as rather a good judge of character.'

Luke sits in silence on the sofa, his head turned away from me.

'Am I your first miscalculation then?'

Frisky's expression is obscured behind a cloud of blue-grey smoke. 'Did I miscalculate? The jury is waiting for the case for the defence.'

'Um.' I know it has to be good. 'It was Dennis's idea.'

'For you to leave without saying goodbye? Or perhaps you were abducted?'

'No, not abducted. He's got a new job, you see, and expected me to go with him. Except he didn't tell me until it was a *fait accompli.* Today. I've just come from Coventry now.'

Frisky's mouth hangs open. 'Gosh. He didn't tell you he was selling the house? Um, forgive me if I'm speaking out of turn, but isn't that absolutely bloody outrageous. Unless you're happy to live someone else's life?'

Someone else's life. I think of that last flashback, of my mother wanting *another life*, where she could make decisions. But I saw what happened when she tried. 'No, I'm not,' I say, very quietly. 'That's why I'm here.'

'Ah . . . '

'I've left him, Frisky. Left Dennis.'

Frisky's eyebrows shoot up. 'Golly. And . . . well done. I know I never met the chap but he sounds like a fruitcake. And not in a nice way.'

His certainty actually makes me question what I've done. 'But he was the only man who ever thought I amounted to anything.'

'Now that's not true at all, Joanna, and frankly I find it rather insulting. I'll forgive you, though, as you do look peaky. Are you hungry, by any chance?'

'Starving,' I admit.

'Right. Decision made. I'm sure the Monday Club can get by without us. Time to celebrate your decision over tea and cake. Oh, and perhaps a tiny slug of my best vintage champagne.'

Frisky goes to order a taxi to take us back, because Luke is still hobbling. 'Entertain the invalid boy, will you, Joanna?' he tells me, before leaving the room.

There's an agonisingly long pause, while I try to think of something appropriate to say.

'I didn't know you came here. To the club.'

Luke examines the backs of his hands. 'First time. Got bored sitting on my ass.'

'And do you like it?'

Finally he looks at me, his eyes cold. 'What is it with the dumb questions? As if you care.'

I feel my face heat up. 'But I do want to know, Luke, honestly –'

'Yeah? That's why you ran off after I spilled my guts to you. You can charm Frisky, but I see what you are. A taker. He was too easy on you.'

'Now hang on a minute. I know you've had a tough time, and I'm very sorry about what happened to your parents, but what about *your* behaviour? The last few months, whenever I tried to talk to you, you clammed up like a sulky child. And you're even ruder to your poor grandfather!'

Luke seems to shrink back into the sofa. 'Yes, well, I admit

I haven't always been too polite. But if you really want to know, Frisky and me, we've been getting along better lately.'

I think of my last words to him, begging him to try harder. 'Really? Why's that?'

'I couldn't exactly run away when he talked to me. Kinda *forced* us to make our peace.'

'Oh. So it wasn't anything to do with what I said, then? I suppose it wouldn't have been, would it, seeing as how I am such a self-obsessed person.'

He looks down at his hands again. 'Maybe it did get me thinking.'

'So if I apologise for going AWOL, will you apologise for being rude and childish?'

'You're calling me childish?'

I nod. Then I stick my tongue out for good measure. 'Yep.'

For a moment, his face is so serious that I think I've gone too far. Then he says, 'Do you want to know the real reason I kept away from you?'

'Not really, but tell me if you must.'

'Same reason I always got tongue-tied around a pretty girl at school.'

'What?' I can't tell where the strange bubbly sensation begins, but it spreads like champagne.

'Yeah, only this time it's worse. Like, a hundred times worse. Number one, because no way am I the kinda guy to hit on a girl who's living with someone. And number two, because when I was at school, I wanted a girlfriend, and now I don't want a girlfriend *at all.*'

'Oh.' The bubbles go flat and I'm rather relieved. It didn't feel that different from indigestion. 'Why not?'

He sighs. 'Like I said before, what have I got to offer a girl? A rusty trailer? A phobia of sleeping indoors.' He allows himself a shy smile. 'Though, you know, I got that fixed. Frisky said he had no intention of coming out to the caravan in the middle of the night to help me take a piss.'

'Bloody hell. And is it OK?'

'Didn't sleep for four long nights but, you know, in the end you can't stay awake any more. But if that's my biggest achievement in the last two years, is it any wonder I can't get a girl?'

'Hang on, though. A minute ago you said you didn't want a girl. Now you're saying you can't get one. Which I would dispute. Girls round these parts aren't *that* choosy. So which is it? Don't want or can't get?'

He frowns at me. 'Have you taken an aggression pill? Only I never heard you talk like this before.'

'Don't change the subject.'

'All right. I guess if I was a girl *I* wouldn't go out with me so how could I expect anyone else to? I mean, would you go out with me?'

I gulp. 'Hypothetically?'

'Uh-huh.'

I scrutinise the overall package. Downsides, a screwed-up life story, no house, the Red Peril for a car (and that's not even his). Upsides, a sense of humour, a great singing voice, the strongest sense of right and wrong I've ever encountered, a wonderful body, a beautiful face.

And something else. How do I describe it, without sounding daft? I've never believed in auras, but there's something about the man sitting opposite me that makes me realise I would trust him with my life.

Something I could no longer do ... no, let's be honest, would never have done with my so-called soul mate.

'Don't keep me in suspense.'

I look away. 'Yeah. I'd consider it.'

'Oh. Right. You'd *consider* it.' He shrugs. 'Well, that's *something*, I guess. I don't fall at the first hurdle.'

'And what about me, Luke? Would you consider me?'

'Shit. That's direct.' He blushes, so deeply that I'm sure every inch of him has turned pink. 'Hypothetically, right?'

I should backtrack now, of course. Save us both the mortification. And anyway, what am I doing discussing dates when I'm only hours out of a long-term relationship?

So I think it comes as something of a surprise to both of us when I murmur. 'No. Not hypothetically. *Really*. Here and now, live for today, for tomorrow we die, would you consider going out with me?'

He freezes and so do I. But it's OK. No harm done, I'll excuse myself from the glass of wine with Frisky, get the train to Newbury, move back home. It's good to follow your gut, sometimes, like Timmy says. Even if it ends in failure, humiliation, self-loathing . . .

'Jo . . . ' Luke is trying to move himself out of his seat. There. I've embarrassed him *so* much that he can't bear to be in the same room. He tries again. 'This is hopeless. Help me up, please.'

I reach for his hand and he grasps it. But instead of hoisting himself up, he pulls me down and it's only when I nearly lose my balance that I realise he's about to kiss me. Our mouths collide momentarily, before I bump my knee against the coffee table and leap back in pain.

'Oh shit,' Luke says. 'That didn't work out how I hoped.'

'So does that mean that your answer is yes?'

'Remind me of the question,' he says, and I groan. 'No. Hang on. I remember. OK, Jo. Hypothetically, would you like me to try that again?'

'No,' I say. 'Not hypothetically. The word you're looking for is *definitely*.'

And this time we're more synchronised. No bump. No clash of teeth. Just a feeling so good that champagne would seem flat in comparison . . .

From: Joanna Morgan
[mailto:scaredycat@headbangers.net]
Sent: Monday 21 August
To: Courtbridge Accident Prevention, Public Protection and Civil Defence Team
Subject: Better to travel than arrive?

Dear ex-colleagues,
Imagine a life with the risks removed.

That's the one I've always led. OK, I could have gone even further: attached bicycle stabilisers to my ankles, worn a helmet and knee-pads to the pub, refused to leave the house without a chemical protection suit. But in every practical way, my life has been worthy of a British Standards Institute Kite Mark.

Not that I'd have dreamed of flying a kite. Think of the overhead power lines.

But my risk-assessed behaviour didn't actually keep me safe, did it? Wrong place, wrong time, and I was never the same again. Thank God.

There will be no more safety bulletins, my friends. I don't know what I want to do with my life right now, but I do know that twenty years of planning for disaster is enough for anyone. No disrespect: it's good to know you're there, doing it for me, but I don't want to be avoiding risk any more, I want to embrace it.

Yes, you never know when the Grim Reaper might come for you, but likewise you never know whether Cupid might get there first.

This is what I've learned about life. Statistics don't keep you safe. Earthquakes happen. Fires burn. Caring makes you vulnerable. People you love *can* leave you or die.

There's every reason to be afraid, but fear won't stop you hurting, though it can stop you living. Oh, and Prince Charming won't rescue you, because the person who loves you when you're scared will probably want you to stay that way.

So, for old time's sake, here are the most important statistics I will ever share:

Chances of dying: 100 per cent.

Chances of regretting things on your deathbed: 99 per cent.

Chances of living the life you want: one.

I'll miss you all, but it's time for me to make the most of my ninth life. Maybe you should get your skates on too . . .

Love,

Jo

Reformed Scaredy-cat

Chapter 40

Ouranophobia – Fear of Heaven

Water laps sweetly against the black-painted wood of the gondola, and I hesitate before stepping in.

'Shouldn't there be a gangplank? It doesn't look very safe.'

Luke laughs. I used to think that because Dennis never laughed at me, that made him my soul mate. But Luke's laugh is like my personal early warning system, alerting me to excessively wimpy behaviour. 'And what would be the worst thing that would happen if you lost your footing?'

'I could fall in the canal.'

'Would you drown?'

I remind myself that lagoons don't have dangerous eddies to drag me under. 'No, because you or the gondolier would rescue me. But I might need my stomach pumped.'

'Not if you kept your mouth shut.' Then he smiles. 'Unlikely, though.'

'I might lose my handbag.'

'We'd buy you another one, in the flea market. A souvenir.'

I know I'm fighting a losing battle. 'Our euros might get washed away . . . '

'Ever heard of cashpoints?'

And now that I can't think of any more dangers, I've no choice but to enjoy the ride.

It would be the fairytale ending, of course, if I'd been

transformed from scaredy-cat to superhero when Luke kissed me. But in truth, it's a slower process. I'm ashamed to admit that even Luke's first properly romantic gesture brought out my killjoy tendencies. When he told me he was taking me to Venice for my birthday, I felt quite faint.

'Italy, in August? We'll melt. And it's number three in the international pick-pocketing league. Birmingham has as many canals, doesn't involve a flight and, as far as I know, is not in peril.' I told him, before groaning. 'Oh shit. That could have come straight out of Dennis's mouth.'

'Well, it's too late anyhow. I already bought the tickets,' he said, 'and booked a place for you on the fear of flying course your dad told me about. Think of it as a dummy run for visiting the States with me – it's not like we can *walk* to San Francisco.'

My next worry was that Venice could never live up to expectations, which distracted me on the plane (along with the visualisation I'd learned on the flying course).

But it'd take a hard, hard heart not to be melted by the city of Cornettos and *vaporetti*. The moment we stepped off the boat, I fell in love . . .

In love with overpriced pizzas; with bank account busting Bellinis at Harry's Bar (we did without dinner last night so we could afford them); with our hotel and its sliding floors and sliding doors that open right on to the canal three feet below (Luke's understandable fear of hotel fires is lessened by the ever-present water); and with the smell of drains and garlic (I wondered whether they might trigger a new set of flashbacks, but I haven't had a single one since leaving Dennis).

I'm in love with the Italian sun that's blasted through my factor twenty-five and turned my nose and shoulders bright pink. In love with the Italian men who whistle despite my sunburn. In love with the strappy, floaty dress Luke bought for me: the first red dress I've ever owned. It matches my hair – well, all but the white streak that I've allowed to grow, a precious reminder of the best thing that ever happened to me. I'm in love with the other couples, of every age and nationality, who float round the swarming city in their own bubble, insulated against the world.

And of course, I'm in love with Luke. It's not always straightforward, navigating his hang-ups and my own, but bloody hell, it's worth it. We spend twenty-four hours a day together, but that doesn't feel enough, even when we're arguing over rock versus pop, or American Budweiser versus European Stella Artois. And if he has the patience of a saint to put up with my daftness, then I like to think I'm good for him too. I arranged for two stars in Ursa Major to be named after his mum and dad, and even though we both know it's a bit barmy, he says he thinks of them every time we look up at the night sky.

I don't believe in soul mates any more (although, if I did, Luke would come pretty close). The whole idea suggests that the gods have matched us all up before we're born, that we never evolve or learn, and it's just not true. If Luke and I had met five years ago, we might never have known how happy we could be together.

That thought makes me feel quite sick . . .

And if that's not evidence enough of the strange nature of true love, there's Dennis and Lorraine, the world's unlikeliest couple. Or maybe not, now I think about it. All that time, she wanted a baby, and I think he secretly wanted someone who'd stand up to him. She took his side instead of mine, sent herself to Coventry to comfort him, and fell in love with Maple Drive. A baby hasn't materialised yet, as far as I know, but the last I heard she was enjoying her new life with the Director of Public Protection.

I bet the two of them are quite a hit in Warwickshire wife-swapping circles.

I'm happy for them, and though I've lost a best friend, I've also lost any residual guilt at walking away from Dennis. You can't stay with people because of what used to be. Look at my parents.

But even their relationship makes sense to me now that I've realised Dad isn't a dastardly villain and Mum isn't a helpless waif. They're bound by their history. Oh, and by Timmy and me: Mum told me when she came to see my new home at the villa that they bicker all the time about which of us makes them proudest. It made me well up. I never realised.

Life in the villa is certainly less comfortable than in Salzburg Avenue. Luke and I sleep in the same room as Frisky and Lucky the goldfish, while we finish the building work. Our relationship hasn't been forged over candlelit suppers and red roses, but over a plastering trowel and paintbrushes.

The villa is the most romantic place in the world . . . even Venice can't compete, though it comes a close second.

'You all right?'

The gondolier makes a sharp turn to avoid a water-taxi, and I wonder whether it's daft to feel seasick on a lagoon. 'Fine.'

Luke rummages in his back pocket for a tiny parcel. 'Here.'

'What's this?' I forget my giddiness as I unwrap the pink tissue paper. Nestling in the centre is a goldfish made of Murano glass.

'I took them a photograph of Lucky and they made it specially.'

The fish's lips are curled in a smile, and no wonder: it has its own little eco-system. Slender glass tendrils of greenery rise from a sand-specked seabed. 'It's gorgeous.'

'Happy?' Luke asks. I think of that round the world funfair ride, on my very first danger date. Of wanting to see Venice, but never believing it could happen.

'Happy as Lucky the goldfish.'

'I know which I'd rather cuddle up to,' Luke says.

The gondolier slows as we approach a limestone bridge with barred windows. 'Is Ponte dei Suspiri, the famous Bridge of Sighs,' he says, pointing. 'Is the final view criminals would see of Venice before going to their prison cells.'

As Luke leans over to kiss me, I think of the snogging hoodies on Court Bridge on Valentine's night, the evening before my life changed for good. When his lips meet mine, I remember how they had to hold on to each other to keep their balance.

And at last I understand how they felt.